Blockchain and the Commons

Recent years have seen a surge of interest in 'the commons' based on a simple yet radical idea: great improvements in production and management could be achieved by reducing barriers to knowledge exchange and power-sharing. Ranging from meadows, forests and parks to language, open-source software (FLOSS and Blockchain) and 3D printers, the commons are distributed or common property resources/infrastructures that are self-managed by their user communities. While acknowledging the significant contributions that can be made through commons-based peer production, this book provides a critical examination of the commons with the aim of contributing to their long-term sustainability. In particular, the book examines the relation of Blockchain to the commons by illustrating the case study of the Commons Stack.

Drawing on a range of interdisciplinary ideas and methodologies, the book argues that there are a number of economic and social barriers that are obstructing the wider reproduction of the commons. Problems with access to capital and training, the lack of entrepreneurial and managerial skills and the absence of institutional support from governments, larger co-ops and NGOs are some of the external difficulties facing the commons today. Meanwhile, localism, gated communities, vested interests, atavism, traditionalism, ideology, conflict, neo-conservatism and techno-elitism represent some of the internal contradictions inherent in the commons. Through overcoming these contradictions, the ultimate goal is to transform capitalism into the post-capitalism of the commons: the creation of a social economy self-organised around the commons.

This book provides vital reading for anyone interested in the commons, from economics, techno-politics and across the social sciences.

Vangelis Papadimitropoulos is a postdoc researcher in the School of Political Sciences at Panteion University, Athens, Greece.

Routledge Frontiers of Political Economy

Economics and Art Theory
Edited by Stratos Myrogiannis and Constantinos Repapis

Capitalism and Agrarian Change
Production and Reproduction in Indonesia
Muchtar Habibi

Capitalist Agriculture and the Global Bee Crisis
Rebecca Ellis

China, Trust and Digital Supply Chains
Dynamics of a Zero Trust World
Warwick Powell

Macroeconomic Modelling, Economic Policy and Methodology
Economics at the Edge
Edited by Mikael Randrup Byrialsen, Hamid Raza and Finn Olesen

Economics, Anthropology and the Origin of Money as a Bargaining Counter
Patrick Spread

Bernard Schmitt's Quantum Macroeconomic Analysis
Alvaro Cencini

Blockchain and the Commons
Vangelis Papadimitropoulos

Globalization and the Decline of American Power
Cyrus Bina

For more information about this series, please visit: www.routledge.com/Routledge-Frontiers-of-Political-Economy/book-series/SE0345

Blockchain and the Commons

Vangelis Papadimitropoulos

Routledge
Taylor & Francis Group
LONDON AND NEW YORK

First published 2023
by Routledge
4 Park Square, Milton Park, Abingdon, Oxon OX14 4RN

and by Routledge
605 Third Avenue, New York, NY 10158

Routledge is an imprint of the Taylor & Francis Group, an informa business

British Library Cataloguing-in-Publication Data
A catalogue record for this book is available from the British Library

ISBN: 978-0-367-48404-0 (hbk)
ISBN: 978-1-032-37890-9 (pbk)
ISBN: 978-1-003-03972-3 (ebk)

DOI: 10.4324/9781003039723

Typeset in Bembo
by Newgen Publishing UK

Contents

Acknowledgements

I would like to thank Jeff Emmett for his significant feedback on the book. I would like also to thank the members of the Commons Stack and the Token Engineering Commons for their participation in the interviews and their kind support in all my queries.

1 Introduction

Blockchain and the Commons

Blockchain is all the rage today for its presumed liberating potential as a technology. Blockchain is a decentralised, tamper-proof, time-stamped and transparent database that comes with a number of affordances and use cases for businesses, institutions, communities and individuals. The main advantage of Blockchain is the elimination of intermediaries and the reduction in transaction costs. Cryptocurrencies such as Bitcoin have been considered to empower start-ups, individuals and communities vis-à-vis centralised institutions such as corporations, banks and governments. On the flipside, Blockchain has been criticised for being technocratic, oligarchic, slow, inefficient, energy-intensive and replete with illicit activity, frauds, scams and speculation.

This book focuses on the relation of Blockchain to the commons, the examination of which still lies on the fringes of the literature. The commons are a mode of peer production, which is based on sharing, openness, co-creation, self-governance and the equitable distribution of value (Bauwens, Kostakis & Pazaitis 2019: 2). The commons are a type of social relations, a technological infrastructure and a new mode of production and property, whereby participants have maximum freedom to cooperate and connect (Bauwens, Kostakis & Pazaitis 2019: 1). Commons-based peer production (CBPP) has the potential to disrupt centralised capitalist production and state management through the decentralised use of the Internet and open-source technologies.

Blockchain is open-source software and, as such, it belongs to the digital commons. Smart contracts developed on top of layer 1 (protocol) of Blockchains enable the creation of decentralised applications such as distributed autonomous organisations (DAOs), which are controlled by the organisation members according to the pre-agreed rules of the smart contract. DAOs are an assemblage of online peer-to-peer communities that seek to coordinate for a common purpose without the need for a central authority. DAOs are sites of algorithmic governance that employ consensus protocols and smart contracts to collect funds, issue governance tokens and vote on allocating funds on various projects. DAOs coordinate today primarily around digital assets such as tokenised funds, code and software, but the goal is to gradually expand into physical assets as well.

DOI: 10.4324/9781003039723-1

This book makes the case that CBPP faces a number of contradictions that go against the sustainability of the commons. Individualism versus collectivism, commerciality versus non-commerciality, competition versus cooperation, private property versus common property, use value versus exchange value and technocracy versus democracy are some of the contradictions that plague CBPP today.

The book employs literature review, semi-structured interviews, participatory observation and digital ethnography to test its hypothesis through the illustration of the Commons Stack case study. CBPP lacks the mechanisms necessary to attract funding, self-govern and process information from the ground up. The Commons Stack is a not-for-profit association that draws on the work of Elinor Ostrom to create a library of open-source Blockchain tools that enable the commons to raise and allocate funding, make decisions and measure impact with the aid of computer-based real-time analytics as well as modelling and simulation.

The book covers, among others, the launch of the Token Engineering Commons (TEC), which is the first deployment of the Commons Stack toolkit. The TEC is the first commons that has used the Commons Stack tools such as the augmented bonding curve (ABC) and conviction voting to raise and allocate funds for the purposes of advancing token engineering, which is a nascent field of crypto-economic design. Crypto-economics uses Blockchain consensus protocols, smart-contract-enabled token issuance and algorithmic governance mechanisms to allocate resources for the purposes of coordinating socio-economic behaviour in decentralised peer-to-peer networks. I put emphasis here particularly on the ABC, which is an adaptation of an automated market maker designed to align individual and collective incentives under a continuous token-weighted voting process called conviction voting.

The TEC made use of the Commons Stack toolkit in the summer of 2021 to raise through crowdfunding the amount of $1,500,000, part of which has been allocated to fund the TEC DAO's operations for the near future. The rest of the funds will be gradually unlocked by the ABC to fund the commons. In the case of the TEC, the community will use conviction voting, among other tools, to vote on submitted proposals aiming to advance the creation of public goods such as open-source software.

What distinguishes the Commons Stack and the TEC from other DAOs that mostly serve their financial interests is their mission to advance the commons. Interestingly, the Commons Stack and the TEC comply with almost all the commons principles, beginning with Ostrom's design principles and expanding on the organisational principles of the digital commons. Transparency, grassroots democracy, sharing, openness, do-ocracy, stigmergy, modularity, ethics, sustainability and the equitable distribution of value are all part and parcel of the Commons Stack and the TEC operations. Of particular importance are the so-called cultural build and praise systems, which nurture a culture of democratic deliberation and gratitude among community members.

However, the Commons Stack and the TEC cannot help but reproduce some of the contradictions of the commons. Compared with larger DAOs operating in the DeFi ecosystem and beyond, the Commons Stack and the TEC have received a limited amount of funding. As a consequence, only core team members receive a meagre salary, while the vast majority of the contributors earn reputation tokens. Precariousness is a common feature of the people involved in the commons, who need also to work in the capitalist economy to make ends meet. People involved in DAOs in particular are usually software developers and highly educated wealthy individuals who have the skills, time and resources to engage in risky ventures. Relying on contributions, grants and donations by wealthy individuals is not a viable business model going forward for CBPP to become a sustainable model capable of challenging capitalism down the road.

The Commons Stack and the TEC have members numbering in the hundreds, but only a dozen or so of them participate in the community calls and vote on proposals. Decisions are mostly debated among the ten to 15 people who seem to be the more knowledgeable over the issues, while the rest remain mere observers. Procedures and tools thus far are too complex for non-geeks to cope with and meaningfully participate in. In the quest for decentralisation, mechanisms span multiple websites and platforms, which becomes overwhelming even for experts to go through.

Techno-economism lurks under the burden of the technical and economic indicators that weigh down on the socio-political foundation of collaboration. Instead of software engineers and social scientists working in isolation, they need to engage in participatory action research. They need to reach out to co-ops and the commons and co-design with the communities their self-governance model in the physical space. Highly sophisticated mathematical models and computer code need to be translated and communicated in plain language for non-experts to understand. Writing software and communicating via computers do not account for democracy. Techno-science can only support, not replace, democracy.

The Commons Stack and the TEC coalesce around several DAOs experimenting with Blockchain-based tools to boost decentralised micro-economies. Their development is co-emergent with the whole Blockchain Web3 ecosystem, which is still in its infancy. The Commons Stack toolkit used by the TEC is written in smart contracts built on the Ethereum platform. Blockchain decentralised infrastructure, especially for DAOs, is not yet ready for large-scale deployment. Ethereum scalability, high transaction fees, flaws in the code, hack attacks, frauds, Ponzi schemes, vote buying, voter apathy, digital illiteracy, standardisation, interoperability, usability, large-scale fair governance issues, legal issues, environmental concerns, applications in the real economy and regulation are all pressing issues that need to be addressed in the long run (Hassan et al. 2020).

Numerous socio-political issues are pending. How would self-governance work for thousands or millions of users online? How would DAOs address the contradictions of online versus offline operation; the digital versus the physical space; algorithmic centralisation versus decentralisation; the tyranny of structurelessness versus grassroots democracy; exploration versus efficiency; paid labour versus reputation; complexity versus simplicity; commerciality versus non-commerciality; fragmentation versus coordination; liminality versus legality?

Additional philosophical and ethical issues arise with regard to the blending of Blockchain with artificial intelligence (AI) and the Internet of Things (IoT). To what degree are humans willing to employ technology to cooperate and communicate? How are humans to strike a balance between online and offline life? Do humans want to financialise life? Do humans want to commodify nature? Do humans want to tokenise value? Do humans want to delegate politics and justice to smart contracts?

Blockchain, AI and the IoT have been often hailed as 'technical fixes' to climate change. However, they have also been criticised for 'greenwashing' rather than being honest efforts to reduce the overall footprint of digital technologies. Sustainability science and political ecology have a critical role to play when assessing the relationship between digital technologies and the environment.

These are all complex issues that cannot be addressed in a decentralised fashion. For CBPP to resolve its contradictions and progress into a self-sustained socio-economic paradigm capable of challenging neoliberalism, a holistic coordination mechanism is a *sine qua non* for creating a chain of equivalence that unites the pluralism of peer production under the post-hegemony of the commons. Local and global commons, the solidarity economy, traditional and platform cooperatives, ethical market entities and Blockchain-based DAOs need to merge into a networked ecosystem of multi-stakeholder cooperatives that can provide their members a steady income, all the while adhering to the principles of openness, sharing, transparency, bottom-up self-management, sustainability science and the equitable distribution of value. This transition presupposes the post-capitalist eco-techno-social transformation of both the means and social relations of production along with cosmo-local intra-regenerative flows of culture, capital, knowledge and resources self-governed by communities.

Book Structure

The book can be read as an update on my first book, which elaborates on the political theories of the commons (Papadimitropoulos 2020). This book focuses on the contradictions of the commons variously playing out at the interface of Blockchain and the commons. The book's structure is as follows.

Chapter 2 begins with a typology of the commons that demonstrates the different types of commons, ranging from local (rural, urban) and global (digital) to cosmo-local and cyber-physical commons. The political economy section examines the commons as a mode of production, while the political theory section approaches the commons from a theoretical perspective. The chapter closes with the contradictions of the commons and the introduction of a post-hegemonic strategy seeking to resolve the contradictions for the benefit of the commons.

Chapter 3 covers Blockchain as a general-purpose technology. It begins with a brief history of the Internet and Blockchain. It then offers an extended synopsis of the technical fundamentals of the two most adopted Blockchains thus far: Bitcoin and Ethereum. Next, it describes the main types of Blockchain and moves on to present Blockchain benefits and risks. The chapter closes with the politics of Blockchain, which serves as the theoretical framework necessary to help the reader smoothly go through the illustration of the Commons Stack case study.

Chapter 4 illustrates the Commons Stack case study. It begins with a description of the Commons Stack's value proposition, goals and activities and the mechanisms put in place to advance the commons. It then delves deeper into the Commons Stack architecture, which breaks down into four layers: the design layer, the governance layer, the production layer and the finance layer. The analysis draws attention to the ABC and conviction voting tools as well as the cultural build and the praise system, which are considered to be the Commons Stack's most significant innovations aiming, respectively, to provide funding for the commons, improve the voting procedure on funding proposals, democratise governance and recognise contributions.

Chapter 4 also documents the TEC hatch, which is the first commons launched by the Commons Stack. It covers the different hatch phases, outlining the different stakeholders and the tokenomics involved in the process. It then describes the TEC organisational structure, explaining how the cultural practices of the TEC intersect with some of the working groups that comprise their governance model. The chapter closes with the technical and social challenges facing the Commons Stack and the TEC in conjunction with the development of the overall Web3 ecosystem.

Chapter 5 summarises the contradictions of the commons that play out in the Commons Stack case study and the TEC hatch. It highlights the pros and cons of crypto-economics in relation to democratic politics. The chapter closes with the introduction of a post-hegemonic strategy seeking to reconcile the contradictions of the commons under a holistic coordination mechanism aiming to unite the pluralism of peer production under the principles of the commons.

2 The Commons

The Typology of the Commons

The concept of 'the commons' originates in the gift economy of primitive societies, Aristotle's republicanism, the feudal commons and modern political philosophy (Dardot & Laval 2014: 25–67; Fourier 1971; Marx 1993 [1858]; Owen 1991 [1813]; Proudhon 1994). The most contemporary elaborations of the commons cover a broad spectrum of disciplines, ranging from political philosophy (liberalism, Marxism, anarcho-syndicalism, critical theory, post-Marxism and existential political philosophy) to sociology, law, crypto-economics, management studies, media and communication studies and computer science (Papadimitropoulos 2020: 5–9).

The most generally accepted definition of the commons has been provided by David Bollier, who defines the commons as shared or distributed resources/infrastructures (natural resources, technology, knowledge, capital, culture), self-managed by user communities in accordance with collectively established rules or norms (Bollier & Helfrich 2015). Thus, the commons consist of three elementary components: (1) a resource; (2) a community; and (3) a commoning activity (De Angelis 2017: 119). A commons can be considered a limited-access pasture or open-access software that can be collectively managed by its users in terms of explicit or implicit rules and/or norms.

The commons depart from the sharing of resources and the production of use value, as opposed to the capitalist economy, which operates on the basis of competition over scarce resources for the production of exchange value (De Filippi & Hassan 2014). In the commons economy, scarcity relates to the material production of local commons such as natural resources and hardware, whereas abundance is most prominent in the immaterial production of intellectual and digital commons (e.g. culture, knowledge and information) owing to information's unique attribute that it can be infinitely copied at zero marginal cost. In the capitalist economy, the abundance of culture, knowledge and information is subject to artificial scarcity, enforced by intellectual property rights.

The commons are premised on a simple yet radical idea: great improvements in production and management can be achieved by reducing barriers to knowledge exchange and ownership of resources (Bollier & Helfrich 2015).

DOI: 10.4324/9781003039723-2

Openness, co-ownership and self-management can result in a constantly improving collective repository of material and immaterial resources (best ideas and practices); hence, the free/open-source technologies of the Internet and the digital commons add up to local (rural and urban) commons, thus forming the cosmo-local commons.

The commons favour decentralisation over central control, bottom-up self-management over hierarchical top-down management, sustainability over growth at no cost, open access over privacy, cooperation over competition, solidarity over self-interest, and distribution of value over profit maximisation (Bauwens, Kostakis & Pazaitis 2019; Bollier & Helfrich 2015; Kostakis & Bauwens 2014). CBPP (Benkler 2006) introduces new and radical forms of ownership, governance, operation and financialisation in a mission to empower communities against the pervasive economic inequalities and power asymmetries of neoliberalism. CBPP is considered to enhance gender balance, increase flexibility, diffuse knowledge and reduce waste and transaction costs, thereby reaching higher levels of social innovation, democratic inclusion and environmental sustainability (Bauwens, Kostakis & Pazaitis 2019). Eventually, commoning and open sourcing become mechanisms to scale the impact of eco-techno-social innovation.

Local Commons

The commons can be classified in two basic types: local and global commons (Kostakis & Bauwens 2014; Bollier & Helfrich 2012, 2015, 2019). Local commons comprise rural and urban commons. Rural commons include ecovillages (e.g. the Cloughjordan ecovillage), community-supported agriculture, community land trusts, biocultural commons (e.g. the Potato Park of Peru) and all types of commons examined by Elinor Ostrom (1990), such as forests, fisheries, pastures, groundwater basins and irrigation fields. Urban commons include community gardens, housing associations, cultural commons, fab labs (digital fabrication laboratories), food co-ops, energy co-ops, neighbourhood budgeting and local currencies, among others (Foster & Iaione 2016).

The Tragedy of the Commons

Garrett Hardin's (1968) famous argument on the tragedy of the commons holds that an open-access commons such as a pasture cannot sustain itself due to the free-rider problem. In the absence of contracts, self-interest induces farmers either to underuse or overuse the pasture. Self-interest prevails over collective action, resulting either in the underuse or depletion of the common-pool resource. A real-world example is the Grand Banks Fisheries off the coast of Newfoundland, Canada. For centuries the supply of codfish was plentiful. In the 1960s and 1970s fishing technology improved and allowed much larger catches. By the 1990s cod populations were so depleted that the Grand Banks Fisheries became bankrupt. The cod stocks had been damaged irreparably (Maples 2018).

The tragedy of the commons is an instance of market failure in which the market fails to allocate resources efficiently, and it can occur almost anywhere value is produced, whether it is a pasture or a digital platform. According to Hardin, the solution to the tragedy of the commons is either government intervention or privatisation and marketisation. Hardin's argument resonates today, with neoliberalism (Brown 2015) championing the privatisation of public assets, including natural resources such as water and forests.

The Comedy of the Commons

In stark contrast to Hardin's tragedy of the commons, Carol Rose (1986) argues for the comedy of the commons, highlighting the 'inherently public property' of goods such as roads, navigable waterways and open squares. She introduced an early version of network effects, which render an open-access resource an anti-rival good. The more that people use the resource, the more valuable it becomes, provided the increased participation outweighs the costs from increased utilisation. When this is the case, efficiency and welfare would suggest opening up resources to public use instead of enclosing them with property rights and state regulation.

Some years later, in 1990, Ostrom illustrated that, under certain conditions common-pool resources can be sustainably managed by local communities of peers. She advocated for a polycentric governance model comprising governments, institutions and communities for managing common-pool resources. Ostrom (1990) has discovered a number of design principles governing traditional commons.

1. Clearly defined community boundaries, in order to define who has rights and privileges within the community.
2. Congruence between rules and local conditions: the rules that govern behaviour or commons use in a community should be flexible and based on local conditions, which may change over time. These rules should be intimately associated with the commons, rather than relying on 'one size fits all' regulation.
3. Collective choice arrangements: in order to best accomplish congruence (principle number 2), people who are affected by these rules should be able to participate in their modification, and the costs of alteration should be kept low.
4. Monitoring: some individuals within the community act as monitors of behaviour in accordance with the rules derived from collective choice arrangements, and they should be accountable to the rest of the community.
5. Graduated sanctions: community members actively monitor and sanction one another when behaviour is found to conflict with community rules. Sanctions against members who violate the rules are aligned with the perceived severity of the infraction.

6. Conflict resolution mechanisms: members of the community should have access to low-cost spaces to resolve conflicts.
7. Local enforcement of local rules: local jurisdiction to create and enforce rules should be recognised by higher authorities.
8. Multiple layers of nested enterprises: by forming multiple nested layers of organisation, communities can address issues that affect resource management differently at both broader and local levels.

Charlotte Hess and Elinor Ostrom (2007) expanded their work over subsequent decades to cover all types of commons, including information, knowledge and cultural commons such as the Internet, scientific knowledge, public libraries, art, etc. (Figure 2.1).

Scholars, civil servants, citizens and activists are working today to apply Ostrom's polycentric model in urban settings (Foster & Iaione 2016). Partner cities such as Amsterdam, Barcelona, Bologna, Naples and Ghent support various commons in the fields of mobility, shelter, food, energy and culture through public–private–common partnerships (Bollier & Helfrich 2015, 2019; Bauwens & Niaros 2017b).

Global Commons

Global commons expand from Ostrom's ecological commons to public goods such as knowledge/intellectual commons and the Internet (open-source software and the digital commons) (Figure 2.1). Public goods are non-excludable and non-rivalrous, meaning that no one can be excluded from speaking a language and one person's speaking a language does not subtract from others speaking the same language as well. Public goods are available in nature, such as Ostrom's common pool resources, and some of them are provided by the state, such as science, culture, health, education, national defence, roads, parks, highways and airwaves. The criterion for distinguishing between public goods and common goods is their type of governance. Whereas the former are managed by state governance, the latter are self-managed by communities (Quilligan 2012).

Public goods such as natural resources and open-source software suffer from the free-rider problem. To tackle the problem, three major solutions have been introduced thus far: (1) turning public goods into club goods excluding free riders, through memberships, copyrights, patents or paywalls; (2) Ostrom's self-management, expanding from natural resources to open-source software; (3) and Hardin's privatisation, resonating with the advent of neoliberalism from 1970s onwards, during which vital parts of the public sector such as energy, infrastructure and education have been subcontracted to corporations to manage according to their interests.

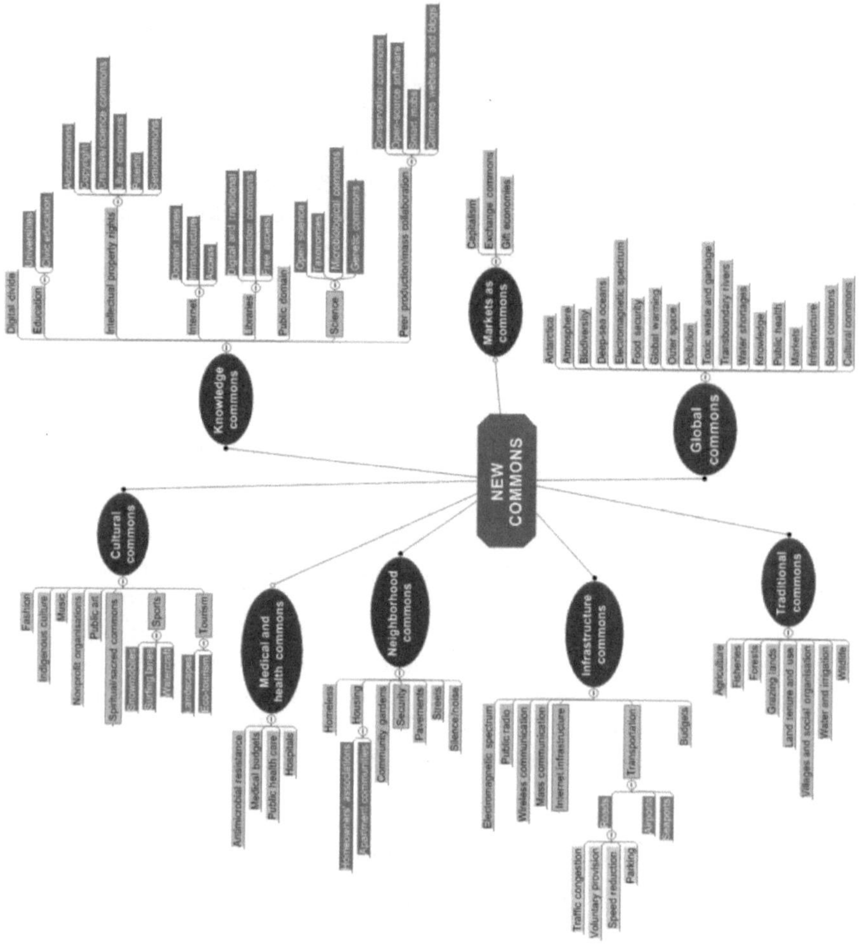

Figure 2.1 A Map of the New Commons

Source: Hess (2008).

The Digital Commons

The development of information and communication technologies (ICTs) in the last few decades has given birth to the digital commons of the Internet. Yochai Benkler (2006) has coined the term 'commons-based peer production' to describe a non-market sector of information, knowledge and cultural production, not treated as private property, but as an ethic of sharing, self-management and cooperation between peers who have free access to online platforms running on open-source software. The term 'commons' denotes a particular institutional form of structuring the right to access, use and control resources, which differs significantly from managerial hierarchies and markets. The distinctive features of the digital commons are: (1) decentralised self-governance through the utilisation of participatory, meritocratic (do-ocracy) and charismatic rather than proprietary or contractual models; (2) the centrality of non-monetary motivations; and (3) the permeation of state and firm boundaries (Benkler, Shaw & Hill 2015: 2–3; Benkler 2017: 265).

In contrast to Ostrom's limited-access commons, the digital commons are open access. They are not confined at a local level, but expand on a global level. The basic code (TCP/IP, HTML, HTTP) that runs the Internet is open-sourced – that is, it cannot be exclusively owned. Open-sourced code allows for decentralised applications and peer-to-peer networks such as file-sharing platforms, citizen media, citizen science, collaborative mapping, P2P currencies, *prosumer* e-communities (Toffler 1980), peer funding, cryptocurrencies, open-data commons, open design, open hardware, gaming communities, critical online public spheres and counter-publics, forums of grassroots digital democracy and the Internet of Things (De Filippi et al. 2013; Fuchs 2011).

FLOSS

Open-sourced code has evolved in the last decades in the form of the Free/Libre Open-Source Software (FLOSS). FLOSS is a hack in copyright law that has all the code on the commons. It permits the access, copy, distribution and remix of the code by all or most users on conditions that it is copied, distributed and remixed under the same licence (Raymond 1999; Stallman 2002; Weber 2004). This is the GNU General Public Licence, or the so-called 'copyleft' licence. Put simply, FLOSS prohibits the privatisation of a digital creation by a sole user. Thus, FLOSS is the main pillar of the digital commons. Some prominent cases of the digital commons are Wikipedia, Slashdot, Loomio, Drupal, Linux, Apache, Mozilla, Wordpress and LibreOffice, and there are hundreds more (Figure 2.2).

Motivations to participate in FLOSS production vary a great deal (Lakhani & Wolf 2005; Lerner & Tirole 2002). Some software developers participate for the pleasure of creation, some for gaining reputation, others for acquiring

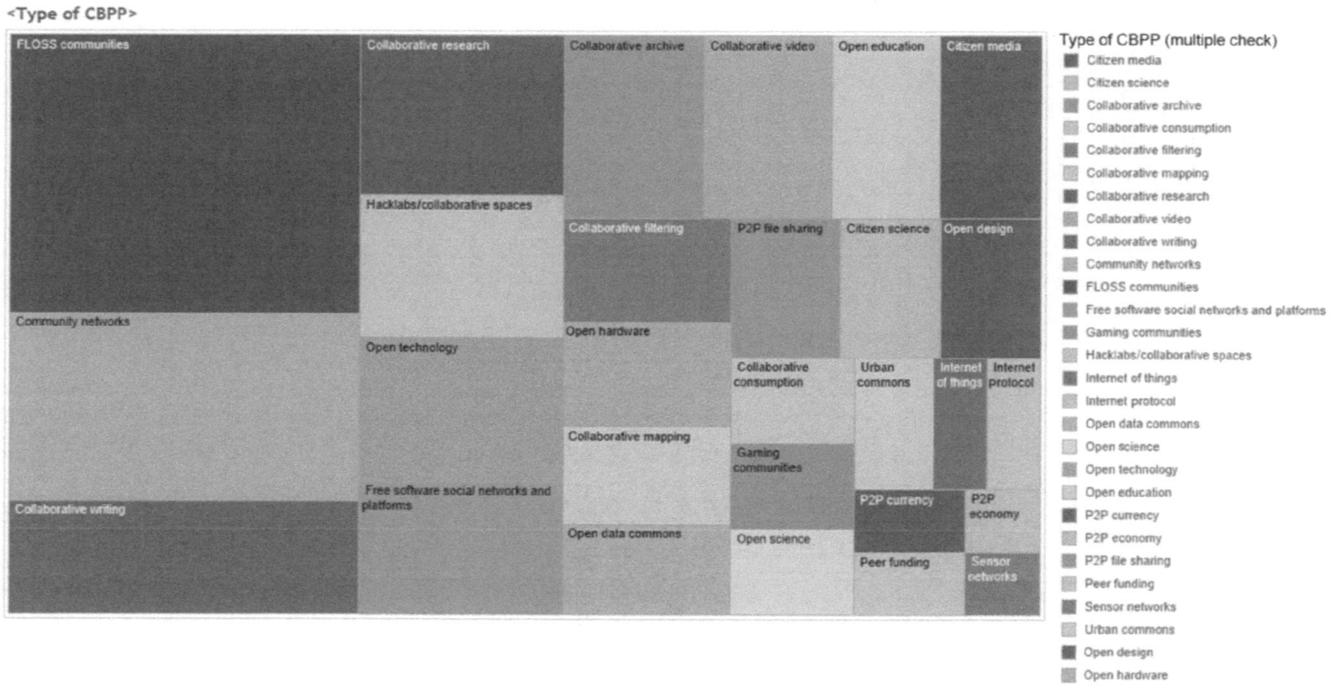

Figure 2.2 The Digital Commons

Source: https://p2pvalue.eu; figure is licensed under CC0 1.0 Universal (CC0 1.0) Public Domain Dedication.

professional experience and others for redeeming voluntary work down the road by receiving a bigger salary. Given that two-thirds of the revenues of the software industry are service-based, the skills indirectly appropriated in free software development can be directly redeemed in proprietary projects (Benkler 2002: 424–425). In short, FLOSS production combines a series of intrinsic and extrinsic motivations.

FLOSS governance in small projects is informal and is based on 'rough consensus' between developers. By 'rough consensus', I mean an indirect coordination and decision-making process, which encapsulates an informal majoritarian or consensus democracy constituted through signals generated by the community posts, forums, online voting systems, polls, and the like. The one who has more sway in the process is often nominated as a 'benevolent dictator for life' to resolve contentious issues, as in the cases of Wikipedia and Linux. When projects scale up to a certain extent, governance turns formal and is assigned to a not-for-profit entity, as in the case of the Mozilla Foundation.

Platform Capitalism

Rose's early version of network effects is manifested today most prominently on the Internet and the digital commons. The definition of network effects is crystallised in Metcalfe's law (Metcalfe 1995): 'The value of a communications network is proportional to the square of the number of its users.' The more people use a network, the more valuable it becomes to its users. Network effects have boosted novel models of production on the Internet such as FLOSS, the digital commons and platform capitalism.

In many cases, FLOSS has developed in the mode of a pro-capitalist commons that benefits both commoners and platform capitalists (Fritsch et al. 2021). A number of capitalist firms have invested in FLOSS for the purpose of outsourcing costs to volunteers, all the while extracting profits from open-source production. On the other hand, software engineers engaged in pro-capitalist commons come to secure the sustainability of their projects by being compensated from various business models built on top of free/open-source software (Birkinbine 2020). Blockchain open-source technology introduces a new sort of contested commons (Fritsch et al. 2021). Cryptocurrencies such as Bitcoin and Ethereum are used by both platform capitalists and commoners, albeit for different purposes.

Platform capitalism – often mistakenly referred to as the sharing economy – is a type of digital capitalism that employs network effects on the Internet to sell products and services online, realise monopoly rents on big data and extract fees from multi-sided markets of interdependent suppliers, producers, consumers and users (Papadimitropoulos 2020: 78–80; Srnicek 2017). Prominent cases are Facebook, Google, Amazon, Airbnb, Uber, Alibaba, Ebay, and dozens more.

Richard Barbrook (1998) considers cyberspace a hybrid terrain of anarcho-communism, which exists in symbiosis with platform capitalism. FLOSS is often sponsored by corporate capital that extracts value from open-source production. The digital commons and the free circulation of information among Internet users depend upon the capitalist production of computers, software and telecommunications, with firms exploiting the precarious labour of global cyber-proletariats (Dyer-Witheford 2006). By the same token, cyber-production depends on the unpaid reproduction of labour, most often undertaken by women (Federici 2012). Anarcho-communism is also symbiotic with the state that subsidises and regulates platform capitalism (Mazzucato 2013). Anarcho-communism coexists with liberal democracy. The Internet user is a prosumer in the digital economy, a citizen of the state and an anarcho-communist in a gift economy (open-source software and the digital commons) largely co-opted by finance capital.

Platform capitalism promises the liberation of communication and the flexibility of creation for prosumers scattered across the globe. However, platform capitalism exacerbates the disparity between private and social returns to information (knowledge) (Stiglitz 2016:48). Not only does platform capitalism extract surplus value from unwaged domestic workers, full-time waged employees and precarious workers; it also transforms profit into rent, turning sociality into the commodification of the general intellect via information disproportionally exploited by corporations enjoying privileged access to it (Žižek 2010). Asymmetries of information, exploitation without coercion and concentrated market power create an oligopoly of knowledge production. Instead of the Internet promoting innovation, creativity and freedom, it often turns into the most efficient censorship and surveillance mechanism, as evidenced in the cases of China, Russia and the United States (Zuboff 2019). Blockchain technology has the potential to oppose centralised power and support novel collaborative models of governance and production. However, it is currently moving towards a libertarian rather a commonist direction (Fritsch et al. 2021).

Platform capitalism has integrated communication and information technologies into a 24/7 global cybermarket. Dallas Smythe (1977, 1981: 22–51) speaks of the 'audience commodity', which portrays the media audience as a commodity sold to advertisers. Platform capitalism is crowdsourced to Internet users, who produce an economy of likes via waged and unwaged digital labour. Whereas waged digital labour is performed on crowdsourcing platforms (Brabham 2013), unwaged digital labour refers to almost any social activity on the Internet, including chatting, posting, searching, reviewing and commenting (Fuchs 2014; Scholz 2012). Thus, digital labour fuels platform capitalism, transforming space and time into a social factory (Tronti 2019 (1962]). Richard Murdock (2013: 164) considers the co-optation of the digital commons by platform capitalism a new enclosure movement.

Big data turns the Internet into advertising real estate (Papadimitropoulos 2020: 250–253). Big data spurs the customisation of demand by advertisers and marketers, who count on analytics to successfully predict consumer behaviour. The Internet and social media serve as agencies of attention and reputation, but only celebrities and superstars can handsomely redeem their reputational currency through social branding. The majority benefit from the services provided by search engines and social media in disproportionate exchange for their privacy. Not only does digital industrialism replicate the core division of industrial capitalism between directors and executants, it further colonises time and space by turning human data into a commodity produced by Internet users themselves, who are classified into a 'mainstream' set of trends, categories and numbers, unwittingly reproducing the dehumanisation of artificial intelligence.

A number of authors have built on the Marxian notion of the proletariat, arguing that digitisation has created a new and more diverse type of proletariat. André Gorz (1980: 69) holds that automation and computerisation have rendered underemployed, probationary, contracted, casual, temporary and part-time workers a 'post-industrial neo-proletariat'. Ursula Huws (2003) speaks of a new class of information-processing workers: the cybertariat. In the same vein, Guy Standing (2011) and Nick Dyer-Witheford (1999: 88, 96) claim that poorly paid, insecure and deskilled service workers constitute a new type of precariat.

Platform capitalism is a technologically advanced form of exploitation, in most cases resulting in a 'race to the bottom' with regard to wages and living standards. Labour alienation, exploitation with or without coercion, precarity (Huws 2014; Standing 2011) and insecurity are the sheer outcomes of the strategic nullification of labour law by corporations making use of legal grey zones to misclassify employees as independent contractors, pay no taxes and violate local laws, labour laws and privacy and anti-discrimination laws (Scholz 2016; Codagnone, Biagi & Abadie 2016: 26–39). Finally, there is strong evidence that insecure employment and precariousness result in psychological morbidity (Virtanen et al. 2005).

Platform Cooperativism

Platform cooperativism opposes platform capitalism by putting the algorithmic design of apps such as Uber in the service of a cooperative business model premised on communal ownership, democratic governance, sustainability and equitable distribution of value (Scholz 2016; Scholz & Schneider 2016; Zhu & Marjanovic 2021). Platform cooperatives cover a broad range of economic sectors (including e-commerce, cleaning services, culture, finance, software development, transportation) and take various forms, such as cooperatively owned online labour brokerages and market places (e.g. Loconomics, Fairmondo), city-owned platforms (e.g. Fairbnb), producer-owned platforms (e.g. Stocksy, Resonate), union-backed labour platforms (e.g. National Domestic Workers Alliance), data co-ops (e.g. MIDATA) and protocolary co-ops enabling peer-to-peer interaction (e.g. Backfeed, La'Zooz).[1]

Platform cooperatives follow in the footsteps of traditional cooperatives to encounter a number of obstacles going forward, such as scaling, competition, democratic governance, financing, regulation, education, member involvement and identity (Nabben et al. 2021). The literature has documented a plethora of shortcomings for traditional cooperatives, such as mismanagement, financial scandals, democratic failure, the lack of transparency and accountability, low member involvement and free-riding (Birchall 2017; De Lautour & Cortese 2016; Malta et al. 2020; Mohamad, Othman & Mohamed 2013; Puri & Walsh 2018; Simon 2019). Traditional cooperatives often assimilate the structure of capitalist companies in order to survive the competition. Either way, they eventually risk being co-opted by corporations (Papadimitropoulos 2020; Restakis 2010).

Similarly, platform co-ops cannot compete with commercial platforms in terms of capital, resources, skills, power, and so on (Philipp et al. 2021; Scholz 2016). They lack the funds necessary to build platforms to the same standards as commercial platforms, thus not meeting consumer expectations in terms of user experience. Funding in the start-up sector stems largely from venture capital, which requires investor control and large future returns. Platform co-ops do not operate on a purely profit-driven business model, and so have difficulty in raising venture capital and embarking on R&D on their own, which is detrimental to their capacity to innovate and produce new lines of products and services (Frenken 2017: 12). Platform co-ops cannot follow the growth strategies of incumbents and build the network effects necessary to fuel market penetration and consolidation. To survive the competition, just as traditional co-ops, platform co-ops succumb to commercialisation and market alienation.

New funding mechanisms (crowdfunding, cooperative banks and credit unions, Blockchain-based tokenomics, alternative currencies) and locally focused commissioning from the public sector could provide vital revenue to platform co-ops (McCann & Yazici 2018: 4). Increased funding would then translate into improved value propositions that could attract more platform users. Platform co-ops need to serve a specific need better than competing platforms, while embodying a concrete set of values for specific consumer categories. Regulation and adequate taxation would be a step further for platform co-ops to gain traction.

To scale up, platform co-ops need to accommodate a wider range of member identities and stakeholder interests, the divergence of which produces conflicts and ideological oppositions (Frenken 2017: 12). Blockchain could address problems of trust and coordination inherent in decentralised decision-making. It may foster transparency and accountability as well as facilitate self-management and the equitable distribution of value (Pazaitis, De Filippi & Kostakis 2017; Rozas et al. 2021). It might enable trust creation and provide automatic and secure coordination of network interactions via open decision-making processes co-administered by smart contracts (Fuster Morell et al. 2017: 60). Blockchain-based funding and governance tools may help platform co-ops scale up into a federated ecosystem of open cooperatives and distributed autonomous organisations. These solutions will be analysed in detail in the course of this book.

Cosmo-Local Commons

The DG-ML model

Vasilis Kostakis and Michel Bauwens (2014) seek to infuse traditional and platform cooperatives with the principles of the commons. They attempt to bridge Ostrom's local commons with Benkler's global (digital) commons under the Design Global-Manufacture Local (DG-ML) model (Bauwens, Kostakis & Pazaitis 2019; Kostakis et al. 2015; Kostakis & Bauwens 2014), which is part of the degrowth movement (Kallis et al. 2018), which advocates a radical political and socio-economic reorganisation based on the reduction of resource and energy use.

The DG-ML model (or cosmo-localism) has been enabled today by the conjunction of ICTs with desktop manufacturing technologies (such as three-dimensional printing and computer numerical machines). Open-sourced code connects design and manufacturing via the Internet and 3D printers. The DG-ML model follows the logic that what is not scarce becomes global (e.g. digital commons of knowledge, design, software), and what is scarce (e.g. natural resources/hardware) is local. Global (digital) commons connect to local commons via transition towns, decentralised communities and fab labs/makerspaces operating on free/open-source software/hardware and powered by renewable energy systems distributed through microgrids on Blockchain and the Internet of Things (Rifkin 2014).

The DG-ML model introduces an on-demand distributed mode of production that connects knowledge and manufacturing cosmo-locally. As such, it differs from mass production in scale, location, operation and consumer–producer relationship. It lowers production costs (no patent costs, no transportation and maintenance costs, no planned obsolescence); it democratises production by unleashing bottom-up value creation, collaboration and eco-techno-social innovation; it blurs production and consumption, thus empowering prosumers; it equitably distributes value to community members; it has the potential to enhance gender balance and non-discriminatory practices via customisation and open access; and it contributes to a sustainable and resilient society and economy (Kostakis et al. 2015: 126). The literature has documented thus far several case studies in the sectors of agriculture, manufacturing and biotechnology, such as AbilityMate, Wikihouse, RepRap, Osvehicle, Farm Hack, Open-Source Ecology, L'Atelier Paysan, Bionics (Kostakis et al. 2015; Giotitsas & Ramos 2017; Papadimitropoulos 2017). Farm Hack, L'Atelier Paysan and P2P Lab, for example, bring together farmers, engineers, roboticists, designers, architects, fabricators, tinkerers, programmers and hackers in order to build and modify tools and machinery with the aim of moving towards sustainable farming. The design of tools and machinery is open-sourced globally for agricultural communities to customise and experiment locally.

Open Cooperativism

The DG-ML model integrates into the model of open cooperativism between the commons and ethical market entities. Open cooperativism aims at the creation of a collaborative economy based on shared resources from which actors can draw and contribute according to their needs and capacities. Open cooperativism is backed by a partner state through taxation, funding, regulation, education, law reforms, and so forth. Some cases of currently existing open cooperatives include Sensorica and Enspiral, which provide hardware and software services respectively based on a commons ecosystem (Bauwens & Niaros 2017a; Bauwens & Pantazis 2018; Pazaitis 2020). Research has identified a three-zoned model of open cooperativism for the core design of a commons-based cosmo-local market interface (Bauwens & Niaros 2017a; De Filippi et al. 2013; Freund & Stanko 2018; Giotitsas & Ramos 2017; Kostakis & Bauwens 2014).

1. The productive commons (PC): the productive community of all members, users and contributors who produce the commons, either for payment or as volunteers. Apart from salaries, contributions can also be valued in Blockchain-issued tokens,[2] which can be exchanged or variously redeemed in the commons network, both offline and online.
2. The entrepreneurial commons (EC): the commercial interface of the productive community of the commons with ethical market entities that transact with or add value to the commons. Ethical market entities do not seek to maximise profits without sufficiently reinvesting surplus in the maintenance of the productive communities (Figure 2.3). They integrate values such as sustainability, knowledge sharing, mutualisation of infrastructure and a more inclusive distribution of value (Bauwens & Niaros 2017a: 21). Profit is not central but peripheral to the social and environmental goals of the community. The EC receives goods and services from the PC to sell in the market and gives funds raised from selling goods and services or from investments to the for-benefit commons in the form of EC tokens.

Productive community	Linux	Mozilla	GNU	Wikipedia	WordPress
Entrepreneurial coalition	e.g. Linux Professional Institute, Canonical	e.g. Mozilla Corporation	e.g. Red Hat, Endless, SUSE	e.g. Wikia company	e.g. Automattic company
For-benefit association	Linux Foundation	Mozilla Foundation	Free Software Foundation	Wikimedia Foundation	WordPress Foundation

Figure 2.3 The Three Institutions that Shape the Model of Open Cooperativism

Source: Bauwens et al. 2017: 13; figure used with permission.

3. The for-benefit commons (FC): the governance infrastructure that sets consensus rules and incentives for both the PC and the EC. The FC fund-raises and sets the exchange rules for the EC and PC tokens within the commons and externally to other ecosystem tokens and fiat, sets the ownership/membership and sharing rules for the commons, defines and enforces reputation, sets collaboration and exchange rules with internal and external entities, acts as the interface to not-for-benefit entities, protects the commons through licences and manages conflicts (Bauwens, Kostakis & Pazaitis 2019: 15). For example, the Wikimedia Foundation collects the funds to support the server space without which access to Wikipedia would become impossible.

The three-zoned model of open cooperativism aims to secure network autonomy and value sovereignty by means of:

1. open protocols and open supply chains that feed into a circular economy designed to eliminate waste;
2. open-value accounting that seeks to equitably distribute value among multiple stakeholders on the basis of tokenised contributions; and
3. value/asset reciprocity between ethical market entities and open cooperatives established via copyfair licensing. (Copyfair licensing differs from copyleft and Creative Commons licensing, in that it requires reciprocity in terms of capital in exchange for the commons.)

Open cooperatives internalise negative externalities, adopt multi-stakeholder governance models, contribute to the creation of material and immaterial commons and are orientated towards a global socio-economic and political transformation, albeit locally based. Ultimately, open cooperativism aims at the creation of a commons-based cosmo-local economy.

However, open cooperatives are still limited in number, occupying small niches in the economy. Blockchain crypto-economics has the potential to widen the scope of the three-zoned model of open cooperativism by allowing for open cooperatives to scale via diverse and hybrid governance models driven by algorithmic design (Fritsch et al. 2021; Rozas et al. 2021). Yet open cooperatives and Blockchain technology are still in their infancy. It is early to estimate if and to what degree they can merge into a broader collaborative economy. These are still hypotheses needing to be tested empirically, before they crystallise into a sustainable socio-economic model.

Platform Socialism

Platform socialism (Muldoon 2022) ranges from strong versions of the state, applying central planning of the (digital) economy, to softer versions of the state, operating as a coordinating mechanism bootstrapping hybrid post-capitalist models of production. Whereas stronger versions of the state favour top-down management of the economy (Dean 2009, 2012; Lenin 1961; Žižek 2008, 2010), softer versions of the state champion the bottom-up self-management of society enabled by the gradual commonification of the state (Cole 2011 [1920]; Dyer-Witheford 2006, 2015; Fuchs 2008, 2011; Kostakis & Bauwens 2014; Wright 2009). Although both versions share the communist goal of the socialisation of the means of production by distributing power to workers, they put forward opposing means in achieving that goal. Central planning is incompatible with decentralised grassroots self-organisation. The realisation of open cooperativism seems more plausible under a softer version of the state, conceived as the enabler of a commons-oriented post-capitalist transition fostered by a variety of policies, such as (Papadimitropoulos 2020):

- multi-stakeholder governance of digital platforms;
- stronger regulation and taxation of platform capitalism;
- transvestment from platform capitalism to open cooperativism;
- participatory planning via concentric models of democracy (representative, associational, direct), expanding from the local to the national and trans-national levels;
- the transformation of intellectual property by limiting its scope and broadening the 'fair use' concept;
- the establishment of a digital rights framework for e-citizens (the right to encryption, the right to computation, the right to an algorithmic opt-out and opt-in);
- the municipal funding of neutral broadband networks, state funding of basic research, and possible strategic regulatory interventions to negate monopoly control over essential resources in the digital environment; free and open-source software could become the default infrastructure in public administration and education;
- the establishment of a public data commons: a digital commonwealth; and
- an alternative Internet, which would contribute to the commons transition through the peer production of open-access projects, open-content projects, free software, open-source projects, alternative online news media, collective digital art projects, cyberprotest, public online media, public access projects, the struggle for net neutrality, the creation of free wireless networks, non-commercial and non-profit virtual communities, and so on.

In this regard, state power would be reduced to a coordinating agency. The main bearer of social change would be a collective subject dissolving across a post-hegemonic chain of equivalence uniting diverse initiatives under the commons principles. By 'collective subject', I mean a set of practices, objectives, discourses and identities that embody the commons principles and apply them across the whole body of society (Kioupkiolis forthcoming). Rather than relying on a central point of convergence being the party, post-hegemony adopts a multidimensional strategy employing macro, meso and micro socio-economics to disperse power into multiple nodes of convergence, which form a chain of equivalence between diverse initiatives and the commons principles represented by a collective subject (Laclau & Mouffe 1985; Kioupkiolis 2019). Holistic coordination meets with pluralism under a networked federation of multi-layered, multi-level prefigurative politics, which transgresses civil society, the economy and the state to form a counter-hegemonic ethics capable of transforming capitalism into the post-capitalism of the commons. This reversed bureaucracy of guild socialism and council democracy would gradually dissolve into the spontaneity of the commons.

The Political Economy of the Commons

Hess and Ostrom (2007) have offered a typology of property that helps situate the commons across the political economy spectrum (Table 2.1). In neoclassical economics, scarcity produces rivalry and exclusion. A good is scarce and, thus, rivalrous if its use by one person subtracts from the total available, thereby excluding others. Goods can be classified in three types: private, public and common goods. Private goods are marked by high rivalry and exclusion. An apple or book cannot be used by two people simultaneously. Property is a legal form of exclusion that renders a good private. Private property is conditioned on contracts, money and the law of supply and demand.

Public goods, on the other hand, exhibit low rivalry and exclusion. All citizens can make use of public education, national defence, parks and highways simultaneously. Some common goods, sometimes also referred to as public goods, can be excludable and rivalrous, while others can be non-excludable and non-rivalrous (Benkler 2006; Kostakis & Bauwens 2014; Ostrom 1990). Grazing lands, fisheries and water can be rivalrous and occasionally excludable.

Table 2.1 Typology of Property

Rivalry			
		High	*Low*
Exclusion	High	Private goods (scarce resources)	Club goods (cinemas, private parks, satellite TV), intellectual property (knowledge, language, software)
	Low	Common-pool resources (forests, irrigation fields, groundwater basins, fisheries, forests, etc.)	Public/common goods (defence, highways, parks, airwaves, knowledge, language, culture, free software, etc.)

Source: Adapted from Hess and Ostrom (2007).

Table 2.2 Moral Economies

Capital, government, civil society			
Goods	Commodities	Public goods	Gifts
Arenas	Markets	Polities	Networks
Payments	Prices	Taxes	Reciprocities
Relations	Personal possessions	Shared access	Co-creation
Identities	Consumers	Citizens	Communards
Ethos	Individual liberty	Equality	Mutuality

Source: Adapted from Murdock (2013).

But nobody can be excluded from walking over a mountain, swimming in the sea or breathing the air. Information, language and knowledge – when not 'enclosed' by intellectual property rights – are both non-rivalrous and anti-rivalrous. The cost of reproducing an additional unit of an e-book or software is near to zero, while their use by more people increases its value.

Public and common goods often blur. The criterion for identifying them is their type of governance. Whereas the former are managed by state governance, the latter are self-managed by communities (Quilligan 2012). We can thus distinguish between two main types of common goods: material/rivalrous (natural resources) and immaterial/non-rivalrous/anti-rivalrous (language, information, knowledge, culture).

Murdock (2013) identifies three moral economies: capitalism, government and civil society (Table 2.2). Capitalism seeks to maximise utility and individual freedom through entrepreneurship, commerce and consumerism. Government regulates capitalism and prevents market failures through the provision of public goods such as public libraries, public parks, public museums and galleries, public service broadcasting, highways and defence. Civil society consists in the myriad amateur cultural and communicative associations self-governed by volunteers on the basis of community and mutuality. The commons identify with the gift economy operating at the intersection of civil society, government and capitalism. Murdock (2013: 157) holds that the potential of a communicative commons represented by the government and civil society is continually compromised by commercial enclosure.

In general, markets are decentralised and non-hierarchical and can scale effortlessly (Emmett 2019a). Yet they are profit-driven, they produce negative externalities and they are often captured by monopolies. States are effective in applying international, large-scale policies. Yet they are hierarchical, centralised and prone to corruption. The commons are community-driven, grassroots and multidimensional in value production. Yet they are difficult to sustain and scale (Table 2.3). Different political economies reformulate the structural relations of the commons with the state and the market differently. Next we discern the differences between neoclassical economics and commons economics.

Table 2.3 The Pros and Cons of Markets, States and the Commons

Pros/cons		
Markets	Efficient, with natural selection through competition Decentralised, non-hierarchical Scale effortlessly	Profit-driven One-dimensional economic models leading to negative externalities Risks of monopolies
States	Able to implement large-scale, targeted incentives (e.g. social and environmental protection Continuously funded organisation	Inefficient (budget bloat) Loopholes in imposed regulation Centralised, hierarchy, information asymmetry (top-down decision-making structure)
Commons	Able to implement community determined incentives to address externalities Emergent, grassroots Multidimensional value optimisation	Hard to set up (multi-stakeholder) Difficult to scale (needs digital infrastructure beyond *c.* 150 people) Lack of sustainable business models

Source: Adapted from Emmett (2019a).

Neoclassical versus Commons Economics

Economics can be classified into orthodox and heterodox economics, or mainstream and non-mainstream. Very schematically, mainstream economics ranges from classical to neoclassical and Austrian economics, whereas non-mainstream economics ranges from Marxist and Keynesian to post-Marxist, post-Keynesian, institutional, neo-institutional, evolutionary and ecological economics (Shaikh 2016). Both branches often intersect variously with behavioural economics, rational choice theory and game theory.

Neoclassical economics is the dominant school of economics today, espousing a type of market fundamentalism grounded on methodological individualism, the utility maximisation principle and relevant supply and demand equilibria. Contrary to classical economics, which considers the cost of production the most important factor determining the price of a product or service, neoclassical economics brings to the fore the consumer's utility as the driving factor of prices.

One of the basic differences between mainstream and non-mainstream economics – and between different non-mainstream economics themselves – lies in the degree of state intervention in the economy. Neoclassical economics sustains the ideological bedrock of neoliberalism, which is a governmental reason that seeks to expand the corporate model into state management (Brown 2015). Commons economics, on the other, seeks to commonify the state towards grassroots self-organisation. In the following

I highlight the advantages of commons economics vis-à-vis mainstream economics.

1. Economics is about the allocation of scarce resources for the purpose of maximising social welfare, which is the mere aggregate of individual preferences. The basic motive of behaviour is self-interest. Each individual aims to maximise utility, which is the pleasure deriving from satisfying one's own preferences (Marshall 2013 [1890]). Markets help match scarce resources with individual preferences via impersonal exchange/trading (Smith 1977 [1776]).
2. Due to scarcity, trading is a more equitable means of allocating resources and maximising social welfare than barter and the primitive gift economy. Unfettered markets are the most efficient means of allocating scarce resources to the highest-valued use, which is set by price signals voluntarily agreed upon and generated by buyers and sellers. Prices are an accurate and sufficient signal of information to allow for decentralisation to match supply and demand and generate social welfare (Hayek 1944). Ultimately, prices are the sole markers of value in the economy.
3. The unintended consequences of unrestricted trade generate social welfare, since in a voluntary exchange both individuals are better off (Smith 1977 [1776]). The more exchanges there are, the better it is for society, since more needs are being met and more individual preferences are satisfied.
4. Firms reduce transaction costs compared to markets (Coase 1937). Hierarchical management of firms and the division of labour increase specialisation, productivity and efficiency. Whereas market exchange moves existing stuff around, division of labour creates stuff, eventually maximising social welfare (Smith 1977 [1776]).
5. Collective action planned either by the state or groups misallocates resources due to the lack of information necessary to coordinate economic activity (Hayek 1944).
6. Property rights guaranteed by contracts protected by the state are necessary and sufficient for the production of knowledge. Property is justified on the grounds of individual labour (Locke 1960 [1690]).
7. Competition is hard-wired in the human species (Hayek 1944).
8. The role of the state is to regulate the economy, reduce transaction costs and promote competition. The state should intervene in the economy only on conditions of market failure (Hayek 1944).
9. Finance performs a number of essential functions for the economy: it allocates capital by recycling surpluses across the globe from surplus countries to deficit countries, in the form of investment and credit; it intermediates between savers and investors, providing credit to individuals and companies; it promotes innovation and job creation; it manages risk; it provides liquidity; and it runs the payment mechanism (Stiglitz 2016: 40). Finance adds value to the real economy by completing markets, thereby propelling the Arrow–Debreu (1954) general equilibrium momentum: if only all

different agents create as many contracts as possible, complete all markets and trade continually between themselves, the economy will reach the Pareto-efficient maximum possibility of human welfare. (Pareto efficiency is similar to a Nash equilibrium, in which all actors benefit – or, at least, are no worse off – from an economic state of affairs.)

10. Capitalism is considered a peaceful economic system that encapsulates the liberal ideal of self-regulating markets, operating as sites of voluntary exchange based on free trade and property rights, designed to foster technological progress and raise labour productivity to satisfy the wants and needs of all (Mazzucato 2018: 63). An ideal capitalism is supposed to produce multiple equilibria, allocating scarce resources under the conditions of perfect competition and information fully accessible to all (Mazzucato 2018: 63–64). The democracy of the market thus comes to represent an ethical pluralism that flourishes in conditions of freedom of choice, tolerance and the rule of law.

Neoclassical economics acknowledges that markets fail under various circumstances. Monopolies, information asymmetries between consumers and producers, externalities not reflected in market prices and the provision of public goods are all instances of market failure (Jacobs and Mazzucato 2016: 16). Governments should intervene and seek to 'correct' market failures, when appropriate, by promoting competition, requiring more available information for consumers, forcing firms to pay for externalities and providing or subsidising public goods. Governments should limit themselves to a minimum regulatory framework of employment, low taxation and consumer and environmental protection. Excessive regulation is considered to slow economic activity to a crawl and precipitously reduce government revenues, eventually 'killing the goose that lays the golden eggs'.

Commons Economics

Non-mainstream economics such as post-Keynesian and leftist economics argue for more radical state intervention in the economy (Papadimitropoulos 2020). However, to tackle the structural contradictions of capitalism that produce immense inequalities and destroy the planet, the commons seek to alter the mode of capitalist production from within the economy. The commons push state-centred democratic rebalances of the capitalist economy towards a post-capitalist commons-oriented transition geared by the self-management of economy and society as a whole. Commons-based economics are anchored on the following premises (Table 2.4).

1. Contrary to neoclassical economics' assumption that collective action is not feasible without clearly specified property rights, Ostrom's work (1990) on local commons has proved that collective action is feasible even among multiple stakeholders (the state, private institutions, individuals, communities) having an interest in self-managing a common-pool resource, be it

Table 2.4 Neoclassical versus Commons-Based Economics

Neoclassical economics	*Commons-based economics*
Self-interest	Diversity of motivations: self-interest, altruism, affect, care, solidarity
Competition (zero-sum game) for scarce resources	Cooperation (win-win game)
Centralised hierarchical top-down management	Decentralised democratic bottom-up self-management
Planned obsolescence; market value created from (artificial) scarcity	Natural abundance; sharing; market value created from scarce resources adding value on top of the abundance of the commons
Imperfect market price signals, overproduction, negative externalities, waste, unsustainability	Open supply chains, mutual coordination by stigmergic collaboration > greater coordination between supply and demand > circular economy, internalisation of negative externalities, sustainability
Centralised research, development and innovation	Decentralised open knowledge and design > optimum participation through modularity and granularity, commons-based eco-techno-social innovation
Intellectual property rights	Copyfair licences and Blockchain-based smart contracts that seek to secure the commons against capitalist co-optation
Information asymmetry, privacy	Holoptism, transparency, open access
Capitalist division of labour > alienation of labour, precariousness, intensification of labour, performance pressure, stress	Open voluntary allocation, equipotentiality = participation conditioned a posteriori by the process of production itself, whereby skills are verified and communally validated in real time > peer-to-peer accountability, creativity, self-realisation
Unjust capitalist co-optation of surplus value through salaries; network effects (Internet) > positive externalities > value crisis > rent seeking, surveillance capitalism > enclosure of the digital commons > capitalist free-riding > the tragedy of the commons	Open value accounting in which incomes are distributed according to one's contribution > tokenisation of 'free labour' (positive externalities) of the general/cognitive/affective intellect across the (digital) commons value chain > fair material and immaterial value flow that recognises reputation, care, affect and reproduction > the comedy of the commons
Profit maximisation among limited shareholders	Equitable distribution of value among multiple stakeholders
Finance and credit	Community transaction mechanisms, such as internal lending, smart contracts, participatory budgeting, common liquidity funds, resource pooling, microfunding, augmented bonding curves
Regulatory state, minimum state, capitalist state, social democratic state	Commons-centric partner state

a river, a pasture, an isolated building, a community garden, or whatever. Ostrom's polycentrism model is today alive and kicking in various multi-stakeholder public/private/common partnerships, as evidenced in rural and urban commons flourishing in Belgium, France, Quebec, Italy, the Netherlands, Switzerland, Japan, and so on.

2. Information comes to challenge scarcity, since it creates an abundance of value owing to its unique characteristics: (a) it is not 'used up'; (b) it can be reproduced infinitely at zero marginal cost. An agent who transmits information can still keep and consume the same information, granting a very low opportunity cost compared to the utility transferred to the receiver. Therefore, given the limits of saturation effects, a great number of agents can consume the same information simultaneously (Brousseau & Curien 2007). The difference between the public goods of information and knowledge and the commons supported by the Internet and open-source software is that the former are managed by the state while the latter are self-managed by communities and peer-to-peer networks. The digital commons expand state-managed public goods into self-managed cyber-physical common goods.
3. Intellectual property rights aim to tackle the contradiction between the abundance of information and the creation of a market for information by creating an artificial scarcity of information. But they eventually lead to the underutilisation of information and the inefficient use of knowledge, with detrimental effects to social welfare (Arrow 1950, 1962).
4. Kostakis and Bauwens' (2014) model of cosmo-localism seeks to tackle the contradiction between scarcity and abundance by means of the digital commons, which build upon scarcity (hardware, resources, infrastructures, capital) to create an abundance of information with respect to which everybody can contribute and draw according to their needs and capacities. The global (digital) commons connect to local rural and urban commons, social enterprises, Blockchain-based platforms and open cooperatives via desktop manufacturing technologies such as 3D printing and computer numerical machines. Glocal commons set up a new socio-economic paradigm that democratises the economy by granting the ownership and management of the means of production to people themselves, assuming people are provided the necessary education to engage in grassroots techno-social innovation (Bauwens, Kostakis & Pazaitis 2019). Blockchain-based funding and governance tools have the potential to further support a post-capitalist commons-oriented transition (Rozas et al. 2021; Fritsch et al. 2021).
5. The digital commons of open knowledge, software/hardware and design promote self-organisation through stigmergy, equipotentiality, holoptism and modularity (Bauwens, Kostakis & Pazaitis 2019). Stigmergy is a form of indirect coordination whereby participants match their skills with the needs of the system, following up on traces left by other participants. Equipotentiality offers equal opportunities for everyone to participate according to their skills. Participation is conditioned a posteriori by the

process of production itself, wherein skills are verified and communally validated in real time. Holoptism grants access to all information necessary irrespective of participants' positional power, thereby limiting information and power asymmetries. Modularity is the degree to which a project can be broken down into smaller components that can be independently and asynchronously produced and recombined (e.g. Wikipedia, Linux). The higher the degree of modularity, the bigger the autonomy and flexibility of peer production.

6. Glocal commons prevent free-riding and the overuse or underuse of common-pool resources by self-monitoring mechanisms reinforced both online and offline: platform moderation and meta-moderation (e.g. Slashdot), technical solutions embedded in the platform (e.g. Slashdot, the NASA Clickworkers project, Kuro5hin); norm-based social organisation (e.g. Ostrom's limited-access commons, Wikipedia, Kuro5hin) (Benkler 2006; Ostrom 1990); and algorithmic mechanism design (e.g. the Commons Stack) (Rozas et al. 2021; Fritsch et al. 2021).
7. Prices, contracts and strict property rights are lossy, sticky and costly (Benkler 2006). The information and allocation gains of glocal commons translate into better, fairer and more sustainable socio-economic outcomes in comparison to price signals and managerial hierarchies. Self-organisation, decentralisation, transparency and sharing supported by open-source code, open supply chains and open-book accounting promote inclusion, distribute value, reduce waste and sustain a circular economy (Bauwens, Kostakis & Pazaitis 2019). Blockchain-based funding and governance tools may align individual economic incentives with the collective production and stewardship of public/common goods. Computer-aided tools introduced by the Commons Stack, such as the augmented bonding curve and conviction voting, can provide liquidity and stewardship of the commons all the while tempering speculation (Fritsch et al. 2021).
8. Competition is not a zero-sum game between rivals but a win-win game between peer producers collaborating on symmetric terms. Rationality does not always translate into self-interest, since humans often rationally pursue non-self-interested goals. Cooperation rather than competition is the evolutionary drive of human species' survival (Bowles & Gintis 2011).
9. Neoclassical economics conceives an ideal form of capitalism that bears little resemblance to capitalism per se. If private property is the product of individual labour, then a large chunk of profit derives historically from the exploited labour of slavery, serfdom and modern wage slavery (Marx 1993 [1858]). Capital has accumulated historically via the raw power of unequal exchange (rents), occasionally reinforced with colonialism, wars, monopolies, oligopolies and cartels, all supported by the entire banking, financial and state–military complex. In short, capitalism has been by and large the product of power, thiefdom and violence, supported by liberalism, which, for some, is the political legitimisation of capitalism. The commons come to address the injustices of capitalism and liberalism by introducing

a post-liberal, post-capitalist ethical economy operating on the basis of affection, solidarity, cooperation and care.

10. In a post-capitalist commons-oriented transition, the state transforms into commons-centric partner states that implement direct democratic procedures to diffuse rather than concentrate power and nurture social transformation from the bottom up rather than engineer it from the top down (Kostakis & Bauwens 2014).

The Political Theory of the Commons

The commons are bound with diverse, entangled and contradictory interpretations. To begin with, the term 'commons' functions as a marketing buzzword for platform capitalism to refer to corporate communities, the so-called sharing economy, the free and open-source movement, consumer tribes, the collaborative economy, flat corporate hierarchies and Blockchain-based crypto-libertarian communities. In short, private ventures are presented as 'commons'.

On the flipside, the commons resonate with a socialist narrative that champions the centrality of the state and the party in the alleged teleological transition to communism (Kioupkiolis 2019). Whereas the commons share with socialism the values of common ownership, egalitarianism and collective self-government, they are at odds with central planning, which has been historically identified with totalitarian control, authoritarianism, violence, terror and the idolatry of leaders.

The commons share with neoliberalism the moral values of maximum freedom and autonomy for the individual, but they part ways with state capitalism in several respects: decentralisation, openness, sharing, community, self-management and the equitable distribution of value. The commons represent multiple versions of the commonification of state capitalism, wherein parties and managers are substituted by 'vanishing mediators' who enlarge the scope for collective self-activity, all the while becoming gradually redundant. By reformatting managerial hierarchies, property rights, contracts and prices, the commons eventually play out in a variety of formats ranging from post-capitalism and anarcho-syndicalism to spontaneous networked anarchism and Blockchain-based DAOs (Benkler 2006; Wright 2009).

Disparate but often entangled strands of thought advocate for a post-capitalist transition driven by commons-based cosmo-local platform and open cooperatives, often merged into cyber-physical DAOs supported by FLOSS, the digital commons and Blockchain technology. Eventually, the discussion on the commons boils down to three basic discourses: liberal (Benkler 2006; Murdock 2013; Lessig 2001; Ostrom 1990); reformist (Bollier & Helfrich 2019; Arvidsson & Peitersen 2013; Kostakis & Bauwens 2014; Rifkin 2014; Rushkoff 2016; Scholz 2016, Scholz & Schneider 2016; Wright 2009); and anti-capitalist (Caffentzis 2013; Dardot & Laval 2014; Dean 2009, 2012; De Angelis 2017;

Dyer-Witheford 1999, 2006, 2015; Federici 2012; Fuchs 2008, 2011; Gibson & Graham 1996, 2006; Hardt & Negri 2000, 2004, 2009; Harvey 2003, 2005, 2010; Kioupkiolis 2019; Laclau & Mouffe 1985; Mason 2015; Söderberg 2008; Žižek 2008, 2010). The above classification covers only the most influential authors in the literature. The three-way classification criterion corresponds to a particular position of the commons in relation to market and state operation, and is overly schematic, since arguments often intersect. This section aims to summarise the main points of the discussion here, as the three discourses have been examined in detail elsewhere (Papadimitropoulos 2020).

Liberalism

The liberals highlight the obstacles that the commons are facing with respect to state and market operation. They claim for a third institutional space through which the commons would peacefully coexist with state and market operation. Liberals often share neoliberal and libertarian viewpoints. Whereas neoliberalism assumes a central role for the state in bootstrapping capitalism and keeping its failures in check, libertarianism abstains from any central authority or adheres to a minimal state that protects the social and economic freedom of the individual to voluntarily reach mutual, consent-based agreements (Papadimitropoulos 2020). Liberals also often share reformist/post-capitalist viewpoints. At times they favour a post-capitalist commons-oriented transformation of capitalism and the state. In general, liberals oscillate between conservatism and radicalism.

Post-Capitalism

The reformists stress the need for the commons to overcome their grave dependence on capitalism and the state. They advocate for a post-capitalist commons-oriented transition driven by ICTs. Reformists often share anti-capitalist viewpoints, combined with both liberal and socialist elements that translate into relevant partner state policies. They abstain from the state centralism of left-wing parties but consider the state an essential component of social change towards the post-capitalism of the commons. They oppose capitalism but they go along with friendly capital transvested into commons-based open cooperatives.

By 'post-capitalism', reformists refer to the creation of an alternative economy not dictated by hierarchical top-down management aiming to maximise shareholder profits through the production of exchange value (Bauwens, Kostakis & Pazaitis 2019; Gibson & Graham 1996, 2006; Mason 2015). Instead, post-capitalism aims at the production of use value, the democratic self-management of production and the equitable distribution of added value among multiple stakeholders such as consumers, prosumers, workers, members and users. In this regard, the state could act as an enabler of commons-based multi-stakeholder open cooperatives. The commons literature portrays multiple variants of a commons-oriented transition, aiming at transforming state capitalism into the post-capitalism of the commons (Papadimitropoulos 2020).

Anti-Capitalism

Anti-capitalists argue for the autonomous development of the commons against capitalism and the state. They seek to transform the social relations upon which capitalism is based. They envisage the commons in terms of self-governed communities that seek to do away with profit, commodity, exchange value, competition, state and corporate power. Anti-capitalists often share anarchist, socialist and post-capitalist viewpoints. Some authors adopt a more anarchist standpoint, opposing both capitalism and the state. Others tilt towards leftist positions, espousing the central role of the state in transitioning towards communism. Others, finally, leave a space open both for ethical market entities and the state to engage in a commons-oriented post-capitalism transition.

The Contradictions of the Commons

The liberals underestimate the potential of technology to decentralise the economy and transform capitalism into post-capitalism (Papadimitropoulos 2020). They adopt a limited version of the commons that seeks to transform neither capitalism nor state operation. They reproduce, instead, the narrative of a liberal democracy intertwined with the commons.

The reformists take a stand in favour of the cooperation of the commons with the state and friendly capital. They call for transvestment from capitalism to the post-capitalism of the commons backed by partner state policies. Yet they cannot address the precariousness and unsustainability plaguing commons-based peer production (Papadimitropoulos 2020). They lack the mechanisms necessary to help peers monetise use value and gain public trust and involvement. Fragmentation and the lack of the political (Kioupkiolis 2019) further reveal the absence of a holistic coordination mechanism necessary to scale up the commons with the aim of becoming the dominant socio-economic model vis-à-vis the state–market nexus. Local, urban and cosmo-local commons often do not cooperate with each other to create a networked ecosystem of open cooperativism capable of challenging neoliberalism (Bauwens & Niaros 2017b).

The anti-capitalists, in their turn, fall prey to the heteronomy of the commons owing to the grave dependence on state and capitalist production (Papadimitropoulos 2020). Reformists and anti-capitalists alike fall short of reaching a critical mass. Finally, leftists rest on an old-fashioned version of statist socialism that needs updating to face the socio-technological challenges lying ahead.

Eventually, all approaches cannot but suffer the contradictions of the commons (Papadimitropoulos 2018). Post-capitalism often alienates commons-based peer production into risky ventures that strive to survive the competition with capitalist enterprises. As a result, the commons extrapolate the Marxian contradictions by the back door:

- commerciality versus non-commerciality
- competition versus cooperation

- private property versus common property
- use value versus exchange value
- profit versus non-profit
- holism, cosmo-localism and internationalism versus decentralisation, fragmentation, localism, atavism, traditionalism, neo-conservatism and ideology
- openness, transparency, accountability and sharing versus privacy, vested interests and gated communities
- everyday libertarianism versus commonism
- the tyranny of structurelessness (hierarchy, techno-elitism, plutocracy, elites, centralisation, benevolent dictators, backroom deals) versus grassroots democracy, transparency, equality, fairness
- technocracy, techno-determinism versus physical space and the political
- inclusion versus exclusion
- individuality versus communality
- liminality versus legality

The very term 'commons' is a contradiction in terms. There are no pure commons, since the commons variously depend on capitalism and the nation state. Thus, the commons reproduce the contradictions of capitalism and the state – that is, the power asymmetries prevalent between directors and executants, capital and labour, elites and the people.

CBPP is often initiated by a bunch of visionaries who act as 'leaders', setting up the manifesto, the roadmap and the milestones going forward. Funding, planning and staffing remains at the discretion of the 'leaders'. Volunteers join in to create a community around the projects. An initial tension, therefore, between centralisation and grassroots democracy creeps in to reveal the risk of private ventures to be presented as a 'commons'.

CBPP is often not open, as its manifesto implies (Schor 2016). Inwards, projects seek to satisfy first and foremost their members. Outwards, they do not cooperate with each other to form alliances. On the other hand, blindly opening up to all runs the risk of being subject to attack vectors and the co-optation of the commons by 'whales' (large asset holders) and capitalist enterprises. Full decentralisation may lead to conflict and disorganisation. The tyranny of structurelessness, loose organisation and the lack of transparency is often debilitating for those seeking to participate in the commons, since they may result in centralisation, hidden oligarchies, plutocracy and backroom deals (Papadimitropoulos 2018). Transparency is critical, since it allows for holoptism, stigmergy, egalitarian democracy and accountability.

CBPP faces multiple barriers: a lack of access to resources and capital; a significant gap in managerial and technical skills; sectoral and operational isolation in a number of subsectors; and a lack of public policy and institutional support, from both state and larger cooperatives (Papadimitropoulos 2020). CBPP still depends largely on financial and technological systems managed by corporate capital and neoliberal state policies (Bauwens & Kostakis 2014: 356).

CBPP has access to a limited amount of funding compared to capitalist firms, not allowing them to compensate all members and contributors adequately. People involved in the local, urban or cosmo-local commons consist basically of core team members, who are paid a salary, and volunteers, who can afford to spare their time and resources. Only core team members are usually paid a salary, with the vast majority of contributors remaining unpaid. Precariousness, therefore, is a common feature of the people involved in CBPP.

In the DAO ecosystem, the vast majority of contributors can afford the risks of engaging in an environment of fluid work, where most compensation is task-based and there is little in terms of a safety net (Ospina 2021). Web3 early adopters have enough savings to cover multiple months of expenses without any income, allowing them an enviable safety net and risk tolerance. CBPP in DAOs revolves mostly around wealthy individuals and software engineers/developers, who make up only a small portion of the people working in the overall economy outside the Blockchain.

Precariousness and the inequity in resources and compensation create conditions of unfairness and exploitation within the commons. The work of the many creates profits for the few – either the core members of the commons or corporations extracting value from the commons. Linus Torvalds, for example, has profited enormously by being the 'benevolent dictator' of the Linux open-source software, either directly through the salary being paid to him by the Linux Foundation or indirectly by the stock options he has been presented by corporations such as Red Hat and VA Linux (Lee 2021). In addition, research has shown that many open-source projects exhibit entrenched leadership and deep inequalities (Shaw & Hill 2014). In many cases, peer production entails oligarchic organisational forms.

Concerns have also been expressed regarding the sustainability of open-source software (Arp et al. 2018; Eghbal 2020). The digital commons and FLOSS are contradictions in terms: the more communist the sharing licence, the more capitalist the practice (Bauwens & Kostakis 2014). Platform capitalism transforms the use value produced by the general intellect on FLOSS and the digital commons of the Internet into exchange value in the form of rent extracted via software engineering, cloud services, advertising marketing and big data management (Srnicek 2017). In particular, cloud technology behemoths such as Amazon, Microsoft and Google tend to gradually enclose open-source software into their premises and sell it as a service, which is to the detriment of FLOSS's long-term sustainability. High-tech corporations such as Microsoft and IBM dig into the production of FLOSS for the purpose of extracting surplus value (Birkinbine 2020). They invest in FLOSS with the aim of outsourcing costs to the crowd and generating profits from enclosing the commons. Ultimately, the commons produce free surplus value for capitalism. As Nathan Schneider (2021a) puts it:

> Rather than diminishing the stature of the firm, as predicted (Benkler 2006, 2017), software peer production may be further intensifying corporate power, lowering the cost of technologies that support mass data collection and user manipulation, such as through Google's Linux-based operating systems and Linux-based server farms.

The unsustainability of CBPP prevents people from exiting capitalism and entering the commons. People need to work for capitalist firms to pay the bills and earn a living. Everyday libertarianism prevails either by necessity or by choice. Capitalism is deeply ingrained in the social imaginary, often serving as the self-fulfilling prophecy that there is no alternative (Ferraro, Pfeffer & Sutton 2005). People are socially hard-wired to behave as self-interested utility maximisers. Eventually, people behave both as *Homo oeconomicus* and as commoners: they are (self-)employed in the capitalist economy, all the while reproducing a gift economy in their working environment, families, friendships, communities, and the like (Benkler 2006).

The contradiction between openness and privacy variously reverberates across the commons. Transparency often opposes the privacy of self-sovereign identities, reflecting a contrast between collectivism and individualism (Dunn 2021). A tension also revolves around commercialising common-pool resources and keeping the open character of the commons (Fuster Morell et al. 2017: 11). Similar is the tension between transactionality and open access, tokenisation and non-tokenisation, quantification and non-quantification. Either way, the commons cannot but depend on venture commonism, crowdfunding, donations and grants to survive. They often need to prioritise their economic sustainability over openness. To the degree that the commons depend on markets, capital and the state, they may additionally have to negotiate their autonomy in exchange for funding. Cooperation is often outweighed by competition due to the skills necessary for participation in software engineering and the digital commons, which reproduces performance criteria, technocracy and techno-elitism. Competition often brings about additional stress and workload compared to capitalist firms. There is, therefore, limited time for intra-commons collaboration.

Not only does capitalism produce immense inequalities, power asymmetries, periodic crises and climate change, it is also inherently racist, since it breeds a social Darwinism in the jungle of capitalism (Balibar & Wallerstein 1991). Instead of cultural difference translating into pluralism and tolerance, it often generates conflicts of interest, censorship, racism and hatred. Everyday libertarianism and the need to survive in the jungle of capitalism often outweigh moral sentiments of solidarity, empathy and compassion. The tragedy of the commons escalates into politics, expanding prisoner dilemma cases from the local to the global level. Competition over global resources produces geopolitical tensions and wars.

The commons are not immune to the inherent immorality of capitalism. Instead of the commons uniting against capitalism, privacy often reverses backwards into gated communities, localism, traditionalism, neo-conservatism and atavism (Bauwens & Niaros 2017b; Harvey 2003: 168, 177–179). The misrepresentation of women is an instance of gender imbalance most prominent across the digital commons and open-source software (Schor 2016: 38–42; Nafus 2011).

The commons seem to follow up with the hippies and leftist movements of the 1960s, supposed to be liberating when it comes to sexual relationships. However, the commons often reproduce a neo-conservative approach. A discourse on sexuality is absent in the commons (Dyer-Witheford 2006). Sexualised language is considered sexist. Sexuality is often identified with labour, thereby reproducing the economism of patriarchic capitalism coupled with neoliberalism, which has transformed sexuality into a transaction. To recall Michel Foucault (1978), the commons follow the mainstream of the rest of society, which seems to have reduced sexuality to a discourse of tact, discretion, prudishness, insinuation and censorship, confined in the 'chat-rooms' of monogamy, pornography and prostitution.

The commons, finally, often operate in the absence of a regulatory framework on commons ownership, copyleft licences, workers' rights, and the like. The contradiction of liminality and legality is especially evident among anti-/post-capitalist versions of the commons, which seek to do away with state regulation.

The aforementioned contradictions prevent the commons from scaling into a sustainable socio-economic model. The commons cannot reach a critical mass. They occupy small niches of socio-economic activity across the global institutional landscape. The commons cannot but rely on philanthropy, state grants, donations, volunteering or venture commonism to survive.

Ostrom's local commons, FLOSS and the digital commons, platform and open cooperatives, Blockchain-based DAOs are just fragmented initiatives that cannot threaten capitalism. For the commons to resolve their contradictions and scale, they need to unite under a networked ecosystem of open cooperatives that provide their user communities a sustainable livelihood along the lines of democracy, ecology and the equitable distribution of value. In short, they need to progress into an autonomous, self-sustained socio-economic model capable of challenging neoliberalism. The Internet and Blockchain technology have the potential to scale the commons via novel tools of governance, monitoring and funding. However, technology alone cannot address the contradictions of the commons.

For the commons to establish a dominant socio-economic model vis-à-vis neoliberalism, a holistic post-hegemonic transformation of society is a *sine qua non*. Post-hegemony is the political strategy that seeks to integrate the different types of commons (local and digital) into a synergetic network of cosmo-local commons, supported by reticular market and institutional mechanisms aligned around the commons. Post-hegemony dissociates from leftist, socialist versions of hegemony (Lenin 1961) that concentrate power on the state. Rather, post-hegemony seeks to distribute power to the people via the commonification of the state and the market. By uniting different projects under a chain of equivalence, post-hegemony formulates a collective subject that incarnates the transformation of *Homo oeconomicus* into *Homo cooperans*. Proper incentive schemes, well-designed policies, financial mechanisms, law reforms, affordable housing, education and sustainability science are all part and parcel of a post-hegemonic strategy aiming to transform neoliberalism into the post-capitalism of the commons, supported by a partner state that represents the interests of the people rather than elites.

Notes

1 See https://platform.coop.

2 A token is a cryptographic derivative that represents a unit of value or asset and is defined by the community in question. Tokens can be programmed to serve different and often overlapping functions (Voshmgir 2020: 152–168). A token can simultaneously convey a voting right, an access right and ownership of a resource. A token can represent shareholder equity, a digital or physical collectible (e.g. a painting), a digital or legal identity (e.g. a national ID) or a certification or attestation by some central authority (e.g. a marriage record, birth certificate, college degree).

3 The Blockchain

The purpose of this chapter is to help the reader come to grips with Blockchain technology before going through the Commons Stack case study. The goal here is not to dive deep into technical details, since this is way beyond the scope of this book and has been done elsewhere extensively (Braun-Dubler et al. 2020; De Filippi & Wright 2018; Quiniou 2019; Schär & Berentsen 2020; Shrivastava, Le & Sharma 2020; Swan 2015). Instead, this chapter presents an extended synopsis of Blockchain's fundamentals to help us smoothly navigate through the Commons Stack case study in the next part of the book. I begin here by outlining the history of the Internet and Blockchain. I then describe from a technological standpoint the two major Blockchains thus far: Bitcoin and Ethereum. I present the different Blockchain types, the Blockchain benefits and risks. Finally, I critically reflect on the politics of Blockchain, which provides the theoretical framework necessary for illustrating the Commons Stack case study.

The History of the Internet and Blockchain

The history of Blockchain dates back to the genesis of the Internet. For the sake of our analysis here, a convenient lens through which to read the history of Internet and Blockchain technology is the polarity between decentralisation and centralisation, which produces diverse theoretical projections with regard to the use of technology per se.

The birth of the Internet originates in Paul Baran's groundbreaking invention of packet-switching technology, which allowed information to be coded into digital bits chopped into packets, which travel simultaneously via many lines across the telephone network, to be reassembled at the end of the lines by other computers (De Filippi & Wright 2018: 13). Initially, packet switching helped researchers and academics to share files and exchange resources with one another. In the late 1950s the ARPANET project, funded by the United States Department of Defense, implemented Baran's packet-switching technology to build a decentralised computer network that would eliminate the possibility of a single point of failure in the event of a nuclear attack (De Filippi & Wright 2018: 13).

DOI: 10.4324/9781003039723-3

Over the decades to come, several layers of protocols were built upon the network, such as the TCP/IP (the Transmission Control Program and Internet Protocol) and DNS (Domain Name System: IP numbers and domain names), which made it easier to identify computers on the network and ensure that information was appropriately coded and routed across the network (De Filippi & Wright 2018: 14). Further developments in cryptography, such as public–private key cryptography, digital signatures and RSA algorithms, helped computer users exchange information in a secure and authenticated manner. Steady advances in hardware, such as semiconductors and optical networking, eventually paved the way for the gradual commercialisation of the Internet.

The public Internet was launched in the 1980s by private Internet service providers (ISPs) operating on the client–server model (De Filippi & Wright 2018: 17). Companies came to own servers (computers) that hosted websites and provided applications, which Internet users could access and use as clients. The client–server model initiated the first stage (Web 1.0) of the World Wide Web evolution in which content was served from the server's file system into read-only static pages. The content was created by a small number of people for the rest of the customers. By the mid-1990s new protocols, such as SMTP (Simple Mail Transfer Protocol) and FTP (File Transfer Protocol), combined with already existing protocols such as HTML (HyperText Markup Language) and HTTP (HyperText Transfer Protocol) to set up the second stage (Web 2.0) of the World Wide Web, featuring user-generated content, usability and interoperability. Applications could now be used to read and write simultaneously. Users could interact with one another, sending emails, transferring files and creating websites linking to other websites. Web 2.0 allowed for podcasting, blogging, tagging, curating with RSS, social bookmarking, social networking, social media and web content voting.

The Internet is actually a design philosophy expressed in a set of protocols. A protocol is an agreed-upon set of rules used to communicate information between machines. The protocols that enabled the creation of both Web 1.0 and Web 2.0 are open standards that make for the core structure of the Internet (Table 3.1). The open design philosophy of the Internet locates intelligence at the ends of the network rather than at the centre, reflecting the end-to-end principle's aim of sustaining a decentralised Internet communication devoid of central control (Lessig 2001: 39, 86–89). The open technical specifications in

Table 3.1 TCP/IP Stack

TCP/IP network protocol layers	
Application layer	HTTP, SMTP, FTP (data packets)
Transport layer	TCP, UDP (data segments)
Internet layer	IP (datagrams)
Link layer	WiFi, Ethernet, LAN, WAN (data frames)
Physical layer	Bits (bit rate)

the network layer of the underlying protocols of the Internet are also referred to as being 'permissionless', in the sense that anyone is free to read, write and share digital information across interactive links without needing to seek permission from a central authority or gatekeeper, whereas previously people were limited to local intranets on private networks (Nabben & Zargham 2021).

Yet TCP/IP, SMTP and HTTP regulate the transmission of data, not how data is stored. Data can be stored centrally or decentrally. Centralisation became the mainstream form of data storage and management by states, banks and universities (Voshmgir 2020: 27–28). The commercialisation of the Internet followed the initial path of institutional centralisation. Web2 platforms such as Google, Amazon and Facebook have used advertising to profit from the 'free' services they provide. Targeted advertising is based on user behaviour and the commodification of private data. Users are paying for services with their private data. Wealth has been mostly accumulated by the companies offering the services, and not by the users contributing content and value to their services. As a result, recent decades have experienced an enormous concentration of wealth and power around Web2 platforms:

> Although the original design of the Internet sought to decentralise power and encourage freedom of communication – even at the expense of spam, fraud, and crime – over the past decade, it has become increasingly concentrated and regulated. The emergence of mobile phones, app stores, and cloud computing platforms has led to the establishment of a more centralised network, dominated by a handful of corporations that control the flow of information and economic transactions ... Currently, most online services generally either act as an intermediary or rely on other intermediaries – such as large cloud-computing providers, search engines, payment processors, domain name registrars, and social networks – to support their services. These intermediaries have the power to impose and enforce laws and their own rules, and to the extent that they are easily identifiable and located in a particular jurisdiction, they also serve as central points of control for regulatory authorities.
>
> (De Filippi & Wright 2018: 6–7)

Some authors even make the case for the emergence of surveillance capitalism, as evidenced in the cases of the United States, Russia and China, with states 'partnering' with corporations to 'trespass' private data in the name of security (Zuboff 2019). Centralisation not only raises political issues of power, democracy, security, trust, privacy and control of personal data but also produces inefficiencies in governance and the supply chain of goods and services (Voshmgir 2020: 27).

Against the mainstream current of centralisation, users have begun applying the end-to-end principle of the Internet in recent decades to transmit information from computer to computer by establishing decentralised peer-to-peer networks that do not rely on centralised servers. Napster, Gnutella, BitTorrent,

Bitcoin and hundreds more peer-to-peer applications have flooded the web, allowing Internet users to freely exchange documents, music and videos without intermediaries (De Filippi & Wright 2018: 17–18).

Bitcoin

Open-source software, cryptography and peer-to-peer networks inspired a number of anarcho-capitalist gurus known as 'cypherpunks' to envisage the creation of decentralised digital currencies and new monetary systems as tools for empowering individuals against the central powers of states and corporations (De Filippi & Wright 2018: 18–20; Nabben 2021a). A major obstacle towards realising that vision was the 'double spending' problem. Since digital cash would be just a series of bits stored in one or more computers, it could be endlessly copied and reproduced, like any other bit of information. Anyone in the possession of a unit of digital cash could make two or more online payments simultaneously. Given the absence of a fixed amount of digital currency in circulation to be issued and controlled by a trusted authority or clearing house – such as a state or a federal reserve that validates transactions and updates account balances – the 'double spending' problem would generate frauds, inflation and currency devaluation, thus wreaking havoc on the economy.

Satoshi Nakamoto (2008) has solved the 'double spending' problem by blending together market-based mechanisms, public–private key cryptography, open-source software, game theory and peer-to-peer networks to create a digital currency named 'Bitcoin'. The initial idea was to create a 'trustless', transparent, censorship-resistant, resilient, tamper-proof digital cash system that is fully peer to peer. Such a system could be run by users themselves, allowing them to send money directly to each other over the Internet without the need for a trusted third party such as a bank or government to control the system.

Proof of Work

Nakamoto created an open-source software known as the Bitcoin protocol that governs the Bitcoin Blockchain ledger, where the transactions of the Bitcoin network are processed and recorded. The software code deploys a market-based, game-theoretical consensus mechanism called 'hash-based proof of work' to validate and group together Bitcoin transactions into separate but interlinked 'blocks'. A cryptographic hash creates a digital fingerprint of the block. Each block contains the hash of the previous block linked along a time-stamped 'chain' going all the way back to the first block ever created by Nakamoto, also called the 'genesis block' (De Filippi & Wright 2018: 23–25; Voshmgir 2020: 39). This ever-growing list of chained blocks forms the Blockchain ledger (Figure 3.1).

The Blockchain is a decentralised global computer 'memory' that records entries and transactions validated by its nodes in a sequential manner. Nodes are computers running the Bitcoin software. They serve as connections to the rest

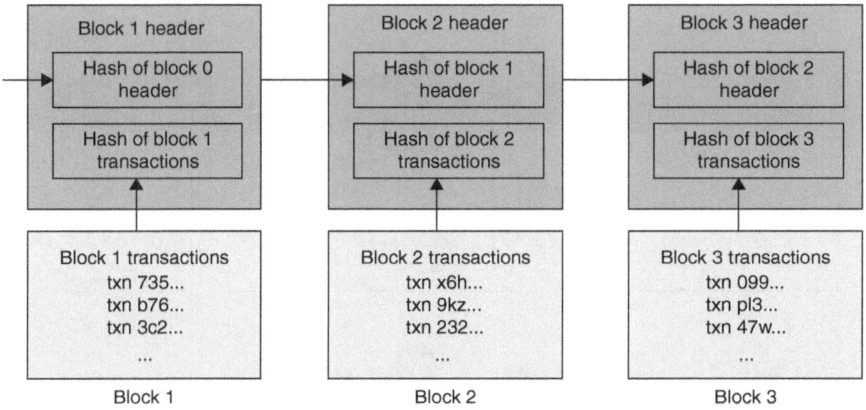

Figure 3.1 A Hash Chain

Notes: The transactions in a block are hashed to generate a fixed-length hash output, which is added to the block header. Every subsequent valid block contains the hash output of the previous block header.

Source: Agbo, Mahmoud & Eklund (2019); figure is licensed under Creative Commons BY.

of the network, sending and receiving information about Bitcoin transactions to and from other nodes. Any computer can become a node in the network and start 'mining' new blocks. There are currently 13,769 Bitcoin nodes scattered across the globe.[1] The Blockchain ledger does not reside on a single computer server. All computers in the network hold an identical copy of the ledger, which is a shared repository of information: an open, low-cost, resilient, transparent and secure storage system that nobody owns but many maintain.

The Bitcoin protocol is a set of rules that define how all nodes in the network can reach an agreement on the true state of the network (Voshmgir 2020: 40). To buy a Bitcoin and engage in a transaction, a user needs to download the open-source software and run the programme or create an account in a crypto-exchange that runs the software on behalf of users. The software employs asymmetric cryptography to allow for transparency of transactions while maintaining the privacy of all network actors (Figure 3.2). It runs one-way hash functions to encrypt information (e.g. A wants to send X bitcoins to B). A one-way hash function takes large amounts of data and converts them into a fixed-length binary sequence that is computationally difficult to reverse-engineer – that is, to generate the original data from the hash. Although it is theoretically feasible to try all possible variations to see if they produce a match, it is time-consuming and therefore expensive (Voshmgir 2020: 82).

Hashing assigns transactions with a private key that generates a public key, which, in turn, generates a public address that represents a pseudonymous digital identity of the token holder (De Filippi & Wright 2018: 37–38). The

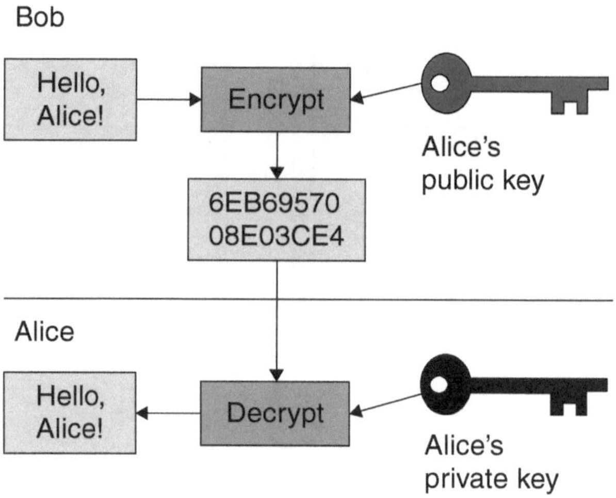

Figure 3.2 Asymmetric Cryptography

Source: Figure is in the public domain via Wikipedia: https://en.wikipedia.org/wiki/Public-key_cryptography.

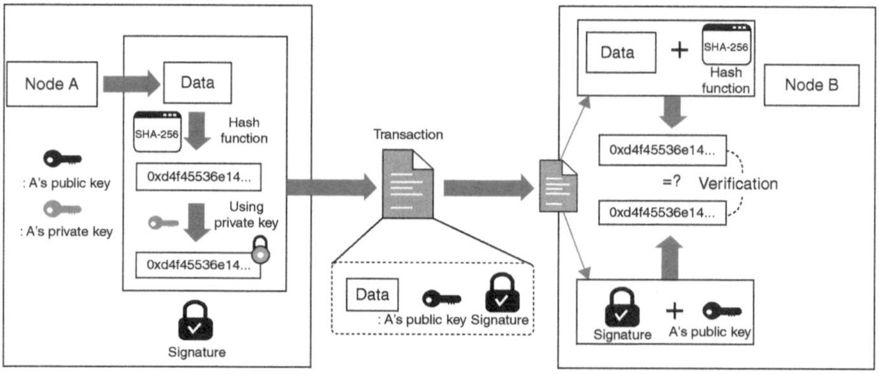

Figure 3.3 A Digital signature

Source: Kim, Kim & Huh (2019); figure is licensed under Creative Commons Attribution 4.0.

public address consists of a long string of letters and numbers visible by anyone on the network, whereas the private key is a password known only to the users engaged in the transaction. The software combines the message with the private key to generate a digital signature, which proves that the user is the owner of the bitcoins she intends to spend without exposing her real identity (Figure 3.3). A digital signature is used for the authentication of the transaction. The private key, the public key and the public address are stored in a Blockchain wallet, which communicates transactions in the Blockchain network. Thus, hashing encodes addresses and transactions stored in blocks. It verifies and validates the account balances of Blockchain wallets and secures the consensus mechanism on the Blockchains (Voshmgir 2020: 74–75).

Nodes, called 'miners', combine hashing with 'proof of work' to record transactions on the Blockchain (De Filippi & Wright 2018: 39–42). The proof of work consensus mechanism was initially developed to slow down spam email messages and denial of service (DOS) attacks (Schär & Berentsen 2020: 148). It is an artificial restriction or complication on performing computations. Its main idea is to slow down computation that can cause congestion on the network. In the case of Blockchain, if blocks are generated too quickly, it takes more time for the network to reach consensus on validating blocks. Proof of work requires that a block's hash begin with a specified number of leading zeros. To generate a valid hash with the required number of leading zeros, nodes in the network engage in a game of trial and error, often referred to as 'mining'. To incentivise nodes to start 'mining', the software rewards each node with a certain amount of bitcoin (De Filippi & Wright 2018: 25). The current block reward is 6.25 bitcoins (BTC) for packaging 1MB of transactions into a block. Additionally, if any transaction has a higher total denomination in its inputs than in its outputs, the difference goes to the miner as a 'transaction fee'. From its inception till 8 August 2022 Blockchain had 748,537 blocks containing 704,643 million bitcoin transactions that were verified, processed and confirmed on the Blockchain.[2]

Proof of work addresses also the 'Byzantine generals' problem', which illustrates the cost of ensuring trust among multiple agents that seek to agree upon a concerted strategy (Figure 3.4). Solving the Byzantine generals' problem

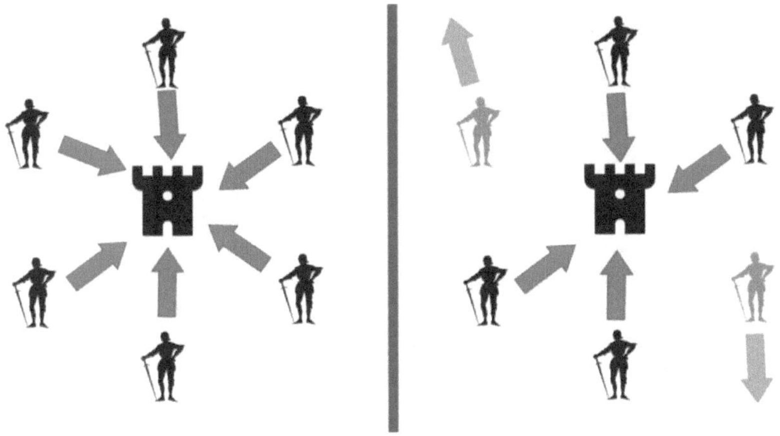

Figure 3.4 The Byzantine Generals' Problem

Source: Figure is in the public domain via Wikipedia: https://en.wikipedia.org/wiki/Byzantine_fault.

by establishing a decentralised consensus mechanism helps solve the double-spending problem. Transparency allows users to collectively update and manage the ledger by freely accessing a Blockchain and verifying that a transaction has indeed occurred (De Filippi & Wright 2018: 38). The network records preceding events or user interaction, resolving the double-spending problem by providing a single source of reference for who received what and when (Voshmgir 2020: 32).

In the case of Blockchain, each block contains the hash function of the previous block. If a node wants to create fake transactions and send others' money to its address, it has to invert all previous hashes along the Blockchain list of records, which is a highly improbable and costly computation (Voshmgir 2020: 41). Even if a malicious node succeeds in altering the details of a past transaction, other nodes in the network will refuse the transaction, since it will differ from the versions held by other nodes in the network, and they will continue mining in the main chain (Figure 3.5).

Once information is recorded on a Blockchain, it is difficult to alter or delete. To do so, miners either need to collude to modify the database or agree to implement a fork on the Blockchain's underlying protocol. Both mechanisms are possible but extremely costly to achieve. Even if a would-be group of attackers had such immense computational power to engage in a '51 per cent attack' and effectively take over the network, they would have to outpace the majority of the honest nodes supporting the network.[3] Given the current scale of Bitcoin's distributed network, such an attack is becoming prohibitively expensive (De Filippi & Wright 2018: 25).

Proof of work ensures that the Blockchain cannot be altered without incurring costs, thereby inducing the nodes to behave honestly (Shär & Berentsen 2020: 148). 'Proof of work' redundancy makes the network resilient and extremely difficult to shut down, since the Bitcoin Blockchain can be copied

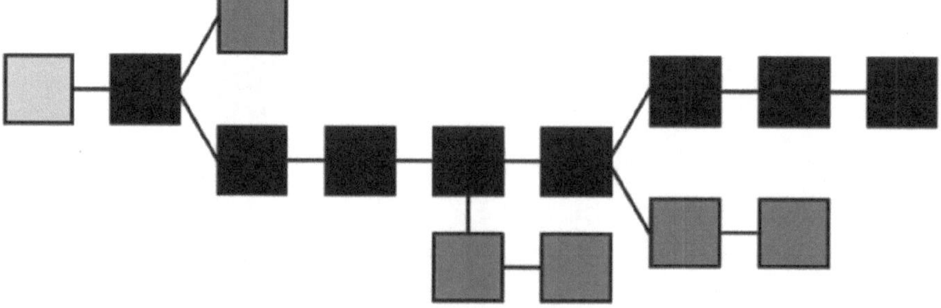

Figure 3.5 Blockchain Consensus

Source: Figure is in the public domain via Wikimedia: https://commons.wikimedia.org/wiki/File:Blockchain.svg; figure is licensed under Creative Commons BY 3.0.

and replicated across the globe in a few hours. In short, proof of work renders the Blockchain a transparent, tamper-proof system of distributed data management.

Monetary Policy

To understand the utility of Bitcoin and any cryptocurrency issued under similar rules, it is necessary to answer the questions of what money is and how money relates to value, which also begs the question of what value is. To begin with, money was invented to solve two basic problems inherent in the barter and gift economy: the double coincidence of wants and the indeterminacy of production and transaction costs (Schär & Berentsen 2020: 6). Money is a general equivalent of commodities that improves price discovery, facilitates trade and renders markets more efficient.

There are three types of money: commodity money, credit money and fiat money (Schär & Berentsen 2020: 9–13). Commodity money, such as metal, shells, cattle and basic foodstuffs, has an intrinsic value in that it can be consumed or used as a factor of production. It has also a liquidity premium, inasmuch as it is flexible to trade for goods and services. Credit money possesses no intrinsic value and carries a promise of payment. It is a piece of paper or digital record, which states that the borrower will make a payment at a specific future date. Credit money includes a liquidity premium in that it can be traded in the market. Fiat money possesses neither intrinsic value nor a promise of payment. Its value derives solely from its liquidity premium backed by central banks and governments.

Money can be created either under competition or under monopoly (Schär & Berentsen 2020: 13). In different regions and eras, different goods were frequently being traded, thereby incrementally becoming a generally accepted medium of exchange called 'money'. Under competition, network effects and demand constitute what money is. The money supply is determined by production costs and aggregate demand. To the extent that there is enough demand to outweigh the marginal benefits over the marginal costs of the money production, anything that can function as a medium of exchange can be effectively supplied as money. Under monopoly, a central bank or government controls the money supply and calibrates demand by expanding or contracting the money supply.

Money can have either a physical or a virtual representation (Schär & Berentsen 2020: 21). Physical money is linked to an object such as cash or gold, whereas fiat money, when not backed by cash or gold, is virtual money recorded in the ledgers of banks and controlled by governments. Bitcoin's fundamental innovation, which serves to disrupt centralised financial institutions, is the decentralised management of owning a virtual asset (Schär & Berentsen 2020: 21). Bitcoin is virtual money issued under competition, the supply of which is determined by computer code, network effects and aggregate demand. It allows a global network to securely transact and exchange value without the need for a costly intermediary and the fear of censorship and confiscation

(Catalini 2017). Bitcoin still has limited exchange value and is mainly used as a store of value. It is mostly considered a hedge for inflation as well as a speculative digital asset.

But what is value? Value comes with different and intertwined connotations. Liberal political philosophy has conceived moral value from the viewpoint of individual freedom and broad consensus over politics (Swift 2006). In post-Marxist political philosophy, value is a discourse and, therefore, intersubjective (Laclau & Mouffe 1985). Value has different meaning in different contexts. Value is interpreted differently in socialism, in capitalism, in anarchism, in the political ecology of degrowth, in crypto-economics, in feminism, and so on. Value relates to power, and power to money, which, apart from representing consensus over the representation of value, has been also used as a form of domination of men over men and men over women over the millennia. Value has been subject to class, nation and gender struggle (Balibar & Wallerstein 1991).

To the extent that monetary value can be separated from moral, social and political value, economics offers two basic answers to the question of value (Mazzucato 2018). Classical economists such as David Ricardo, Karl Marx and Adam Smith defined value in terms of the labour expended in the production of one unit. A car is more expensive than a chair, because of the larger amount of time invested in its production. Labour translates into time and time into money. According to the Marxist labour theory of value, the value of Bitcoin consists in the computational power/energy (proof of work) expended to mine the digital coins along with the precarious labour of workers across the globe to extract the minerals and construct computers and mobile phones (Dyer-Witheford 2015; Kleiner 2018).

Neoclassical economists such as Alfred Marshall, Léon Walras, Stanley Jevons and Carl Menger inverted the objective theory of value measured by labour into the subjective theory of value measured by consumer utility (Mazzucato 2018). Utility translates into the price a customer is willing to pay for the chocolate. Money is not concealed labour, as Marx would have it, but the measure of utility, which varies between individuals, corresponding to the evolution of human preferences over time. Value is, therefore, subjective. Anything that is divisible, portable, durable and uniform can be agreed upon to function as a unit of account, a means of exchange or a store of value, whether it is metal or shells or cigarettes or digits in a computer, as is the case with Bitcoin. The value of Bitcoin derives from its expected utility as a speculative asset and a store of value. As long as there is demand for bitcoins, the positive feedback loop between investors and miners will go on spiralling across the cryptosphere, or will be operating in reverse if and when the bubble contained in the speculation bursts.

Nakamoto (2008) modelled Bitcoin as a kind of fiat money with an arbitrarily fixed supply, following the Austrian theory of money. With the exception of commodity money, money is a derivative or representative of value. In neoclassical economics, value derives from scarcity, since, if the money supply was infinite, it would have no value whatsoever (Mazzucato 2018). There would be no incentive to produce and sell to make a profit. There would be no efficient allocation of resources to the highest-valued use. Markets would not exist and society would return to barter and the gift economy.

Scarcity lies at the core of the Bitcoin protocol, which is programmed to allocate a fixed supply of 21 million bitcoins, with each one of them to be 'mined' every ten minutes (De Filippi & Wright 2018: 26). Blockchain constantly updates itself to represent the latest state of the Bitcoin ledger. Given that computers will probably get better at solving proof-of-work problems in the long run and may reach the capacity to mine blocks twice as rapidly, the software is set to automatically increase the difficulty of the hash function so that block creation adjusts to the programmed rate of ten minutes. The more nodes there are on the Bitcoin network attempting to enter the 'mining' process, the harder it becomes to generate a valid hash with an appropriate number of leading zeros. A miner's probability of finding a valid hash for a block is roughly proportional to the percentage of a Blockchain-based network's total computational resources that the miners contribute (De Filippi & Wright 2018: 40). The difficulty adjustment is related to the total mining power estimated in the total hash rate per second (TH/s), which is increasing over time.[4] On large networks such as Bitcoin, the probability of any individual mining a block using non-specialised hardware is low, thus leading to the centralisation of mining by big companies equipped with expensive hardware.

The bulk of the Bitcoin supply has already been created (*c.* 18.7 million), with the remainder to be mined until 2140.[5] Every 210,000 blocks (roughly every four years) the block reward gets cut in half. Bitcoin halving lowers inflation to stimulate demand, which in turn increases the price. In the event that halving does not increase demand and price, the difficulty of mining will be reduced to keep miners incentivised (Conway 2021). The quantity of bitcoins released as a reward is still smaller, but the difficulty of processing a transaction is reduced, thereby increasing the rate of mining and the subsequent rewards per total mining. As the report of BofA Securities states:

> Capped supply, coupled with accelerating adoption, will likely put upward pressure on bitcoin prices over the medium and long term. The main drivers of adoption are institutional investment; decreasing barriers to entry, mainly for retail investors; and growing acceptance of bitcoin as a store of value and inflation hedge in Developed Economies and Developing Economies, respectively.
>
> (Shah & Moss 2021: 48)

Blockchain is a digital commons that is accessible to all but the resource it produces is finite (Voshmgir 2020: 269). Scale comes at a cost to the network, since more transactions means more data to process and more records to store. Blockchain is thus subject to the tragedy of the commons. Proof of work is essentially a market-based, game-theoretical consensus mechanism to prevent underuse or overuse of the commons by incentivising contributions and disincentivising exploitation. Competition and pay-off structures incentivise actors to 'mine' and exchange a scarce supply of tokens. The more actors participate, the more the value of the token appreciates, thus enticing more actors to join the club. Bitcoin converts, therefore, into an actor–club good that is elastic to actual demand.

Bitcoin is 'cheat-free' because the entire protocol is in a self-reinforcing Nash equilibrium (Staggs 2020). In game theory, the Nash equilibrium, named after the mathematician John Forbes Nash Jr, is a proposed solution of a non-cooperative game, involving two or more players in which each player's strategy is optimal vis-à-vis others' optimal strategy. Since altering the data on Blockchain is highly improbable and expensive, players are disincentivised to do so. Bitcoin protocol requires that users stay honest and play by the rules of the game. No player can benefit by unilaterally changing her strategy.

To sum up, asymmetric cryptography, open-source software, peer-to-peer networks, game theory and crypto-economics weave in to address the Byzantine generals' problem, solve the double-spending problem and prevent the tragedy of the commons. Put simply, Bitcoin's technological innovation consists in the creation of a digital signature that is impossible to counterfeit. Immutability and pay-off structure combine with competition over scarce resources to allow for value transfer across the decentralised network of Blockchain in a permissionless, censorship-resistant and transparent manner.

Ethereum

Proof of Stake

The Bitcoin Blockchain has a number of limitations. It is slow, energy-intensive and favours those who can afford to buy the hardware necessary to mine bitcoins, thereby leading to the centralisation of the network (Voshmgir 2020: 56). Bitcoin can process only a limited set of transaction types, data types and data storage sizes. Bitcoin is highly volatile, thus keeping away merchants and banks. Bitcoin limitations minimise the sorts of potential applications. In addition, the Bitcoin protocol is hard to update and improve due to the lack of formal governance. Therefore, Bitcoin comes with a number of debilitating effects in scaling up and turning into mainstream.

Second-generation Blockchains such as Ethereum launched in the last decade to address these limitations (Buterin 2015, 2017; De Filippi & Wright 2018: 27–31). Like Bitcoin, the Ethereum virtual machine is governed by a consensus-driven, open-source protocol. It uses a native digital currency (ether), which is allocated to miners maintaining the network and can be transferred just like bitcoins. Unlike Bitcoin, which is designed for the sole purpose of maintaining and facilitating the issuance and circulation of the bitcoin currency, Ethereum is a general-purpose Blockchain that allows for multiple other programmes (applications) to be written in terms of smart contracts and uploaded on the ledger. Just as Bitcoin has been designed to disrupt finance, Ethereum is poised to disrupt networked computing by replacing centrally controlled code with decentralised applications operating on Blockchain.

The Ethereum Blockchain is currently upgrading to a proof-of-stake mechanism (Ethereum 2.0) so as to update the state of the network. Whereas, in proof of work, miners expend energy (electricity) into computing power 24/7 to mine blocks into existence, in proof of stake validators commit stake – that is, a certain amount of money denominated in ether – to attest (or 'validate') blocks into existence (Buterin 2020). Instead of vast amounts of electricity, proof of stake requires coins (ether) to run the system. Validators sign messages with coins. Ethereum validators accrue rewards for making blocks and attestations, just as Bitcoin miners receive rewards for the costs of using electricity and expensive hardware to validate bitcoin transactions.

In proof of work, for attackers to take over the network they need to control more than 50% of the network's mining rate, that is to own 51% of the nodes on the network, which makes a 51 per cent attack expensive (Buterin 2020). In proof of stake, for attackers to take over they need to have more coins than the rest of the network, which makes a 51 per cent attack also expensive. Both proof of work and proof of stake are subject to centralisation and plutocracy owing to rich stakeholders (whales) gaining an advantage in governing the state of the network. To become a validator in Ethereum, one needs to stake 32 ether, which is the equivalent of $54,496 at the time of writing.[6] Ethereum 2.0 is putting to the test a number of mechanisms, such as quadratic voting (QV), to mitigate plutocracy (Buterin 2019).

The transition to Ethereum 2.0, an improvement on the Ethereum Blockchain, began in December 2020 and is scheduled to be completed in the next few years. Currently the Ethereum Blockchain experiences high transaction fees and slower transactions due to high demand. The Ethereum Blockchain is also approaching 1TB of data, which is impractical for one node to store. The transition to 2.0 will shift the protocol from proof of work to proof of stake, with the aim to increase storage, reduce power consumption, improve scalability and lower transaction fees. The main challenge of scalability is to increase transaction speed (faster finality), and transaction throughput (high transactions per second), without sacrificing decentralisation or security.[7]

There are two options when it comes to scaling a Blockchain: increasing the hardware parameters (computing power, bandwidth, storage) and changing the rules of the protocol for the software to process more transactions per second; or applying primary technical fixes on the protocol itself and adding secondary improvements on top of the protocol (Buterin 2021a). The main challenge with the first option is that bigger blocks are more difficult to verify and are prone to centralisation and insecurity. Ethereum adopts the second option, deploying advanced mathematical and cryptographic techniques on the protocol itself (layer 1) and on top of it (layer 2), such as sharding and roll-ups, respectively.

Instead of increasing the size of the existing Blockchain database, sharding is a layer 1 solution that breaks up the main Blockchain into many chains in order to spread the load of data horizontally (Buterin 2021b). Code and computing are executed on the main Blockchain while data is split across shard chains. Validators (nodes) who download and run the client software need only to store/run data for the shard they are validating, not the entire network. Individual shards provide proofs to the main Blockchain and interact with one another to share addresses, balances and general states using cross-shard communication protocols. Sharding thus reduces network congestion and increases transactions per second.

Roll-ups are a layer 2 solution that add up to on-chain sharding by moving computation and state storage off-chain, but keep some data per transaction on-chain (Buterin 2021a). Essentially, they roll up a bunch of transactions into a single one, compress it cryptographically and post it on the main Blockchain, which simply verifies it. The main Blockchain thus processes only deposits and withdrawals, and verifies proofs that everything happening off-chain is following the rules of the protocol.

It would be helpful here to provide a simplistic analogy. Let us consider the Blockchain as a highway and the cars running on it as tokens that can be sold and traded in the market. Let us also consider that four large companies manufacture and sell the cars and design how big the highway is, how fast the cars are, how high the toll fee is, etc. The problem is that the highway can get congested and the tolls are high. To make the highway bigger, the cars faster and the tolls cheaper, the four companies could simply redesign the highway and the cars. However, this centralised design would make the companies vulnerable to theft. Hackers could 'break in' and steal the cars.

The alternative solution presented by Ethereum 2.0 would be to create parallel sideways and split the manufacturing, design and monitoring of the cars to thousands of decentralised validators. This way, the system preserves its decentralisation and scalability while remaining secure. However, for this solution to be viable at least several hundred of the validators – depending on the number of sideways and cars – should be constantly active, to manufacture and design cars as well as regulate traffic. Otherwise, the whole system would be subject to collapse.

Consensus protocol improvements such as proof of stake combined with sharding are layer 1 scaling solutions, and roll-ups are layer 2 scaling solutions. Layer 1 and layer 2 scaling solutions combined may allow for hundreds, or even millions, of transactions per second with the full decentralisation and security of Blockchain. Yet, for both solutions to be attack-resistant, at least a few hundred clients are required to run the software.

Smart Contracts, DApps and DAOs

Ethereum leverages the power of a Blockchain not just to store information related to the transfer of a digital currency but to host decentralised applications (DApps),[8] utilising sophisticated smart contracts (De Filippi & Wright 2018: 27–28). DApps consist of a back-end smart contract and a front-end web interface. A smart contract is a computer algorithm designed to automatically execute, control or document events according to pre-set rules. Smart contracts operate in the sequence of 'If A, then B' and are immutable: once deployed they cannot change retroactively (Szabo 1997). The most commonly used example of a smart contract is a vending machine. If you insert a coin in the slot of a vending machine, it releases a product of your choice. Smart contracts can be used to generate and transfer tokens (associated with physical or digital assets), verify signatures, record votes and implement new Blockchain-based applications and governance systems (De Filippi & Wright 2018: 72–89).

The unique value proposition of Blockchain-based 'smart contracts' is the creation of a permanent public record of agreed-upon transactions that cannot be changed retroactively.

> Through simply downloading an app on your smartphone, you can choose your code of law, your preferred arbitration method, write a smart contract, and get married, title your land, notarize a will, incorporate a company, get health insurance, and much more, in just a few minutes for a couple of dollars. It is backed by an ID and reputation system, dispute resolution, and an app library where people can upload and share or sell their own do-it-yourself governance apps.[9]

Smart contracts further enable the creation of decentralised applications such as DAOs, which are controlled by the organisation members according to the pre-agreed rules for the smart contract (De Filippi & Wright 2018: 148). DApps and DAOs introduce the third version of the web (Web 3.0), which represents a new vision for web applications: from centrally owned and managed applications to applications built on decentralised protocols. Whereas Web 2.0 brought a front-end revolution, Web 3.0 brings a back-end revolution (Table 3.2). Ethereum 2.0 becomes a general-purpose computer infrastructure utilising smart contracts and DAOs to open up an unimaginable space of diverse applications across all sectors of the economy, ranging from finance and business to law and governance.

Table 3.2 From Web 1.0 to Web 3.0

Web 1.0 (1980 to 2005)	*Web 2.0 (2005 to 2020)*	*Web 3.0 (2020 onwards)*
Open protocols	Siloed services	Open protocols
Decentralised	Centralised	Decentralised
Dedicated infrastructure	Cloud computing	Distributed computing
Community-governed	Governed by companies	Community-governed
Static content	Interactive content	Interoperable assets
Content owned by users	Content owned by companies	Content owned by users
Read-only	Read–write	Read–write–own
Banner ads	Interactive ads	No ads
Page views	Cost per click	Tokenomics

Blockchain Types

Blockchain can be considered an improvement on the Internet from the standpoint of decentralisation, among others (Buterin & Weyl 2018). It is a distributed software ledger programmed to produce consensus about facts – whether it is a transaction, a vote, a smart contract, a registry, a DApp, or whatever – and to support applications without relying on central third-party verification mechanisms employed by governments and corporations. It deploys a software protocol that predetermines how computers (nodes) store information, engage in transactions and execute software code such as smart contracts. Decentralised consensus mechanisms such as proof of work and proof of stake apply a set of rules with predefined incentives and cost structures to secure the sustainability of the system against unilateral exploitation. Blockchain leverages mass computation and connectivity to create 'governance markets' at scale and reward those who contribute to consensus. A 'market' is created to award coins to those who enforce the governance rules of the protocol. Cryptography weaves in to secure the pseudo-anonymity and validation of transactions.

There are two main types of Blockchains: public (permissionless) and private (permissioned) (Voshmgir 2020: 53–63). In a public Blockchain, anyone can read, write, validate transactions and use the network without permission. Public Blockchains such as Bitcoin and Ethereum use a native token tied to a consensus mechanism (proof of work or proof of stake). Although tokenised incentives keep the network safe from manipulation and attacks, they also render it slow. Large-scale applications with high transaction volumes still cannot run on public Blockchains, since the latter can process a few transactions per second. Layer 1 and layer 2 solutions such as sharding and ZK-Rollups are currently being tested on Ethereum 2.0 to address the issue of scalability. These are, essentially, mechanisms that seek to lighten the Ethereum Blockchain via side-chain and off-chain data storage and processing.

In a private Blockchain, on the other hand, only invited members can read, write, validate transactions and use the network upon permission (Voshmgir 2020: 53–63). Private Blockchains such as banks, institutions and industry consortia have a federated set up with bilateral agreements. They are clubs that allow participation only to members. They do not need a token to incentivise behaviour and protect themselves against 'Sybil attacks', since they know each other beforehand and every member is subject to binding contractual agreements. They can settle a large amount of transactions per second, as they do not have to deal with an indefinite amount of anonymous nodes. They also provide more privacy compared to public Blockchains, since the ledger data is not publicly accessible. Few businesses are keen to lay their back-office functions bare to the world, so most enterprise Blockchains are private and 'permissioned', meaning that access is restricted to trusted users. For instance, Corda, a finance-focused Blockchain developed by r3, a consortium of banks, and Hyperledger Fabric, originally developed by IBM and a firm called Digital Asset, work this way (Gerard 2018).

Blockchain Benefits

Decentralised technologies have gained significant momentum in the last decade with the advent of platform ecosystems such as Ethereum Blockchain, Cardano, Solana, Polkadot, and the like. There have been more than 10,000 Blockchain publications in the literature during the last decade, spanning all Blockchain potential applications (Wang et al. 2021). The reach of Blockchains has rapidly expanded beyond payments and financial products to support novel applications across various fields, ranging from decentralised games and logistics to reputation systems and the Internet of Things (Nascimento & Pólvora 2019). At the present time the hype around innovative Blockchain-based projects has driven the market capitalisation of 20,726 cryptocurrencies to $1,046 trillion.[10] An EU Commission report has identified 131 Blockchain-based projects currently operating across almost all sectors of the economy (Figure 3.6). Latest research has documented 1,049 projects using Blockchain to create a positive impact and solve social and environmental issues across the globe.[11]

The Blockchain is designed to disrupt centralised institutions that are rife with corruption, periodic crises, fiat currencies, instabilities, power asymmetries, concentrated risks, single points of failure, economic rents, clearing and settlement costs and counterparty risks (Buterin & Weyl 2018; Gensler 2018; Swan 2018). However, Blockchain applications are still in their infancy, representing an extremely fast-moving field, with little established theory and plenty of exuberant speculation and fraudulent practices. There are many challenges yet to be solved, such as security, performance, interoperability,

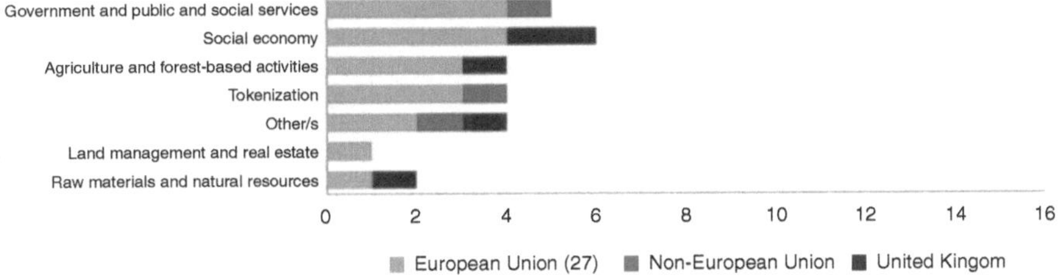

Figure 3.6 Relations between Sectors of Activity and Region

Source: Hassan et al. (2020); figure is licensed under Creative Commons Attribution 4.0 International.

legality and scalability. Analysts anticipate significant growth as digital asset use cases move beyond Bitcoin's store of value thesis to an industry characterised by product innovation, regulatory clarity, increased institutional participation and mainstream adoption (Shah & Moss 2021). However, sceptics draw attention to potential risks related to Blockchain technology (Atzori 2017). Blockchain thus comes with both benefits and risks.

Intermediaries

Ronald Coase (1937) showed that uncertainty, asymmetric information and the risk of moral hazard undermine the ability of markets to effectively complete contracts due to increased transaction costs, thus giving rise to firms operating as a nexus of contracts between multiple stakeholders (Catalini 2017). The main benefit of storing and keeping track of data on Blockchain is the reduction in verification and networking costs, which bypasses intermediaries such as firms, governments and banks, lowers barriers to entry, facilitates trade and asset management, enhances innovation and catalyses new business models (Catalini & Gans 2019; Braun-Dubler et al. 2020: 120–122; Tapscott & Tapscott 2016; Swan 2015).

The cost-effectiveness of Blockchain is co-extensive with three exponential cost curves: (1) Moore's law (the cost of processing digital information – i.e. speed, which halves every 18 months); (2) Kryder's law (the cost of storing digital information, – i.e. memory, which halves every 12 months); and (3) Nielsen's law (the cost of shipping digital information – i.e. bandwidth, which halves every 24 months) (Davidson, De Filippi & Potts 2016: 3; 2018). Cost reduction opens up opportunities for the design of digital platforms that offer new approaches to data ownership, privacy and licensing; the monetisation of digital content; and auctions and reputation systems (Catalini & Gans 2019: 2). The Blockchain is poised to further increase security, efficiency and transparency in the economy. It can enhance financial inclusion by bringing two billion 'unbanked' people, some 25 per cent additional 'consumers' and 10 per cent more 'new merchants' into the global economy.

Finance

Blockchain could address a number of payment system deficiencies, such as costs, delayed settlement, chargebacks, fraud, privacy, financial inclusion, cross-border payments, centralisation of ledgers and complexity (Gensler 2018). Blockchain could be used to facilitate international payments, which are slow and expensive because of the many layers of intermediation obstructing computer systems from smoothly communicating with each other. Blockchain could relieve much of the administrative burden. Some banks are experimenting with Blockchains to improve their systems. Santander Bank, for example, has launched a smartphone app called One Pay FX that allows customers to send international payments in a matter of seconds. One Pay FX uses a closed, permissioned, quasi-Blockchain system operated by Ripple, an American firm (Gerard 2018).

Smart Contracts

The Blockchain technology currently applies in numerous use cases: digital currencies, securities, derivatives, insurance, private markets, equity, trade, exchanges, escrow accounts, crowdfunding (or initial coin offering: ICO), digital identity, public e-voting, public registers and gambling (Braun-Dubler et al. 2020: 143–222). Smart contracts are used to define payment tokens or financial instruments, manage memberships, monitor token transfers and grant or withdraw access permissions to systems (Braun-Dubler et al. 2020: 102–104).

Smart contract use cases range from simple to complex. They can be used for simple economic transactions such as sending money from A to B. Smart contracts can also be used for registering any kind of ownership and property rights, such as land registries and intellectual property, or managing access control for the sharing economy. Use cases can be found in banking, insurance, energy, e-government, telecommunications, the music and film industry, fine art, mobility, education, and many more. Each agreement, process, task or payment can be collectively managed. Many traditional intermediaries, such as lawyers, brokers and bankers or public administrators, and Internet platforms might no longer be necessary, or, at least, some of their services might become obsolete: Cars could use smart contracts to pay their own bills upon fuelling up at the petrol station, or charging up at an electric charging pole. Invoices could be settled upon arrival of a product shipment (Voshmgir 2020: 107–108).

Blockchain applications are pertinent for all industries and can be customised to suit the needs of each industry (Shrivastava, Le & Sharma 2020: 37–38, 240–241; Swan 2015). The Blockchain can apply to supply chains and logistics to verify signatures, ensure the quality of goods and automate shipping processes and production. It can provide risk-free asset management and transparency in record-keeping for businesses and governments alike. Tangible and intangible assets such as property titles, company shares, patents, cars and houses can now be registered on Blockchain.

E-Government

The permissioned tokenless Blockchain can have numerous applications in the public sector. It can introduce participatory e-voting, streamline government processes, reduce waste, eliminate bureaucracy, ensure data security, integrity and reliability in storing school, medical records and certificates of birth, death, anniversaries, college degrees, and so on. It can also improve healthcare, education and social services, prevent tax fraud and reduce the cost of regulation, since the risks of fraud and monitoring costs decrease (Akins, Chapman & Gordon 2014; Shrivastava, Le & Sharma 2020: 38). In short, the permissioned tokenless Blockchain can enhance participatory democracy, transparency, efficiency and justice.

The Internet of Things

The Blockchain can combine with 5G, real-time bid data analytics, machine learning, artificial intelligence and the Internet of Things to provide security, privacy, integrity and efficiency in the emerging technologies (Shrivastava, Le & Sharma 2020: 99–121; Zhang & Wen 2015). A network of Internet-connected devices such as mobiles, home appliances, thermostats, sensors and cars is called the IoT:

> The Internet of Things will connect everything with everyone in an integrated global network. People, machines, natural resources, production lines, logistics networks, consumption habits, recycling flows, and virtually every aspect of economic and social life will be linked via sensors and software to the IoT platform, continually feeding Big Data to every node – businesses, homes, vehicles – moment to moment, in real time. Big Data, in turn, will be processed with advanced analytics, transformed into predictive algorithms, and programmed into automated systems to improve thermodynamic efficiencies, dramatically increase productivity, and reduce the marginal cost of producing and delivering a full range of goods and services to near zero across the entire economy.
>
> (Rifkin 2014: 11)

5G is the fifth generation of wireless networks. The 5G technology brings a high data rate, reduced latency, energy savings, cost reduction, higher system capacity and massive device connectivity (Shrivastava, Le & Sharma 2020: 43–54). Blockchain can combine with 5G on the Internet of Things to unleash value creation across all sectors of the economy. Smart cities, smart governments, driverless vehicles, smart homes and all sorts of sensor-driven devices can leverage the security, transparency, decentralisation, immutability and consensus arbitration of Blockchain as foundational layers of operation. Smart contracts, in particular, are considered the missing component of IoT to install secure, self-executable, automated machine-to-machine processes. For example, each time a printer runs low on ink, it can automatically order cartridge from any shopping website.

> Blockchain technology can be used in tracking billions of connected devices, enable the processing of transactions and coordination between devices, and allow for significant savings for IoT industry manufacturers. This decentralised approach would eliminate single points of failure, creating a more resilient ecosystem for devices to run on. The cryptographic algorithms used by blockchains would also help make consumer data more private. The benefits of decentralising IoT are numerous and currently

> superior to current centralised systems. However, blockchain is a newer invention and, similar to IoT, current applications fall short when it comes to scalability and integration.
>
> (Shrivastava, Le & Sharma 2020: 174)

DApps, DeFi, ReFi, NFTs and DAOs

Blockchain protocols and smart contracts are the basic components laying the foundations for the different layers of Blockchain infrastructure (Figure 3.7). Applications built on top of layer 0 (the physical layer) and layer 1 (the protocol layer), such as DApps, DeFi, ReFi, NFTs and DAOs, are poised to reshape the future of organisations. I briefly go through them in the following.

DApps

Blockchains such as Ethereum, Cardano and Polkadot enable the creation of DApps,[12] which are software programmes built on top of Blockchain layer 1 that combine a smart contract and a front-end user interface.

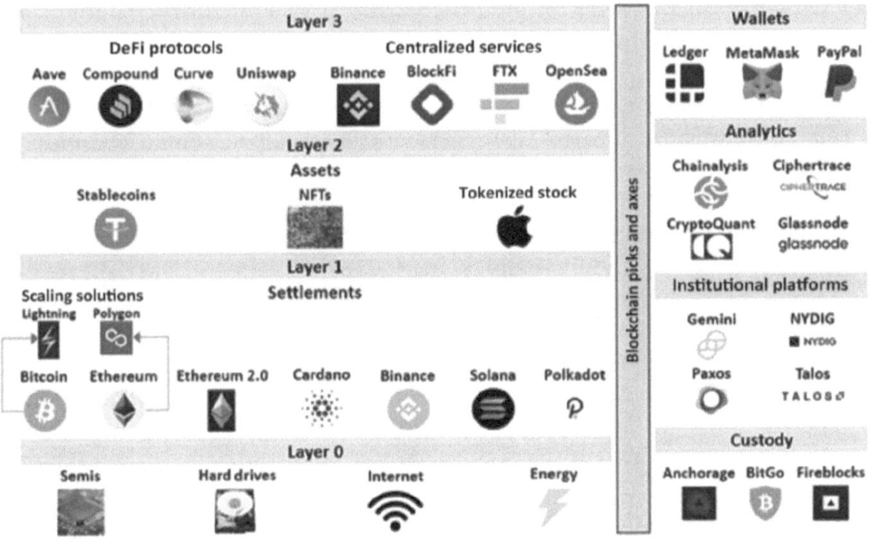

Figure 3.7 Blockchain Layers

Source: Shah and Moss (2021); reprinted by permission. Copyright © 2021 Bank of America Corporation (BAC). The use of the above in no way implies that BAC or any of its affiliates endorses the views or interpretation or the use of such information or acts as any endorsement of the use of such information. The information is provided 'as is' and none of BAC or any of its affiliates warrants the accuracy or completeness of the information.

Traditional centralised Web2 applications such as Twitter, Trello and Slack use HTML, CSS or javascript to create a webpage or a mobile app. The front end of a webpage or a mobile app communicates through the HTTP protocol with one or more centralised web servers. When using a service such as Twitter, Facebook, Amazon or Airbnb, for example, the webpage will call an application programming interface (API) to authenticate user ID, passwords and relevant personal data with low levels of security, since personal data is stored on centralised servers.

In contrast to the Internet, which channels data through centralised servers, the Blockchain consists of thousands of computers that process data over a distributed network. On the front end, DApps use the same technology to create a page on the Internet. However, on the back end, DApps communicate with their respective Blockchain networks through a 'wallet',[13] which serves as a bridge to the Blockchain ecosystem. A wallet is an application (computer programme with an interface) that allows users to read their crypto balance, send transactions and connect to other applications. Wallets manage Blockchain addresses and cryptographic keys necessary to identify and authenticate users in the network. Instead of using the HTTP protocol to communicate with the network, DApp wallets trigger smart contracts that interact with the network and execute transactions.

Decentralised applications such as BitTorrent and Napster utilised peer-to-peer networks on the Internet long before the advent of Blockchain. For an application to be classified as a DApp, it must adhere to the following criteria.[14]

1. It must be open source and changes to the protocol must be decided via consensus on the part of its network users. Open-source technology allows for developers to build on top of each other's work, to combine and recombine different elements from various projects to create new types of applications and services. This encourages techno-social innovation.
2. Data must be stored on the Blockchain.
3. DApps must generate digital assets that act as a proof of value.
4. Digital assets such as tokens are distributed as rewards on the network.
5. Transactions are executed with smart contracts, which are key element of DApp technology. A smart contract is essentially a DApp that brings a back-end functionality on the Blockchain, which is coupled with a front-end user interface capable of making calls to the back end.

The vast majority of DApp development is on the Ethereum Blockchain. Ethereum was designed to be a general-purpose Blockchain capable of building and supporting all kinds of applications by deploying a Turing-complete language called Solidity.[15] Smart contracts on Ethereum network are typically written in Solidity, but they can be written in any other programming language. Smart contracts can be forked and combined to create software, which can be applied across different industries. There are already several industries in which DApps are showing great potential, such as decentralised finance (DeFi), regenerative finance (ReFi), enterprise solutions, gaming, NFTs (non-fungible tokens: digital collectables), and more.

DeFi

DeFi is a decentralised alternative to centralised financial services offered by banks and hedge funds (Schär 2021). It offers similar services, such as saving crypto, sending crypto around the globe, accessing stable currencies, borrowing funds with or without collateral, staking, liquidity mining, yield farming, trading tokens 24/7, buying insurance, and many more. DeFi services offered by several platforms such as Uniswap,[16] MakerDAO[17] and AAVE[18] are a fast-growth segment of Blockchain, with total value locked of $71.63 billion in February 2022.[19]

However, research has shown that DeFi is a category of unlicensed, unregulated and non-custodial financial services the governance of which is based on plutocratic tokenised voting rights that introduce a minority rule in the 'digital Wild West' (Barbereau et al. 2022). DeFi governance brings to the fore a new class of 'shadowy' elites that reproduces the oligarchies of the centralised status quo they purportedly wish to abolish. Thus, the Ethereum Blockchain that supports much of the DeFi ecosystem seems to be currently co-opted by libertarian finance rather than fostering a decentralised culture and economy.

ReFi

ReFi is an alternative to DeFi that seeks to tackle climate change and empower individuals and communities across the globe by employing a number of Blockchain-based tools, such as ecological state protocols, ecological state contracts, satellite-powered remote sensing verification data used for global carbon accounting, market-driven carbon credit issuance used for monetising ecosystem services such as permaculture and carbon sequestration,[20] natural-capital-backed assets,[21] carbon-backed cryptocurrencies and algorithmic climate protocols,[22] carbon credit exchange, carbon credit NFTs and carbon sequestration cryptocurrencies,[23] online marketplaces for NFTs that fund animal and environmental conservation efforts,[24] crypto-backed renewables,[25] crypto-backed biodiversity,[26] artificial intelligence to measure and reward sustainable nature stewardship,[27] and many more.[28]

In short, ReFi uses Blockchain to transfer part of the carbon credits used in the existing carbon offset market into the crypto-market, thereby disincentivising carbon production by making it expensive through hoarding and speculation, all the while incentivising ecological practices by pouring money into carbon sequestration and renewables aiming to reduce carbon emissions and tackle climate change. ReFi thus seeks to bring together the compliance market and voluntary carbon offset projects under a crypto-market generating profits for all actors, ranging from state, corporations, NGOs, individual farmers and communities, at the same time as tackling climate change.

However, it seems that ReFi reproduces the ever-growing commodification of natural resources, which revives the worst nightmare of crypto-biotech neo-liberalism. It would be interesting, instead, to push towards transvestment from libertarian crypto-capitalism to a cosmo-local post-capitalist economy using open-sourced eco-friendly technologies to democratise economic activity and tackle climate change.

NFTs

DeFi and ReFi have the potential to combine with non-fungible tokens to create a new economic paradigm that provides more opportunities for individuals, communities and businesses. An NFT is a cryptographic token minted and stored on the Blockchain that certifies the ownership and authenticity of a digital asset such as art, collectibles, audio or photos (Nadini et al. 2021). Whereas bitcoin is divisible into smaller units that can be equally exchanged in the crypto-market, an NFT is a unique certificate of ownership that can be attached to a digital asset and traded in crypto, just as bitcoins are. It is a non-replicable digital signature that authenticates a one-off association, typically with a digital file. Its value derives from its ability to prove ownership and authenticity of the asset it represents, whether it is a meme, a video, a song, a ticket, a licence, a degree, a conference presentation or even a house. An NFT itself is not the asset it represents but the ability to algorithmically confer rights over a digital asset just as an ordinary contract does (Lewis et al. 2021). The difference lies in it being written in a smart contract on the Blockchain and decentrally verified.

To fully understand the potential utility of NFTs, we should first revisit some fundamentals of copyright law (Casey 2021; Lewis et al. 2021). According to the first sale doctrine, people can rent or resell a physical book or CD they have bought and thus transfer partial or total ownership to others, but they cannot make copies of them and distribute them without copyright owners granting them a licence to do so. On the Internet, anonymity coupled with the low cost of digital reproduction allowed for the free copy and distribution of almost anything digital, from e-books to MPEGs and MP3s. People can easily right-click on a JPEG or an MP3 and save it on their computer for personal use. It is possible to go even go further and distribute for free digital files using peer-to-peer platforms such as Vuze and BitTorrent.

The utility of an NFT is to provide a vital building block for a better system of rights enforcement by establishing provably unique, scarce digital markers of ownership over anything digital or analogue. The Ethereum Blockchain is the most widely used platform for creating and launching NFTs.[29] The development of NFTs was pioneered with the invention of the ERC-721 token, which sets a standard for the creation of an NFT. The ERC-721 token standard implements an API for tokens within a smart contract. The ERC-721 standard helps register a token on the Blockchain with unique values such as metadata and information about ownership. It can be used in various platforms guaranteeing the provenance of art or collectibles, or along the supply chain of other goods and services.

Any producer can mint any amount of NFTs attached to almost any product, from digital art and videos to rooms in an apartment, and sell them or rent them (Casey 2021). Most digital files sold as NFTs can be downloaded by anyone, but only the purchaser of the NFT owns the product and can sell it. The purchaser of this NFT is granted the proprietary right not to every copy or version of the underlying product but to the specific copy or version of the product that the NTF represents (Lewis et al. 2021). For example, a songwriter may create a song, link it with an NFT file in a predetermined number of copies and sell it on an NFT market. The purchaser can then resell or trade this NFT in secondary markets, while the songwriter is earning royalties each time the song is downloaded or traded in a platform. In essence, an NFT is a derivative of value that can be publicly validated and recorded on the Blockchain as well as traded on secondary DeFi crypto-markets.

NFTs are currently used to represent digital artworks, collectibles, video game assets, photos, videos, domain names and virtual land. Speculation is the biggest use case for NFTs at the moment (Chohan 2021). A digital artist called Beeple sold the digital work *Everydays: The First 5000 Days* for $69.3 million at Christie's in 2021. CryptoKitties is a Blockchain game on Ethereum in which users can trade virtual cats. Genesis, the first high-selling cat, was sold for $117,712. An NFT of a video clip of LeBron James dunking sold for more than $200,000 on NBA Top Shot. Jack Dorsey, the CEO of Twitter, sold his first Tweet, which simply read 'Just setting up my twttr', for $2.9 million.

Notwithstanding current speculation, NFTs are said to open up unimaginable opportunities (Wilser 2021). The essential utility of an NFT lies in its capacity to create markets for reselling value that is costly to register and validate in the physical world. It can help businesses, communities and individual producers such as artists claim royalty rights in every future sale of their products. NFTs can introduce fractional ownership of property, thereby fostering financial inclusion and pouring liquidity into real estate markets. NFTs can constitute self-sovereign identity along with privacy protection that can link with almost anything digital or analogue, from DeFi platforms and social media accounts to university degrees, licences, diplomas, healthcare, insurance, events, ticketing, brand names, marketing, and so on. NFTs will allow multiple users to own a single piece of digital content such as a meme, a game, an article or a movie. They can secure compensation for and the monetisation of user-generated digital content. NFTs can eventually blend with DAOs and support a remix culture of content creation, self-governance and collaboration.

However, we should note that the recent craze for NFTs is moving in a centralised direction: the top 10 per cent of NFT traders account for 85 per cent of transactions and trade 97 per cent of all assets, and 10 per cent of buyer–seller pairs have the same volume as the remaining 90 per cent (Nadini et al. 2021). Critics stress that NFTs do not subvert the structure of property rights underpinning the capitalist exploitation of the many by the few (Varoufakis

2022). At present, NFTs are a compelling example of how Blockchain technology is being co-opted by crypto-capital in ways that increase scarcity and enclose the commons.

DAOs

DAOS' POTENTIAL

DAOs have been referred to as sites of algorithmic governance (Buterin 2014). They are an assemblage of online peer-to-peer communities that seek to coordinate for a common purpose without the need for a central authority (Nabben 2021b). DAOs have their rules of operations collectively agreed upon and encoded on smart contracts running on Blockchain. They are commonly Internet-native 'decentralised applications' deployed on top of the layer 1 protocol Blockchain, mixing Web3 tools with Web2 platforms. Basically, DAOs comprise a group chat on platforms such as Discord and Telegram, a multi-signature (multi-sig) account (Bronkema 2020), a smart-contract-enabled token issuance and self-governance mechanisms. Since they rely on a Blockchain, DAOs inherit some of its properties, such as transparency, cryptographic security and decentralisation (Hassan & De Filippi 2021). Indeed, Samer Hassan and Primavera De Filippi (2021) offer a comprehensive overview of the current literature on DAOs, which covers a number of issues ranging from computer science and economics to law, governance and politics.

DAOs coordinate today primarily around digital assets such as tokenised funds, code and software, but the goal is to gradually expand into physical assets as well. DAOs employ in varying degrees both on-chain and off-chain governance (Nabben 2021b; Voshmgir 2020), most often involving consensus mechanisms, crowdfunding, token engineering and fund allocation for various projects. DAOs span multiple centralisation versus decentralisation frameworks and ecosystems according to varying degrees of on-chain and off-chain governance. DAOs spin up with multiple use cases: some offer financial services (DeFi), others provide grants, others build protocols, others build software, tools and infrastructure. DAOs exist for purposes such as shared investment vehicles, special-interest hobby groups or software development (Faqir-Rhazoui, Arroyo Gallardo & Hassan 2020, 2021; Nabben et al. 2021: 11). Different types of DAOs often interoperate via forking or DAO2DAO operations such as open-sourcing or selling Web3 services, tools and components to receive back stake or allocation of tokens from DeFi applications, stable coins, yield farming, and more. Irrespective of the heterogeneity of DAOs, most of them are currently moving in a libertarian direction rather than a collectivist one.

> In short, a DAO can be defined as people with common goals that join under a blockchain infrastructure that enforces a set of shared rules. Typically, the members of a DAO are registered, each with a unique address. They also have an amount of 'governance' tokens linked to that address, which

> are usually required for participation, and may take a role in the DAO decision-making system. It is also common that DAOs manage resources, e.g. cryptocurrencies. DAO members may decide how to allocate them through a decision system.
>
> (Faqir-Rhazoui, Arroyo Gallardo & Hassan 2020)

2021 witnessed a sevenfold year-on-year increase in DAOs summoned, reaching a total of nearly 2,000 DAOs today[30] – nearly 150 DAOs summoned each month.[31] More than $6 billion worth of digital assets are held in the 20 biggest DAOs, according to a report from ConsenSys.[32] There are now more than 190,000 DAO members across crypto. DAOs pop up every month, to the extent that is almost impossible to keep up with all innovation happening in the field. Protocols, tools, services and modules are constantly under experimentation and change.

DAOs may get their initial funding to launch their operations from various sources: crowdfunding, crypto-angel investors and firms such as Consensys and Ethereum, bounties on Gitcoin, crypto earnings, bonding curves, retroactive airdrops, successful ICOs, donations and grants. Governance is executed via token-weighted voting, quadratic voting, conviction voting, tao voting, and the like. Labour contributions can be recognised and measured in tokens such as 'cred' or CSTK score. Dispute resolutions can take place in decentralised courts such as Celeste and Kleros.[33] And insurance can be supplied in the case of hacks or bugs in the code that lead to losses. Funding, voting, labour, dispute resolution and insurance break down into modular, composable, multi-layered tools for executing specific governance processes that transition between physical space and cyberspace (Nabben 2021b).

DAOS' VULNERABILITIES

However, DAOs come with a number of challenges and vulnerabilities with regard to technical and governance issues, among others (Samman & Freuden 2020: 28–33). To begin with, smart contracts may contain bugs that make them susceptible to technical attacks, as in the case of the famous 'The DAO' hack in 2016. Smart contracts also cannot reflect the complexity that characterises human decision-making. Nor can they adapt rapidly enough to unforeseen situations. It is questionable whether governance mechanisms such as voting may be efficient and scale at a decentralised level. Currently, most DAOs consist of no more than 150 members. A challenge arises with regard to encouraging participation and tackling voter apathy when it comes to scaling into hundreds, thousands or even millions.

DAOs are not as decentralised as they are claimed to be, since major decisions are most often taken by core developers or benevolent dictators (Tai 2022). Decentralisation is threatened by oligarchies, plutocracy and cartel-like behaviour (collusion attacks, Sybil attacks, shadow voting), which need to be addressed ex ante by the rules embedded in the smart contract for a DAO to be attack-resistant.

Transparency may be contradicted by the right to privacy, since many DAO members, especially of libertarian origin, want their identities to be kept secret. Moreover, decentralisation and scaling falter on the high transaction costs on the Ethereum platform, which may become cheaper as soon as the scaling solutions of Ethereum 2.0 are deployed in the platform. Accounting, taxation and government regulation are also issues to be considered in the near future.

DAOs promise to democratise culture, society and the economy. However, writing software and communicating via computers in the digital space do not account for democracy. DAOs can be used in the service of democracy inasmuch as they connect to the physical space and the real economy to support a broader socio-political movement capable of challenging neoliberalism across all spheres of society. A first step in that direction would perhaps be the merging of DAOs with platform co-ops.

DAOS AND PLATFORM CO-OPS

For the sake of argument here, I distinguish between DAOs that have a more libertarian orientation and DAOs that have a more commonist orientation. Commonist DAOs have the potential to support the transformation of capitalism to post-capitalism by evolving into worker-owned cooperatives and commons-based organisations that prioritise the production of use value over exchange value (Fritsch et al. 2021). Traditional as well as platform cooperatives could use Blockchain to become a more sustainable social enterprise. Platform co-ops could upgrade their platform to merge with DAOs (Mannan 2018).

Platform co-ops and DAOs come with similarities as well as differences (Robey 2021, 2022). They both share the principles of self-ownership, self-management, concern for community and the equitable distribution of value among multiple stakeholders. However, platform co-ops are based on 'one member, one vote' governance, while DAOs are based on 'one token, one vote' governance. Platform co-ops, therefore, are said to be democratic, while DAOs are plutocratic. DAOs seek to address plutocracy by collectively accrediting member identity as well as by applying alternative governance models, such as community staking DAO allocation (Regen Network), quadratic voting, conviction voting (the Commons Stack,[34] 1hive[35]), and more (Fritsch et al. 2021). Although DAOs are still underdeveloped with regard to legal issues and accountability concerns, they are better suited for organisations aiming to scale globally. Platform co-ops have several applications to the real economy, but they are less successful in securing funding and scaling (Table 3.3). Unlike shares in cooperatives, tokens used in DAO governance can be sold to secondary markets. This makes entrance to newcomers easy but renders a DAO susceptible to short-termism. DAOs can learn from cooperatives' emphasis on long-termism and establish more cultural patterns around token vesting, limited transferability or more experimental mechanisms (Kreutler 2021).

Table 3.3 Platform Co-ops and DAOs

	Co-ops	*DAOs*
Governance	One member, one vote; democracy	One token, one vote; plutocracy
Ownership	Legal	Alegal (De Filippi, Mannan & Reijers 2022)
Finances	Bank account	Smart-contract based treasury
Funding	Not suitable for equity-based venture capital investment	Crowdfunding
Use cases	Real economy	Digital economy
Scaling	Difficult	Easy
Vision	Long-termism	Short-termism

Platform co-ops and DAOs can learn from each other (Robey 2021, 2022). Platform co-ops can use the Blockchain to increase transparency and accountability, automate their database and scale by allowing members to remotely participate in decision-making. Platform co-ops can benefit by adopting token engineering in fields as diverse as governance, reputation systems, voting and crowdfunding. Token airdrops can be a way of distributing rewards and dividends within loose and large networks and attracting more decision-making members to an organisation (Robey 2022). Platform co-ops can turn into open co-ops and mutualise resources and know-how, just as DAOs development builds on open-source software.

DAOs can learn from the collective practices of platform co-ops. They can take the advantage of cooperatives to find legal footing, increase legitimacy and achieve mass adoption (Raymond 2021). DAOs can share tools and resources with each other in a DAO2DAO model.[36] DAOs can apply to the real economy by upgrading the already existing infrastructures of platform co-ops. Some examples would be agriculture and food production, wherein farmers could use the blockchain to track the produce from farm to market, and even produce metrics that could reverse climate change.[37]

Interestingly, there are examples of organisations operating on different sectors of the economy, such as feminist economics,[38] governance,[39] riding and delivery services,[40] finance,[41] housing,[42] art[43] and insurance,[44] which employ Blockchain technology for their own purposes (Davila 2021; Robey 2022; Samman & Freuden 2020). Eventually, the merging of platform co-ops with DAOs has the potential to create a networked ecosystem of open cooperativism capable of transforming capitalism into the post-capitalism of the commons (Freund & Stanko 2018).

However, there are significant challenges when it comes to scaling these organisations. It is not technically possible yet to include tens of thousands of stakeholders such as workers and consumers on the platform (Raymond 2021). Critical questions are the following. How would platforms actually engage people? What would platforms do with their attention span? What would happen if platforms get 1,000 people to vote every day? How would online operations relate to offline operations? How would algorithms interact with the fluidity and richness of social relationships? What are the dystopias involved in AI and human interaction?

Traditional cooperatives operate on a 'one member, one vote' system. Although this is theoretically possible in the DAO landscape too, DAOs normally operate on a 'one token, one vote' system, which is susceptible to plutocracy and whale attacks. Problems of hidden costs and hoarding power are persistent. Identity is much harder to keep track of in a DAO and there are ways of gaming the network (Raymond 2021). Moreover, passing hundreds or thousands of votes on the Ethereum main net would be prohibitively expensive for a cooperative, since votes on Ethereum Blockchain are transactions, and a transaction carries a $30 fee, on average. Ethereum-based DAOs are currently testing various scaling solutions and tools to address these issues, such as sharding, roll-ups, multi-sig wallets, self-sovereign identities and quadratic and conviction voting.

Even so, the challenges facing the merging of DAOs with cooperatives are not solely of a technical nature. Algorithms can be racist and sexist (Heilweil 2020). They cannot reflect the uniqueness and quality of human relationships. Technical decentralisation does not necessarily imply the political decentralisation of power that comes with unions, strikes, minimum wage campaigns and other forms of labour and community organising. There are DAOs that seek to be more political by building DAO2DAO infrastructures and offering safety nets to members, just as states do. Opolis[45] is an example of a member-owned digital employment cooperative currently utilising DAO technology to offer independent workers access to high-quality group-rate employment benefits such as healthcare insurance, a (crypto) payroll and tax compliance, among other things. But these initiatives still focus mostly on the individual rather than the collective. Building individualistic, niche and fragmented alternatives for freelancers does not suffice for collective liberation. The latter requires disrupting the overarching constitutional pattern of neoliberalism in which these technologies are embedded (Varoufakis 2022). DAOs may blend with DApps, NFTs and existing organisations running off Blockchain. Some DApps, NFTs and DAOs may be independent, autonomous and crypto-native while others may need to connect with existing institutional infrastructures and property rights.

> In such scenario, it would be possible, for instance: to have public institutions using freedom-respecting software providing services without compromising user's privacy (e.g. through the mathematical method of zero-knowledge proofs); to have large-scale co-operation across non-profits validated by a network of trust in which each vouches for their known 'friends'; to have new crowdsourced metrics of the multiple forms of value created by communities and social actors; to customise services beyond the current

> uniformity imposed by monopolistic software platforms, lowering the barriers for competition and opening the door to new forms of innovation by multiple non-profit and for-profit actors; appropriate automatic rewarding of work, including previously invisible reproductive work. And all these forms of co-operation would be facilitated without having an owner of the infrastructure with absolute control over the network and its resources.
>
> (Hassan et al. 2020: 102)

Blockchain protocols and smart contracts have unleashed enormous levels of value creation and exchange, as well as fraud and speculation. DApps, DeFI, ReFi, NFTs and DAOs are the interconnected building blocks of the Web3 ecosystem, which is growing, with new applications and use cases popping up every month. Combined with IoT and AI, the Web3 ecosystem has the potential to sustain a new socio-economic paradigm to the degree that it connects to the real economy. However, the whole ecocystem is moving in a libertarian rather than a collectivist direction. Either way, mainstream adoption is still a long way off, due to the inefficiencies and risks associated with Blockchain technology, among other factors.

Blockchain Risks

Blockchain technology has been hailed as the missing link to settle scalability, privacy and reliability concerns on the IoT (Shrivastava, Le & Sharma 2020). However, Blockchain bears similar risks to the IoT. Blockchain applications so far offer marginal benefits over state-of-the-art centralised solutions. At times Blockchain reproduces the very anomalies it purports to eliminate: centralisation of miners and crypto-exchanges, corruption, manipulation, fraud, money laundering, tax evasion, illicit actions and scams (Hu et al. 2019; Nizzoli et al. 2020; Vasek & Moore 2018). For all the technology's potential, most attempts to use it remain tentative. The advantages of Blockchains are often oversold. Blockchain is still slow and overhyped (Odiljon & Gai 2019). As David Gerard (2018), a Blockchain sceptic, puts it: 'Blockchains don't solve the underlying problem of agreeing on what you want to do and how.'

Complementary innovations such as scaling mechanisms, multi-sig wallets and oracles may secure transactions, increase adoption and ensure that distributed data management on the Blockchain is kept in sync with critical offline information and events. Blockchain applications may have far more benefits, inasmuch as a number of technical, ecological, legal and socio-political challenges are addressed (Braun-Dubler et al. 2020: 103).

Monetary Policy

Critics claim that Bitcoin has no intrinsic value, since it is not a unit of account, a stable store of value, a scalable means of payment or a safe asset backed by some form of collateral (Krugman 2018; Roubini 2021). Bitcoin and crypto are considered a speculative bubble fuelled by irrational exuberance accompanied by hack attacks, Ponzi schemes, pump and dump schemes, spoofing, wash trading, manipulation, and the like. In fact, Bitcoin has a negative value, given its environmental impact from its enormous energy use. Even if Bitcoin is to be widely accepted as a means of payment in the long run, it is subject to deflation, since its quantity is limited by default and, therefore, it is impossible to reflate the economy in times of recession by increasing the quantity of money (Varoufakis 2017).

> Many economists remain sceptical that cryptographic tokens can permanently replace conventional currencies since: (1) there are strong network externalities that favour existing conventional currencies; (2) the lack of sophisticated token supply rules leading to socially desirable stability and liquidity of tokenized economies. Furthermore, (3) from a classic economic perspective, it seems impossible to pre-specify socially optimal 'lender-of-last resort' rules in a smart contract. Lender-of-last resort refers to a safety-net institution, usually provided by central banks, to reduce the risk of a lack of liquidity of financial systems as a result of financial panics and bank runs. It represents government-guaranteed liquidity to financial institutions. The lack of such a lender-of-last resort makes financial systems susceptible to financial crises and systemic panics.
>
> (Voshmgir 2020: 184)

One could counter-argue that the real value of Bitcoin is the dematerialisation of scarcity and the denationalisation of money, steered by decentralisation powered by an algorithmically sound technology that could be reprogrammed ad hoc to stimulate multiple equilibria of supply and demand. However, pseudo-crypto-abundance depends on the scarce minerals, energy resources and labour power put into the production of the hardware used by miners – let alone the social reproduction of production itself included in household labour most often performed by women. Dmytri Kleiner (2018) applies the Marxist labour theory of value to assess Bitcoin:

> Not only has Bitcoin failed as money, but the asset bubble it has created has diverted investment from real production of goods to speculation, and the mining process consumes a phenomenal amount of energy, with catastrophic environmental effects. Meanwhile, it has done nothing in terms of making the economy fairer or reducing the power of either governments, banks or any of the intermediaries it was meant to displace … If there is value in the original vision of Bitcoin, to have a form of money that can be used to make payments across the internet in a way that makes government unnecessary and doesn't reveal real names or physical location, it needs to be programmed differently. Such a currency would need to work in such a way that the supply of the currency increases when more mining capacity

> is added to the pool. This allows the market to regulate its exchange value by the natural increase and decrease of investment in mining relative to demand for the currency. It is possible to create a cryptocurrency with a stable value by simply eliminating the feedback loop, creating a rational cryptocurrency with a consistent work:coin ratio. Bitcoin could be made rational by increasing and decreasing the number of Bitcoins produced per block along with the increase and decrease of the difficulty of the proof of work. This way, the number of Bitcoins produced would scale in proportion with the investment in mining. However, there may not be much interest in doing this. As miners would need to choose to use their hashing power to make a standard rate of profit mining the rational cryptocurrency instead of chasing speculative returns by mining bubble-prone, intentionally irrational cryptocurrencies. Another obstacle would be get attention for it, as a rational cryptocurrency would not attract hype, because it would not have fantastically skyrocketing exchange rates.

Much depends on how high-tech corporations and states are going to react to the surge in the value of Bitcoin and crypto as a whole. To the extent that traditional institutions tolerate or adopt Bitcoin as a digital asset, it is likely that the next decades are going to experience niche crypto-markets sailing along high-tech whales in the state-regulated ocean of platform capitalism. An alternative or even parallel scenario would entail the competition between centralised and decentralised markets, the latter comprising DApps, DAOs and platform and open cooperatives (Freund & Stanko 2018). So long as there is demand for decentralised digital currencies, Blockchain-based networks will continue to operate (De Filippi & Wright 2018).

Performance, Scalability and Security

For Blockchain to scale and achieve mainstream adoption, it needs to be fast, interoperable and secure. Existing Blockchains are not as fast and secure as centralised data management systems (Braun-Dubler et al. 2020: 107–108; De Filippi & Wright 2018: 56). High transaction costs, traffic jams, hack attacks and front running are some of the bottlenecks of the Blockchain. Trade-offs boil down to the famous trilemma, according to which Blockchain can maintain only two of the following properties: decentralisation, scalability and security (Braun-Dubler et al. 2020: 108). Scalability is a supply and demand problem, whereby the amount of people who want to engage in transactions surpasses the disk space available for transactions on the chain. Only the ones who can afford to outcompete the rest by paying the most can send transactions.

Decentralisation adds to the security of the system, since it eliminates single points of failure and a 51 per cent attack. Yet it hinders scalability, as each redundant node consumes disk space and adds delays due to the required synchronisation of the blocks. Redundancy means the same task is done in parallel by many nodes, which check on each other whether the results are the same. Less redundancy means that potential hackers need control over fewer nodes to have greater than 50 per cent control and be able to manipulate the database. Decentralisation is, therefore, a factor of security, since it is extremely difficult for a bad actor to control more than 50 per cent of the network. Centralisation could scale the Blockchain but it makes the network vulnerable to a manipulation by a 51 per cent attack. The real challenge lies in the Blockchain consensus process becoming faster and more efficient without compromising on decentralisation and security. As mentioned above, several mechanisms are already being put to the test in Ethereum 2.0 to resolve these issues, and research on new technical solutions is ongoing (Braun-Dubler et al. 2020: 108–110).

Decentralisation is a key design principle of Blockchain. However, like the Internet, the Blockchain is highly vulnerable to centralisation (Torpey 2019). Cryptocurrency exchanges such as Binance and Coinbase are centralised intermediaries that take custody of user assets and conduct most of their transactions off the Blockchain. Protocols and applications built on Blockchain are designed by a small core of developers funded by venture capitalists. Proof of work is highly centralised. Today, four mining pools control over 50 per cent of the Bitcoin Blockchain, and two mining pools control more than 50 per cent of the Ethereum Blockchain (De Filippi & Wright 2018: 180; Vigna 2021). Proof of stake reinforces plutocracy, since the ones who own more stake exert more power in the system. Therefore, major developers, companies and corporates can manipulate the system to their interests. Thus, a major challenge to be addressed is how to incentivise stakeholders to play by the rules while eliminating concentrations of power (Braun-Dubler et al. 2020: 96).

Interoperability

A Blockchain serves as a distributed accounting machine that performs computations and records all token transactions. It is a processor for decentralised applications that run on top of the Web3 (Voshmgir 2020: 32). For Web3 to replace Web2, a number of additional protocols are required. Apart from computation, Web3 needs file storage, messaging, identities, external data (oracles) and many more. Data needs to be portable and protocols interoperable to sustain a decentralised network. Many of these protocols and services are still in development (Voshmgir 2020: 33).

Energy Usage

Crypto-energy usage is a much-contested issue. Relevant research is still lacking to offer reliable information on different non-proof-of-work Blockchains and the quantification of their energy-saving potential for specific use cases (Sedlmeir et al. 2020). Admittedly, Bitcoin and Ethereum consume significant amounts of energy (Truby 2018). Bitcoin's electricity consumption is 0.29 per cent of total world electricity consumption, while the amount of electricity used for Ethereum is more than the annual consumption of Croatia or Jordan

(Braun-Dubler et al. 2020: 242). The impact of Blockchain on the environment may be gradually countervailed by the employment of renewable energy resources as well as compromises to be made between the degree of decentralisation, security, performance and energy consumption. The Blockchain technology might actually benefit nature if it increases accountability in the global supply chain, and even solve market failures if externalities can be better monitored (Braun-Dubler et al. 2020: 242).

Public Policy and Legal Frameworks

The advent of the Internet and Blockchain technology marks the potential passage from the liberal rule of law to the rule of code. From the law passed from elected governments to the code written by software engineers. Lawrence Lessig (2001) has coined the dictum 'Code is law' to demonstrate that code enables certain forms of social activity, while disabling others. As code evolves, it turns into the algorithmic engineering of social norms. Thus, code transforms into a sort of politics.

> As the technology further matures, blockchains could accelerate a structural shift of power from legal rules and regulations administered by government authorities to code-based rules and protocols governed by decentralised blockchain-based networks. Code-based protocols and decisions related to their development would ultimately dictate how these systems work and shape our means of interaction. We could increasingly subject ourselves to the 'rule of code' – code that may not be controlled by any one party and that may or may not operate in accordance with the 'rule of law'.
>
> (De Filippi & Wright 2018: 7)

The Internet was initially considered an anarchic medium, the unregulatability of which would undermine the power of governments and national courts over people. Yet the Internet had centralised points of distribution (the ISPs), which might ultimately be controlled by governments (De Filippi & Wright 2018: 50–51). ISPs operate within the jurisdiction of a state and, therefore, should comply with national laws. Over the past 20 years governments have been imposing regulations on ISPs and high-tech corporates. ISPs are often forced to filter Internet communications and block certain sites that violate the law, such as those hosting copyright-infringing material or child pornography. Online payment processors are obliged to deter unlawful activities such as money laundering. E-commerce is attentively monitored by authorities to prevent platforms from dealing in drugs or illegal arms. Google and Facebook are required to police their services, secure private data and report criminal activity. Countries such as Russia and China even ban certain websites and applications, thus directly controlling the type of information their citizens can view.

In short, although the Internet eliminated old intermediaries, it enabled new intermediaries to come to the front, which could be regulated (De Filippi &

Wright 2018: 179). The same is likely to occur in Blockchain. Just like the Internet, governments could impose regulations on crypto-exchanges and platforms, ISPs, end users, software developers and hardware manufacturers, which operate in particular jurisdictions and so can be regulated by local, state or national governments (De Filippi & Wright 2018: 173).

Government intervention on the Blockchain carries a major trade-off between strong versus soft regulation (De Filippi & Wright 2018: 173–192). Whereas strong regulation incurs the risk of stifling Blockchain innovation, the unfettered development of Blockchain could facilitate fraudulent practices such as money laundering, tax evasion, child pornography, drug trafficking, and the like. Pseudo-anonymity on Blockchain does not fully preserve identity privacy. Sophisticated IoT data analytics and AI machine learning could map out the relationships of transactions recorded on the Blockchain and combine them with contextual data (metadata) to reveal the identities of end users and detect illicit behaviour. Governments could require ISPs operating within their jurisdictions to discriminate between transactions on the Blockchain. Governments also could apply regulations to search engines and social networks to avoid indexing or distributing links to illegal Blockchain-based applications. Governments could regulate big centralised mining companies that operate on the Blockchain. They could also regulate hardware manufacturers (such as Intel or Samsung) to track or halt specific Blockchain-based applications that allow unlawful acts. Governments themselves could employ permissioned Blockchains to overcome bureaucracy and improve state governance overall.

There is much discussion these days in the United States as to whether cryptocurrencies should be considered commodities, securities or derivatives (Schonberger 2022). Public officials hold that cryptocurrencies and Blockchain platforms should be regulated accordingly to protect investors from scams, hack attacks, manipulation, and the like. To strike the right balance, governments should carefully examine the technology's benefits and drawbacks on a case-by-case basis.

Ultimately, the transnational nature of Blockchain is a double-edged sword. On the one hand, decentralisation wipes out intermediaries, potentially distributing power to the many. On the other, the transparent and tamper-proof database of Blockchain could transform into a powerful tool for global surveillance and control (De Filippi & Wright 2018: 33–34). Compared to the Internet, Blockchain is prone to greater centralisation by multinational corporations operating in concert with governments and organisations to control the database. Blockchain centralisation would revive the Orwellian nightmare of surveillance capitalism, a glimpse of which we are already witnessing in the development of China's 'social credit' system. By managing the allocation of labour and behaviour among humans and machines, Blockchain could spit out various technological dystopias, as manifested in sci-fi novels, movies and series such as *1984*, *Brave New World*, *Matrix*, *Startrek* and *Black Mirror* (De Filippi & Wright 2018: 55). Code could either liberate humanity from toil and drudgery or enslave it deeper into techno-feudo-capitalism.

However, the distributed scope of Blockchain makes it difficult to tame. Even if governments manage to regulate the activity of crypto-exchanges, platforms and miners in a handful of jurisdictions, Blockchain operations could migrate to other Blockchain-friendly jurisdictions (e.g. Switzerland) or introduce a fork on the network to bypass the regulation in question (De Filippi & Wright 2018: 181–183). The 'end-to-end' principle of the Internet renders online activity immune to absolute control. Perhaps we are likely to experience in the decades to come a cat-and-mouse game between regulators and libertarians, crypto-commoners, and the like.

The in-built absence of an overarching authority on Blockchain creates a legal vacuum that bears additional socio-political complications. Mainstream approaches to Blockchain are often biased. They disregard that technology is not value-free; it comes imbued with affordances that constitute a prefigurative politics (Husain, Franklin & Roep 2020; Leach 2013), as manifested, for example, in the contrast between decentralisation and centralisation and the delusionary tendency to replace politics with Blockchain (Dicker 2021; Faustino 2019; Swartz 2017). Technology is first and foremost a social construct embedded with moral values that correspond to core socio-political categories. Thus, proper assessment of the disruptive potential of Blockchain requires a critical examination of the different political interpretations of Blockchain.

The Politics of Blockchain

To fully come to grips with Blockchain, it is essential that we engage in the public debate over the technology, since different political theories project different Blockchain perspectives. The hype around Blockchain is fuelled by a diversity of actors and political factions: computer geeks, fraudsters, start-ups, corporations, banks, governments, institutions, media, anarcho-capitalists, cypherpunks, neo-institutionalists, Marxists, socialists, ecologists, conservatives, liberals and digital communitarians all contemplate and experiment with Blockchain technology for their own purposes (Husain, Franklin & Roep 2020; Tan 2022).

Much of the present literature on Blockchain technology lacks the necessary critical scrutiny and analytical depth, producing often biased, overly optimistic and libertarian statements. Consequently, there is a significant lack of definitional clarity when it comes to Blockchain politics. The theoretical landscape is hazy and conceptual elaborations are frivolous. The Blockchain comes with a diverse set of political imaginaries that play out in different patterns (Husain, Franklin & Roep 2020). As with the commons literature, political theories of the Blockchain technology range from libertarian, liberal and neo-liberal accounts to neo-institutional, post-capitalist, anti-capitalist and socialist accounts.

Key to mapping out the discussion is the contrast between decentralisation and centralisation that runs through the history of the Internet. The debate over decentralisation versus centralisation is one of the most recurrent themes in political philosophy, raging since Plato, Aristotle, Thomas Hobbes and John Locke up until contemporary political theory. However, decentralisation alone is a limited standpoint. Politics reflects foundational concepts of political theory, such as democracy, freedom, power, equality and justice, that cannot be reduced into a simplified contrast between centralised and decentralised governance. Rather, the contrast between centralised and decentralised governance plays out at the foreground of various discourses over democracy, freedom, power, equality and justice.

One of the most common themes on the Blockchain literature concerns the role of the state in modern liberal democracies. The classical liberalism of Hobbes and Locke considers the state a progression from nature to civilisation (Swift 2006). The state constitutes a central authority that represents the people on the basis of consent granted upon a hypothetical social contract, which legitimises the few to rule over the many. In this regard, the state has historically been introduced as a coordination mechanism to advance the evolution of the human species from tribes to large-scale constitutional patterns, such as villages, towns, states, and so on. Thus, the state has, essentially, been hailed as the solution to the problem of scale for the evolution of the human species. Marxism, on the other hand, considers the state the historic outcome of class struggle, enslaving the many to the exploitation of the few, which goes all the way back to slavery and evolves into serfdom, proletarianisation and modern wage slavery. In this regard, the state is the indispensable institutional backbone of capitalism.

Libertarians meet with Marxists in their critique of the state. Whereas for libertarians the advent of Blockchain technology represents the natural progression from centralised institutions to self-regulated markets, for Marxists the demise of the state signals the natural progression of state capitalism towards communism (Swift 2006). Although for classical Marxism the natural progression of state capitalism to communism passes through state socialism, for autonomous Marxism state capitalism is rife with contradictions that can be overcome only by the self-management of production by workers themselves (Papadimitropoulos 2020). Whereas for classical Marxism the contradictions of capitalism revolve around the division between owners (capitalists) and non-owners (workers) of the means of production, for autonomous Marxists the contradictions of capitalism expand on the division between directors (managers) and executors (workers) of production. The latter is orthogonal with the core division of society between rulers and ruled, exercised par excellence by the state. Whereas for orthodox Marxism the socialist state is the natural or teleological stage of the transition from capitalism to communism, for anarchists and autonomous Marxists the state is an unnecessary and oppressive means of power. Right-wing libertarians espouse a Blockchain-based techno-capitalism that does away with the state, but left-wing libertarians, post-liberals, anarchists and autonomous Marxists often meet in envisaging a Blockchain-aided commons-based transition to post-capitalism, supported or not by a partner state.

Crypto-Libertarianism

A line of argument, drawing often on Jürgen Habermas (1996), reasons that the development of ICTs such as the Internet and mobile phones can bootstrap a model of participatory democracy anchored in public deliberation, transparency and accountability of decision-making process. A number of authors have advocated for digital democracy or tele-democracy supported by ICTs (Arterton 1987; Coleman & Gotze 2001; Grossman 1995; Hague & Loader 1999; Hill & Hughes 1998; van Dijk 2006; Ward 1996). The Internet and mobile applications, it is claimed, can bring about the massification of discourse and prototype the democratisation of media. Push-button voting, tele-referenda, tele-polling and free access to online databases and registers can now provide a higher degree of citizen involvement in political and legislative procedures. Technology can now ensure greater transparency, openness and inclusiveness (Vesnic-Alujevic et al. 2019). A number of analysts argue that ICTs facilitate the participation of citizen-amateurs in formerly professionalised activities, thus signalling the 'open sourcing' of journalism (Gillmor 2004), politics (Castells 2007; Jenkins 2006), science (Benkler 2002) and culture (Jenkins 2006; Lessig 2004). The power of 'everybody' (Shirky 2008), the 'crowd' (Surowiecki 2004) or the 'mob' (Rheingold 2003) is giving rise to a new populist renaissance of democratic participation and inclusion.

Blockchain technology represents the latest trend in the rationale to employ ICTs to democratise politics and the economy (Buterin & Weyl 2018). Crypto-libertarians advocate that the state is an illegitimate, bureaucratic, corrupt, inefficient and irremediably obsolete agent of power. Central coordination and the state are the products of a patriarchal, hierarchical and gerontocratic model. In concert with elites and multinational corporations, governments exert asymmetric power and pervasive control over their citizens, in the style of Big Brother (Magnuson 2020: 10). Elections held every four years misrepresent real-time information. Representative democracy perpetuates the tyranny of the 'majority' over minorities. Justice is fine-tuned to the interests of elites. State capitalism is prone to periodical economic crises. Populism emerges as the coefficient of distrust to modern liberal oligarchies, masterfully orchestrated by the manufacturing of consent by mass media.

The Blockchain, instead, is poised to secure individual privacy from rapacious governments and corporations, eliminate information asymmetries and render the Internet truly democratic. It is supposed to grant individuals more degrees of freedom and power. Personal responsibility, self-promotion, self-government and smart contracts take precedence over top-down policies, paternalistic central institutions and 'faceless government bureaucrats'. DAOs could now self-organise on flat structures, thus challenging the very core hierarchical structure of corporations and governments (De Filippi & Wright 2018: 1; Frank 2015; Patron 2014; Robinson 2015; Thorp 2015). Blockchain allows a more distributed diffusion of authority, in which the source of legitimacy stems from individuals themselves (Atzori 2017: 48). The freedom, transparency and efficacy of decentralised self-governance make up for coercion, misuse of power, friction and single points of failure on the part of corporations, banks and governments (Atzori 2017: 47). Collective relationships between individuals, corporations and governments are replaced by computer-based atomic interactions (Atzori 2017: 48). Some even go further, to argue that algorithmic-based distributed consensus, perfect information and decentralised market mechanisms may solve the problem of societal organisation by transforming politics into computer engineering (Garrod 2016: 66). The rule of law gives way to the rule of code.

Blockchain overcomes the geographical limits of nation states, thereby fostering cosmopolitanism and globalisation (Swan 2015). Libertarianism prevails over state-centred politics. The state becomes useless and withers away due to lack of consent.[46] States turn into business-engineering mechanisms and society is run by Blockchain-based smart contracts and free-market rules. Private corporations, DApps and DAOs compete to provide private and public goods and services. Society transforms into a global prediction market, speculating through cryptocurrencies and tokens. Citizens first vote on specific proposals or targets, then on the means to achieve them. They gain or lose tokens, depending on the proposal acceptance or rejection. Vote buying, a practice considered anathema to legacy political systems, transforms politics into prediction markets (Buterin & Weyl 2018). The libertarian dream of self-regulating markets becomes a reality. Society is reduced to the zero-sum game of the survival of the fittest among self-interested utility maximisers competing in the Darwinian jungle of anarcho-capitalism.

Crypto-Scepticism

Crypto-sceptics cover a broad spectrum of approaches, ranging from liberals and social democrats to post-capitalists and Marxists. Moderate voices hold that Blockchain is not going to abolish the state but to ameliorate governance, reduce power asymmetries and provide more granular legal frameworks tailored to citizens' needs (Swan 2015). Others are more critical and stress the risks that could overweigh the benefits of Blockchain technology (Atzori 2017). To begin with, the quest for profit leads to the centralisation of miners, who could further merge into conglomerates that could expose citizens' records and essential rights to private interests and unpredictable market dynamics (e.g. uncertainty of mining profitability, volatility of prices, discontinuity of investments, speculative attacks, etc.) (Atzori 2017: 51). Centralisation thus could exacerbate risk concentration and periodic capitalist crises.

Decentralisation, on the other hand, is not exempt from drawbacks. In a distributed architecture with thousands or millions of nodes on a global scale, to modify a protocol may result in a complex and time-consuming procedure, which can be highly debilitating for real-time politics (Atzori 2017: 53). The open-source nature of Blockchain, allowing it to be forked or dismissed by the community at any time, renders it insecure when it comes to preserving contracts and government services, which may become susceptible to invalidity due to obsolescence or boredom, or shift towards a new system. Open-source systems also suffer from bugs and flaws in the code, which could compromise the security and the civil rights of millions of citizens (Atzori 2017: 52).

Open-source software provides neither equal opportunity nor inclusiveness. In practice, decisions are executed by a small number of core developers on a consensus-based policy, which represents a shrunken version of passive democracy. Despite the much-vaunted egalitarianism of peer-to-peer networks, Blockchain is prone to techno-elitism, with code developers, miners, fintech professionals and techno-preneurs assuming a privileged role in society, to the detriment of the big mass of computer-illiterate or low-skilled individuals (Atzori 2017: 57; De Filippi & Hassan 2018). The digital divide prevents the majority of people from participating in the Blockchain-based cosmopolitan governance. Despite the incorruptible nature of algorithms, subtle or hidden points of control emerge on cyber-space, either directly managed by start-up founders, key executives, chief scientists and core developers or indirectly shaped by diffused, charismatic powers (Atzori 2017: 58). Blockchain experts become the new policy-makers.

Blockchain is producing the demise of bureaucracy, in one form, and its apotheosis in another (Laul 2019). Power does not 'float freely' on Blockchain. Decentralisation replaces old intermediaries with new intermediaries, who occupy novel centres of power. And whereas, for libertarians, inequalities may pose a meritocratic indicator of justice in the jungle of crypto-capitalism, in the real world inequalities bring to the fore the potential anti-democratic use of Blockchain. Under the guise of fixing 'technical' issues, 'benevolent dictators' impose their anti-democratic power over government services and essential citizens' data, without any formal legitimacy (democracy) or control. The 'transparent' control of personal data by novel oligarchies could exacerbate surveillance capitalism along with numerous dystopian scenarios, famously depicted in series such as *Black Mirror*.

Blockchain further bears the risk of economism and techno-determinism (Hayes 2016; Swan 2015). The 'gamification' of politics through nudging token-based incentives may have detrimental effects on citizens' fundamental rights (di Zerega 2013). It can depoliticise society, turning politics into a zero-sum game among apolitical, nihilistic, self-interested utility maximisers. It can impose a 'crypto-Leviathan' on society by enforcing a social contract between profit-driven and power-seeking individuals (Reijers et al. 2021). Blockchain can be used as a novel speculative tool for modern liberal oligarchies, transforming citizens into profit algorithms (De Filippi & Loveluck 2016). The reduction of politics to code and profit is unmindful of the cultural, social, institutional and ethical complexity of human interactions, and it may lead to a technological dystopia (Atzori 2017: 54). Technology cannot but be subject to *the political* – that is, the moral ground that forms the rationale behind coding and algorithms (Papadimitropoulos 2020).

Critics of Blockchain admit that Blockchain technology can greatly improve the structure, management and decision-making processes of both states and markets (Nguyen 2016). However, they claim that Blockchain-based algorithmic governance cannot replace politics. Rather, what is expected to be seen is permissioned Blockchains fostering better governance and making legal frameworks more granular and tailored to the needs of citizens (Swan 2015).

> A reasonable conclusion is that the blockchain-based governance should be seen as an organisational theory – with significant technical and managerial advantages for markets, private services, communities, and e-government itself – while it is not meant to be a stand-alone political theory. Likewise, blockchain technology and decentralised platforms are not hyper-political, but rather pre-political tools. If not balanced out by the functions of centralised, democratic institutions, the blockchain-based governance risk falling within the concept of amoral antipolitics, justified by the rhetoric of inevitability of globalisation, free-market and individual power (Marden, 2003). And these antipolitical forces are able to disrupt those very democratic values that today many libertarians strive to defend.
>
> (Atzori 2017: 59)

Neither crypto-libertarian nor liberal approaches are liberating enough, since they do not question the power asymmetries inherent in capitalism. When libertarians do so, they reproduce an individualistic stance, which abstracts from society's underlying collective substance. On the other hand, liberals do not call into question either capitalism or liberal democracy as such. Discussions revolve around the degree of state intervention in the capitalist economy. Both libertarians and liberals of all sorts (centre and left-wing) assume that managerial hierarchies and/or the sheer coincidence of individual preferences are the sole normative pillars of the human species, establishing cross-sectional 'tribes' and 'clubs' on the Internet and beyond.

Finally, critics claim that Bitcoin and the like reflect an anarcho-capitalism that is neither apolitical nor satisfies the needs of the planet and society (Kostakis & Giotitsas 2014; Varoufakis 2022). Bitcoin and crypto as a whole would be more useful for the planet and society if they were integrated into a broader political transformation of state capitalism into the post-capitalism of the commons (Papadimitropoulos 2020).

Neo-Institutionalism

A more radical line of reasoning departs from neo-institutionalism to navigate its way around post-capitalist accounts of Blockchain. Neo-institutionalists employ the analytical framework of transaction costs theory (Alchian & Demsetz 1972; Coase 1937; Williamson 1985), Austrian economics (Hayek 1944) and public choice economics (Buchanan & Tullock 1962; Olson 1965; Ostrom 1990) to envisage the functionality of Blockchain beyond a payment system. The basic idea is to use the Blockchain to move away from centralised capitalist markets and the state. The Blockchain should not be seen through the lens of a Schumpeterian innovation process alone but as a general-purpose technology that facilitates novel types of socio-economic self-management, such as DApps and DAOs running on smart contracts (Davidson, De Filippi & Potts 2016, 2018).

DApps and DAOs are Blockchain-based decentralised organisations that combine transaction cost reduction with price-driven coordination and collective decision-making to resolve the principal–agent problem and compete with centralised managerial hierarchies (firms and state) and markets (Berg, Davidson & Potts 2017). DApps and DAOs are, basically, distributed governance models running on Blockchain that may improve on current democratic systems, which suffer from lobbyism, corruption, information/power asymmetries, centralisation costs and rent-seeking.

Crypto-democracy is supposed to mitigate the tyranny of the majority, the exploitation of organised minorities and rational voter ignorance through transparent polycentric governance of self-organising communities adapting to the most efficient information and incentive context (Davidson, De Filippi & Potts 2016: 14–15; 2018). To the extent that DApps and DAOs may reduce transaction costs and manage to self-organise around price discovery and collective decision-making, they may outcompete managerial hierarchies and markets in the long run (De Filippi & Wright 2018).

However, crypto-democracy is token-weighted, meaning that one needs to own tokens in order to vote on a proposal. The more tokens one has, the more voting power one has. Plutocracy and vote buying run counter to the egalitarianism of the commons. Additional mechanisms should be employed to mitigate plutocracy and/or dissociate crypto-economics from democratic procedures for communities willing to fully adhere to the principle of egalitarianism.

Ostrom's Commons 3.0

Many authors with neo-institutional tendencies take a step forward to applying Ostrom's design principles to the Blockchain (Bollier 2015; Cila et al. 2020; Davidson, De Filippi & Potts 2016, 2018; O'Dwyer 2015; Pazaitis, De Filippi & Kostakis 2017; Rozas et al. 2021; Rozas, Tenorio-Fornés & Hassan 2021). Ostrom's work on the commons has developed over two basic stages: Commons 1.0 covers the polycentric self-management of natural resource commons (e.g. forests, fisheries and irrigation systems). Ostrom identifies a set of design principles in the operation of the natural commons that often render the commons superior neo-institutional solutions to market or government institutions.

Ostrom's work expanded in the last decades to cover the digital Commons 2.0 (open-source software, open science, peer production, open innovation). Ostrom's design principles for the natural commons have been applied also to Commons 2.0 (e.g. Wikipedia, Drupal) (Hess & Ostrom 2007; Hess 2008; Fuster Morell 2010; Forte, Larco & Bruckman 2009; Rozas 2017; Viégas, Wattenberg & McKeon 2007). Ostrom shows that publicly observable reputation mechanisms can offer a solution to the free-rider problem and generate cooperation in the production and maintenance of quasi-public goods such as the intellectual commons of knowledge, information and culture. However, Commons 1.0 and 2.0 are functional only on fragmented, small-scale offline and online communities.

Blockchain technology has the potential to expand the application of Ostrom's design principles to Commons 3.0. It provides a technical solution to the problem of scale by blending local with global commons under algorithmic governance. Blockchain decentralisation may diffuse power over shared distributed accounting ledgers around which open collaborative networks can organise the production of both material and immaterial goods and services in a common-centric and cosmo-local model (Manski & Bauwens 2020; Rozas et al. 2021; Rozas, Tenorio-Fornés & Hassan 2021).

When commons-based projects start to grow substantially they tend to resort to more explicit and rigid organisation processes, and even formal institutions, such as the Wikimedia Foundation and the Drupal Association. Blockchain decentralisation may help loosen control without losing control, since it allows for communal ownership and horizontal control of shared resources. Blockchain transparentisation builds on the immutability of open-source code to facilitate negotiation, install accountability, increase legitimacy, help resolve conflict and create a culture of openness and participation. Blockchain decentralisation and transparentisation combined may help the commons scale on a global level (Rozas et al. 2021; Rozas, Tenorio-Fornés & Hassan 2021).

The digital representation of value through tokenisation may help define the boundaries and governance rules of a commons as well as readdress power dynamics within the community in a more inclusive and transparent manner. For example, care labour may now be represented by reputation or labour tokens (Rozas et al. 2021). Similarly, tokens may confer certain rights over one aspect, all the while disabling rights over other aspects of a project. Shermin Voshmgir (2020: 266) distinguishes between simple and complex, purpose-driven tokens. A simple token is a cryptographic derivative that may be programmable money or represent real-life assets and rights. Purpose-driven tokens are micro-, macro-economic tools for steering complex token-driven communities. They incentivise individual behaviour to contribute to a collective goal. However, tokenisation exhibits the risks of extreme quantification and data fetishism (Sharon & Zandbergen 2017). It is up to communities themselves to decide upon the extent to which they may incorporate tokenisation in their socio-technological artefacts.

Smart contracts – that is, the self-enforcement of rules based on preset algorithms – may have numerous applications to commons-based DApps and DAOs (Rozas et al. 2021):

- setting boundaries;
- formalising governance rules;
- settling negotiations;

- establishing clear mechanisms for conflict resolution;
- regulating monitoring procedures and graduated sanctions;
- redistributing, pooling, capping, allocating or mutualising resources;
- creating layers of nested DAOs; or
- sharing agreements and different forms of tokenised value among various communities in interoperable ways.

For example, in the case of a community Wi-Fi network, Blockchain transparency would help identify the use of resources by community members. A smart contract could automatically enforce a previously negotiated Internet bandwidth limit and penalise a potential misuse of the commons network (Rozas et al. 2021). In the case of nested entities of community Wi-Fi networks, smart contracts may ensure the autonomy of local DAOs jurisdictions vis-à-vis certain respects of higher DAOs jurisdictions. However, given the ex ante nature of smart contracts and their still limited capacity for upgrading, it is up to communities themselves to decide on the aspects to remain in/off the Blockchain code. Similarly, the impersonality and the technical expertise necessary to programme a smart contract should be subject to direct democratic control and deliberation. Finally, DAOs open up multiple legal challenges that still need to be resolved (De Filippi & Wright 2018).

Inspired by Ostrom, neo-institutionalists advocate Blockchain-based polycentric models of federated governance in which companies, governments, start-ups, DAOs and communities participate in hybrid commons-based post-capitalist models of economy, aiming to overcome the stringent dichotomy between capitalism and the state. They combine Ostrom's institutional analysis and development framework – which can be classified as a model of cooperative game theory – with systems theory and crypto-economics to produce highly sophisticated mathematical models and software that apply Ostrom's design principles on the Blockchain. Governable stacks (Schneider 2022a) and modular politics (Schneider et al. 2021) are instances of software being currently designed to be used by communities to self-organise on the Blockchain.

However, Ostrom's polycentric model builds on rational choice theory, which reproduces the methodological individualism and the utility-maximising principle of neoclassical economics. It reintroduces an incentive-based cost–benefit analysis to solve complex coordination problems in cooperative contexts such as the self-management of common-pool resources. As such, it reduces the collective interconnectedness of individuals to cooperative games that discard the power asymmetries inherent in the actors (governments, companies, NGOs) participating in the governance of a common-pool resource.

Neo-institutionalists seem at times to oscillate between right-wing and left-wing libertarianism. On the one hand, they bring in Austrian economics to Commons 3.0. On the other, they claim that the introduction of capitalist market rules in Commons 3.0 distorts the mission of the latter (De Filippi & Hassan 2014). On the one hand, they praise Blockchain technology for its liberating potential. On the other, they alert us for the pitfalls of a trustless dream (De Filippi 2019).

Like Ostrom, neo-institutionalists often go along with friendly capitalism by not calling into question the undemocratic structure of capitalist firms and the unjust expropriation and inequitable distribution of value. They do not overcome the grave contradictions residing at the core of capitalist production – that is, the division between directors and workers, owners and non-owners of the means of production. They do not challenge liberal democracy wherein the very contradictions of corporate management penetrate the core of state management. Thus, they often oscillate between radicalism and conservatism, eventually reproducing the contradictions of capitalism and the state within the commons themselves.

To avoid these contradictions, neo-institutionalists need to engage in participatory action research. Rather than well-paid computer scientists and academics working in the 'comfort' of capitalist enterprises and neoliberal universities to produce highly sophisticated mathematical models and software, it would be better for them to reach out to platform co-ops and the commons to understand the needs of the community and co-design the parameters of their self-governance model together. Sophisticated mathematical models and computer code should be translatable in simple language for non-experts to understand and should be communicated in physical space. The solutions to the problems of society and the planet will not come from computer scientists and academics working alone in their offices to produce highly sophisticated mathematical models and software but from interdisciplinary teams cooperating primarily in physical space to alter the social relations of production from the ground up.

Crypto-Commonism

A convenient lens through which to read the neo-institutionalist oscillation between conservatism and radicalism is the major division between crypto-libertarianism and crypto-commonism (Fritsch et al. 2021; García-Siñeriz 2018). Whereas the former and most dominant is inspired by libertarianism or anarcho-capitalism (Buterin & Weyl 2018), the latter comprises a great deal of often disparate and entangled branches of radicalism, ranging from left-wing libertarianism and neo-institutionalism to anarcho-syndicalism, autonomous Marxism and crypto-communism (Alizart 2020; Davila 2021; Fritsch et al. 2021). The boundaries are uncertain and often overlap. Vitalik Buterin, for example, the founder of Ethereum and one of the most prominent advocates of the crypto-economy, would rather be considered a republican libertarian than a right-wing libertarian, since he argues for the creation of a better world through the proliferation of decentralised self-regulated communities, often with the aid of the state apparatus.

There is a tendency in the grey literature to relate crypto-libertarianism to anarchism. However, there is a fundamental difference between anarchism and libertarianism. Very broadly, anarchists and libertarians share their opposition to both state and corporate coercion along with their advocacy to voluntary association (García-Siñeriz 2018). Yet they differ in their conceptualisation of freedom. Libertarians adhere to a negative account of freedom, according to which the individual should be free from 'outside interference' when choosing an action or belief. Negative freedom stipulates freedom of individual choice and the neutrality of the state over citizen ethics. Anarchists, on the other hand, aspire to a positive account of freedom according to which every action and belief feeds upon a shared meaning that penetrates individuality (García-Siñeriz 2018). This is not to reduce the individual to the collective but to stress the ontological interconnectedness of 'being-with-together'. The individual goes along with the co-emergence of the political – that is, with the social structure of human existence and interaction.

Whereas crypto-libertarians defend the freedom of capitalist markets from the interference of non-market forces, anarchists expose the exploitative nature of capitalism, which is the domination of capital in labour, ecosystems, working conditions, etc. Anarchism resonates more with crypto-commonism than with crypto-libertarianism. Crypto-libertarians adopt an individualist approach to human interaction, a capitalist approach to economic organisation and a market-based approach to governance, but crypto-commonists hold a collectivist view of social interaction, a commonist approach to economic organisation and a democratic approach to governance (García-Siñeriz 2018). Whereas crypto-libertarians consider the invisible hand of the free market to be the privileged agent that drives the trustless technology of Blockchain on the principles of neoclassical economics, crypto-commonists regard the Blockchain as a trust-enabling technology that could facilitate democracy on the principles of commons-based economics. Crypto-libertarians champion market fundamentalism; crypto-commonists espouse economic democracy (Table 3.4).

Blockchain Commons, Crypto-Libertarianism and DAOs

Blockchain is a contested commons. As open-source software, it belongs to the digital commons produced by online communities in terms of commoning. At the same time, Blockchain commons is used by market forces in the vein of crypto-libertarianism. The very contradiction between use value and exchange

Table 3.4 Crypto-Libertarianism, Crypto-Commonism and Post-Capitalism

Crypto-libertarianism, crypto-commonism, post-capitalism			
Ethics	Individual freedom	Egalitarianism	Aligning individual with collective interests
Economic organisation	Exchange value	Use value	Aligning exchange value with use value
Governance	Market forces	Democracy	Aligning market forces with democracy

value that features on FLOSS and the digital commons expands on Blockchain. Exchange value lies at the core of Blockchain, in the form of the scarce native protocol token that introduces a crypto-derivative market operating on the capitalist principles of commodification, financialisation, collateralisation, speculation, tokenisation, and so on. Some authors come to see the Blockchain commons as a positive externality of crypto-libertarianism (Voshmgir 2020). In this regard, the Blockchain commons is considered the coefficient of the profit incentive.

Others see it as another instance of the co-optation of FLOSS from crypto-capitalism that extracts value through tokenisation, seigniorage and transaction fees (Vercellone 2013). From this viewpoint, the crypto-sphere opens up ample space for the 'becoming-rent' of profit. In effect, the crypto-sphere adds an additional layer of fictional capital, as Marx would have it, into a zero-sum game in which use value is co-opted by exchange value being sucked up by whales in whirlpools of speculation, eventually expanding accumulation by dispossession (Harvey 2003). Bitcoin is often portrayed as a DAO, but it is better viewed as a DLO (distributed lobbying organisation), given that the 75 million currently existing wallets – as of January 2022 – comprise a number of whales (early HODLers) with preferential interests.[47] (A Bitcoin HODLer is a paraphrase of a crypto 'holder', used to stress the determination not to sell the cryptocurrency until it becomes mainstream.) As such, Bitcoin is an innovative peer-to-peer technology co-opted by a new type of hyper-imperialist techno-feudalism that seeks to colonise time and space (Linares 2021). It represents the crypto-enclosure of the digital commons into ownable, tradeable assets (Schneider 2021b: 5).

Crypto-commoners strive to resolve the contradiction between use value and exchange value by tokenising use value and introducing crowdfunded markets into the models of DApps and DAOs operating on the principles of the commons. They seek to steer Blockchain towards the post-capitalism of the commons via the collective production, consumption and circulation of use value. Blockchain-based crowdfunded DAOs could be considered anti-capitalist insofar as they challenge private ownership of the means of production and competition over one-directional capital accumulation, which leads to monopolies or oligopolies. What differentiates crypto-libertarian DAOs from crypto-commonist DAOs is that the latter are oriented towards an aim external to money in and of itself (Fritsch et al. 2021). Whereas in the former profit is central, in the latter profit is peripheral to community goals.

Crypto-commonist DAOs seek to resolve the scaling problem inherent in Commons 1.0 and 2.0. Platform co-ops operating in the real economy can now utilise the shared distributed accounting ledgers of Blockchain to organise the production of both material and immaterial goods and services in a common-centric and cosmo-local model. Blockchain thus supports the production of a new type of cyber-physical commons that links local with global commons under the rule of code (Fritsch et al. 2021). Blockchain-based federated scaling interconnects a clustering of DAOs that incorporates cultural heterogeneity, all the while remaining attentive to non-linear dynamics between interlinked common-pool resources on different scales.

Cyber-physical commons differentiate from past efforts at commoning inasmuch as they innovate upon market relations, money forms, the production of value, capital accumulation and distribution, digital identity and governance processes to bridge to nascent post-capitalist markets, rather than oppose market relations altogether (Fritsch et al. 2021). They aim to redefine markets, labour and money so as to become more conducive to nurturing and maintaining commons value(s). They employ novel tools of grassroots self-organisation, such as:

1. crowdfunding;
2. interoperable open protocols and supply chains for a circular economy;
3. open-value accounting engineered by token issuance;
4. contribution-based distribution of value among multiple stakeholders;
5. value/asset reciprocity among ethical market entities and commons-based open cooperatives established via copyfair licensing;
6. reputation tracking and impact assessment;
7. the integration of social and ecological externalities, including thermodynamic accounting, which gives direct access to flows of resources and energy usage;
8. collective sense making;
9. social signal processing;
10. peer-to-peer mutual credit issuance;
11. self-sovereign identity management, based on reputation and mutual attestation; and
12. testing and validation of holistic design principles through simulation and modelling.

Some go even further, to envisage post-Blockchain commons-based ledgers that do not rely on a single chain of blocks but may have multiple chains and incorporate different security and consensus protocols. Holochain,[48] for example, rather than relying on a single ledger of transactions, in which each transaction needs to be verified by all other nodes, allows for local and contextual open ledgers to connect with each other and become interoperable (Manski & Bauwens 2020: 9) (Table 3.5).

Cyber-physical commons aim to prioritise use value over exchange value and address the problem of scale by interconnecting Commons 1.0 and Commons 2.0. However, it is still unknown how the contradictions of the commons are going to play out across the emerging ecosystem of Blockchain-based cyber-physical commons. Next, I take a snapshot of how the contradictions of the commons are crystallised in the tension between crypto-libertarianism and crypto-commonism, showcased in the Commons Stack DAO.

Table 3.5 Libertarian versus Commons Blockchains

Ledger projects	
Libertarian	**Commons**
One world ledger (Bitcoin, Ethereum)	Interoperable P2P ledgers (Holochain, Faircoin, EcSA)
Commodity-based	Contribution-based, mutual credit
Tokens and cryptocurrencies	Asset-backed tokens
Competitive games	Cooperative games
Smart contracts	Ostrom's social contracts
Oligarchic proof of consensus (one dollar, one vote)	Distributed and contributory proofs
Market value	Value sovereignty
Extractive systems	Generative, nature-friendly ecosystems
Profit-driven	Impact, purpose, benefit-driven
Trustless	Trustful (web of trust)

Source: Adapted from Manski and Bauwens (2020: 10).

Notes

1 See https://bitnodes.io.
2 See www.blockchain.com/explorer.
3 See www.investopedia.com/terms/1/51-attack.asp.
4 See www.blockchain.com/charts/hash-rate.
5 See www.blockchain.com/explorer?view=btc.
6 See https://ethereum.org/en/staking/#:~:text=Requirements,the%20process%20and%20hardware%20requirements.
7 See https://ethereum.org/en/developers/docs/scaling.
8 See https://ethereum.org/en/dapps.
9 See https://blog.bitnation.co.
10 See https://coinmarketcap.com.
11 See https://positiveblockchain.io.
12 See https://ethereum.org/en/developers/docs/dapps.
13 See https://ethereum.org/en/wallets/#main-content.
14 See https://ethereum.org/en/developers/docs/dapps/#top.
15 See https://ethereum.org/en/developers/docs/smart-contracts/languages/#solidity.
16 See https://uniswap.org.
17 See https://makerdao.com/en.
18 See https://aave.com.
19 See www.defipulse.com.
20 See www.regen.network.
21 See https://celo.org/alliance.
22 See www.klimadao.finance.
23 See https://saveplanetearth.io.
24 See https://project-ark.co.
25 See https://farm.vc.

26 See https://blockchain-biodiversity-foundation.org.
27 See www.gainforest.net.
28 See https://refidao.com.
29 See https://ethereum.org/en/nft/#main-content.
30 See https://daohaus.club/review.
31 See https://app.daohaus.club/explore, https://snapshot.org/#.
32 See https://consensys.net/reports/defi-report-q2-2021.
33 See https://kleros.io.
34 See https://commonsstack.org.
35 See https://1hive.org.
36 See www.prime.xyz.
37 See www.regen.network.
38 See https://disco.coop/manifesto.
39 See https://estoniadao.org//.
40 See https://eva.coop/#.
41 See www.robinhoodcoop.org.
42 See www.commonlandsnet.org/; www.lasuitedumonde.com.
43 See https://songaday.world/songadao.
44 See https://nexusmutual.io/; https://opolis.co.
45 See https://opolis.co.
46 See https://blog.bitnation.co.
47 82 addresses account for 14.15 per cent of the total supply. See https://bitinfocharts.com/top-100-richest-bitcoin-addresses.html.
48 See www.holochain.org.

4 The Commons Stack

Introduction

This chapter intends to put theory into practice. It investigates whether and to what extent the contradictions of the commons apply to the Commons Stack in this case study. The Commons Stack is a Blockchain-based liberal version of the digital commons, aiming to scale the commons by piecing together Ostrom's design principles and crypto-economics. The Commons Stack is a not-for-profit association that draws on the work of Ostrom to help launch commons aiming to sustain public goods (Fritsch et al. 2021; Emmett 2019b). The commons lacks the mechanisms necessary to attract funding, self-govern and process information from the ground up. The Commons Stack builds on the work of pioneering DAOs such as 1hive,[1] Aragon,[2] SourceCred[3] and Moloch[4] to create a library of open-source Blockchain tools – governance tools, signalling tools, reputation tools, capital accumulation and distribution tools, voting tools – that enable purpose-driven communities to raise and allocate funding, make decisions and measure impact with the aid of computer-based real-time analytics as well as modelling and simulation.

The Commons Stack seeks to address collective action problems at the local level and then help communities scale into cyber-physical commons at the global level (Emmett 2019b, 2020). Cyber-physical commons attempt to bridge local and global (digital) commons by means of crypto-economics, which is an emerging branch of economics that introduces algorithmic design to coordinate socio-economic behaviour in decentralised peer-to-peer networks (Buterin 2018; Voshmgir & Zargham 2020; Zamfir 2015). Crypto-economics combines institutional economics, behavioural economics, computer science, game theory and token engineering to innovate in a number of fields:

- real-time preference signalling (Beck, Müller-Bloch & King 2018; Reijers et al. 2021);
- novel voting systems, such as conviction voting, negative voting and quadratic voting (Emmett 2019c; Karjalainen 2020);
- incentive alignment (Beck, Müller-Bloch & King 2018; Karjalainen 2020);
- algorithmic dispute resolution (Barnett & Treleaven 2018);

DOI: 10.4324/9781003039723-4

- on-chain transparency, accountability and distribution of benefits (Beck, Müller-Bloch & King 2018; Cila et al. 2020);
- self-enforcing security and censorship resistance (De Filippi, Mannan & Reijers 2020); and
- self-sovereign identity (Duffy 2017; Manski & Manski 2018; De Filippi & Wright 2018).

Drawing further on ecological economics, complex systems theory, interdisciplinary research and advances in data science, the Commons Stack employs token engineering to allow purpose-driven communities to effectively manage shared resources by aligning individual incentives with community goals. Shermin Voshmgir and Michael Zargham (2020) consider multiple different types of resources that can be managed by crypto-economic networks, from the physical (hardware, electricity) to the financial (tokens, fiat money) and the social (attention, governance participation, code contributions, evangelism). Managing these resources towards achieving shared goals is the same challenge that Ostrom was studying in commons initiatives around the globe.

> In all cases the design goal is strong emergence around some objective (Klein et al. 2001). It is also possible to envisage the objective selection process as dynamic consensus (Kia et al. 2019). Broadly speaking purpose-driven token design lives at the boundary of behavioral economics and dynamic decentralised coordination in multi-agent systems which bridges with institutional economics (Coase 1998), and in particular platform economics (Rochet and Tirole 2003).
>
> (Voshmgir & Zargham 2020: 10)

The Commons Stack's objective is to overcome the contradiction between individual incentives and community goals and scale human coordination towards the production of public goods (Emmett 2019b). The main idea echoes the liberal principle that every actor, when acting in her own best interest, actually benefits the system. Thus, the Commons Stack gives a commons twist to Adam Smith's ideal of self-regulated markets by seeking to reconcile markets and the commons. Paradoxically, the Commons Stack brings together Hayekian economics of information signalling with Ostrom's economics of collective action and Marx's economics of communism. As such, the Commons Stack constitutes a commons-based neo-institutional organisation.

> While current blockchain networks like Bitcoin could be considered digital commons, our plan is to extend the purpose of these networks into the management of real-world public goods, in a cyber-physical commons. The killer application of these systems lies within their capacity to restructure the way we incentivise, monitor and govern shared resources. Because of the trustful nature of blockchain technologies, they are uniquely able to sustain CBPP within communities of incentive-aligned people at scales

that extend beyond physical trust networks. By bridging the impact of these systems to the physical world, we can improve the way we collaborate, make decisions, and manage shared resources as a collective.

(Emmett 2020)

Communities around the globe could use the open-source, token-engineered killer application of the Commons Stack to fund, govern, customise, simulate and test their own ecosystems. The Commons stack of open-source tools is composed of four layers: economics, accountability, governance and feedback (Emmett 2020). Each layer breaks down into four components: (1) the augmented bonding curve, which seeks to provide sustainable funding for communities; (2) the Giveth DApp, which offers proposal and escrow services; (3) the conviction voting tool, which introduces a continuous decision-making governance process; and (4) the Commons Analytic Dashboard, which allows communities to measure impact and determine to what degree the desired value is produced within the community (Figure 4.1). Each of these components is modelled out of mathematical first principles and integrates several parameters that have been collectively designed and beta-tested before being turned into computer code to be applied in the real world.

The Commons Stack will be launching these components in an iterative engineering approach, testing out how these components work in a beta-environment. These four components will be open-sourced, interoperable and modular so as to be forked and used in any commons initiative or open-source project. The final goal would be to constantly improve upon these components

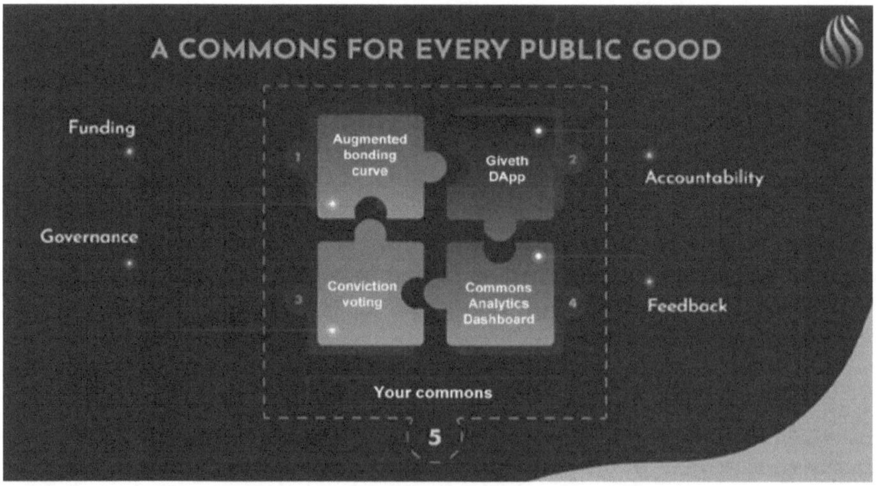

Figure 4.1 The Four Basic Components of the Commons Stack Toolkit

Source: Commons Stack website.

and synthesise them into a minimum viable commons that would introduce a new standard token network design.

In iteration 0, the Commons Stack initialises the cultural and technical components required to make these systems succeed, beginning with the launch of the Trusted Seed community, which consists of early backers and members of community projects. In the community-building phase, the team embarks on onboarding and educating members. Funds are collected through crowdfunding, and the apps, finally, go live.

In parallel runs, the open sourcing of cadCAD, which is a modelling framework and simulation tool for complex adaptive dynamics computer-aided design, is used to support more rigorous token engineering processes (Zartler 2022). CadCAD is deployed to improve upon the conviction voting module as a means of continuous preference signalling, as well as the augmented bonding curve as a source of continuous funding for cyber-physical commons. In each phase the model updates itself to fit the specific conditions in the commons. In subsequent iterations the Giveth DApp transforms into an interoperable framework for funding proposals. It helps refine the Commons Analytic Dashboard as a digital twin of the commons, the latter being simulated in cadCAD to help communities discern the health of the commons through the display, monitoring and analysis of raw data. In the last phase, when funding works and is stable, it is left for the community to be governed, providing ongoing funding to the projects.

Ultimately, the Commons Stack intends to innovate at least at four fronts.

1. The design layer, which consists in the scientific and engineering work put into the Commons Stack toolkit.
2. The governance layer, which builds upon Ostrom's eight principles to constitute the cultural build of the commons.
3. The production layer, which creates, measures and rewards value in the commons.
4. The finance layer, which seeks to accommodate individual incentives with the goals of the commons via crowdfunding and taxation.

All four layers feed into each other across the Commons Stack architecture (Figure 4.2). The finance layer pools capital into the commons via crowdfunding and in-built taxation. The governance layer determines the technical parameters of the design and finance layer all the while the production layer measures and rewards value creation across all layers. As such, the Commons Stack exemplifies a decentralised token-engineered organisation that builds the tools necessary for cyber-physical commons to grow into a sustainable federated ecosystem. The Commons Stack is a DAO growing alongside other DAOs for the purpose of helping DAOs grow and connect to the real economy in the model of cyber-physical commons.

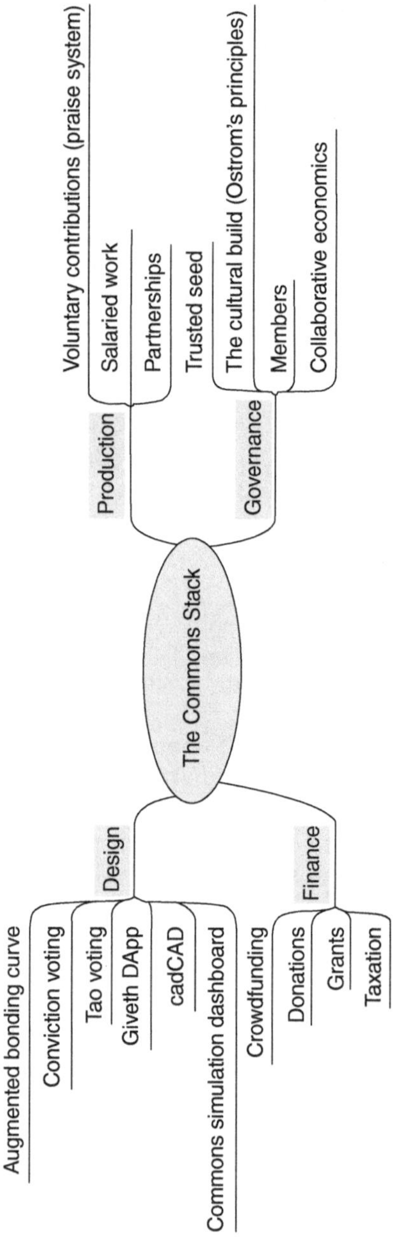

Figure 4.2 The Commons Stack Architecture

Methodology

The Commons Stack is a complex and multidimensional DAO. Transparency is a core feature of the DAO, having all resources such as code, budgets, documentation and handbooks available online on various platforms, such as the Commons Stack website,[5] Zenhub, Medium, Github, Telegram, Twitter and Discord. The methodology adopted for carrying out research on the Commons Stack case study comprised digital ethnography, literature review, participatory observation and semi-structured interviews with core team members of the team as well as a part-time contributor and a member of the Trusted Seed.

The core team members interviewed are the following: Jeff Emmett, who is a token engineering researcher at the Commons Stack and BlockScience; Livia Deschermayer, who is the leader of the cultural build in the Commons Stack and the Token Engineering Commons; Kristofer Lund, who is coordinating the development of the praise system; and Chuy Garcia, who is the steward of the communications working group of the TEC. The part-time contributor interviewed is Maria Cordova, who is the gardener of the Trusted Seed in the Commons Stack, and the member of the Trusted Seed interviewed is Felix Fritsch, who also runs the Crypto Commons Hub[6] in Austria. I also participated in several community calls as an observer and met in person with core team members of the Commons Stack in the first Crypto Commons conference, held in Austria in 2021.

The purpose here is not to go into the nitty-gritty of the Commons Stack operations. The objective is to explain the value proposition, goals, activities and mechanisms put in place to advance the commons. The Commons Stack is a project in progress that interoperates with the overall Web3 ecosystem, with experimentation lying at the core of the project. This case study, therefore, cannot but come with a number of limitations. Although it covers all four layers of the Commons Stack architecture, it does not go deep into political science issues related to democratic leadership, governance frameworks, conflict resolution and power dynamics among stewards and community members. Future research may also delve deeper into the technical components of the Commons Stack library as well as the so-called cultural build and praise system, considered to be the core innovation of the Commons Stack.

The Design Layer

The Augmented Bonding Curve

Bonding curves are price discovery mechanisms that introduce liquidity into both liquid and illiquid markets (Balasanov 2018; de la Rouviere 2017a; Truong 2018). They require collateral in exchange for a given token, predetermining supply and demand interaction and multiple equilibria. A bonding curve is an alternative to the initial coin offering model. Whereas ICOs are based on a supply-side predetermination of fiat token value and maximum quantity, a bonding curve is a demand-side mathematical curve predefined by an algorithm written in a Blockchain-based smart contract along two dimensions: price and token supply. The smart contract issues a token at a spot price depending on demand. The spot price is the value of a single token at a point along the curve; the supply is the tokens issued in exchange for collateral. Token supply grows or shrinks based on the collateral tied to it. Thus, a bonding curve is a correlation of token supply and demand at a spot price. It is a constant that you define along two variables (price and token supply), the predetermination of which increases or decreases the space of governance (Fritsch et al. 2021).

Bonding curves allow for the creation of decentralised markets, since they are not launched by a central authority or company or institution issuing a number of tokens and distributing them to the public (Kohlhaas 2018, 2019). Instead, the rules of minting and burning tokens are agreed upon by a group of people or a community and are written in a protocol implemented by a smart contract on Blockchain. In comparison with a multi-sided market, in which price discovery is open among multiple agents buying and selling orders, a bonding curve constitutes an automated market maker that operates outside cryptocurrency exchanges, matching supply and demand along a price curve preconditioned by the terms indicated in the smart contract. When an actor buys a token at a spot price, the smart contract creates the token from scratch, stores the received payment as collateral and moves the spot price up along the curve. When an actor sells a token, the smart contract buys it back at its spot price with funds from the reserve, destroys (burns) the token and moves the price down along the curve. The more tokens are bought, the higher the spot price rises. The more tokens are sold, the lower the spot price drops.

In general, bonding curves are automated market makers that allow for price discovery, thereby opening up a vast design space for new incentive mechanisms. They provide a Hayekian point of economic interface with the real economy, with price becoming the signal of information necessary to create a market. Yet, just like ICOs, bonding curves are susceptible to front-running, pump and dump schemes, manipulation, and the like.

Curation Markets

Simon de la Rouviere (2017b, 2017c, 2018) has built on the bonding curve innovation to introduce the concept of 'curation markets'. Distributed communities utilise bonding curves to participate in tokenised crypto-economic curation games and produce novel signals in information markets. They mint tokens around any topic or idea as a quantitative representation of its affective capacity. Tokenising, for example, a joke represented in a meme could produce a market around it. Essentially, curation markets create a new class of derivative assets through the monetisation of affect towards common themes. In Marxian terms, they transform the use value of the general intellect circulating on the Internet into exchange value to be traded between communities.

De la Rouviere's contribution goes even further, since he introduces the option of taxation for the sake of a common cause. A community could tokenise affect via demand-driven bonding curves and tax trades to directly fund common causes. Not only does taxing trades with the bonding curve introduce novel fundraising opportunities for the commons, it also discourages short-term speculation and market manipulation. Thus, curation markets could function as prediction markets for the commons. Bonding curves could serve as intermediate tools for coordination mechanisms, systems interfaces, configuration spaces, funding mechanisms, voting, community currencies and micro-economies. Paradoxically, bonding curves bring Hayekian economics and Ostrom's collective action together by allowing for communities to set up micro-economies on their own rules.

The Commons Stack builds on de la Rouviere's concept of curation markets to introduce the augmented bonding curve, which is one of the main pillars of the Commons Stack's infrastructure (Titcomb 2019). The ABC is a combination of crowdfunding and polycentric governance over funds allocated to achieve the Commons' goals. Combined with conviction voting, it serves as a new tool for collective preference estimation and shared resource allocation (Zargham, Shorish & Paruch 2020). The ABC augments existing bonding curves by deploying conservation principles to generate returns while balancing speculation and subjectivity. It issues fungible governance tokens (DAI) allocated to a reserve pool and a funding pool at a percentage predetermined by the community. (DAI is a stablecoin cryptocurrency issued by Maker DAO.) Although the reserve pool serves as collateral for the tokens in circulation, the funding pool is generated via taxation and is used to fund proposals submitted by token owners, who also bear the right to vote over submitted proposals.

The ABC launches in two phases: (1) the hatch phase, which is a crowdfunding initialisation period during which the Trusted Seed community – founding members, devoted contributors, initial investors of the Commons Stack – comes together to fund a commons; and (2) the open phase, which is open to the public to purchase and sell from the bonding curve.

In the hatch phase (Figure 4.3), members of the Trusted Seed (hatchers) participate in a hatch crowdfunding process during which they pool capital to fund a commons. Hatchers may contribute either financial capital or intellectual/sweat capital, or both. All hatchers receive newly minted tokens (xDAI) relative to their contribution, a percentage of which are allocated to the reserve and the funding pool. Tokens allocated in the reserve pool are locked in a vesting process that combats early speculation/arbitrage. Tokens allocated in the funding pool are used to curate options for future capital allocation through novel governance mechanisms such as conviction voting and quadratic voting.

In the open phase (Figure 4.4), the vesting process is initialised and anyone can contribute DAI and become member of the commons. Contributions return newly minted unlocked tokens, which are allocated directly to the reserve pool and can be traded and burned or used to vote within the system.

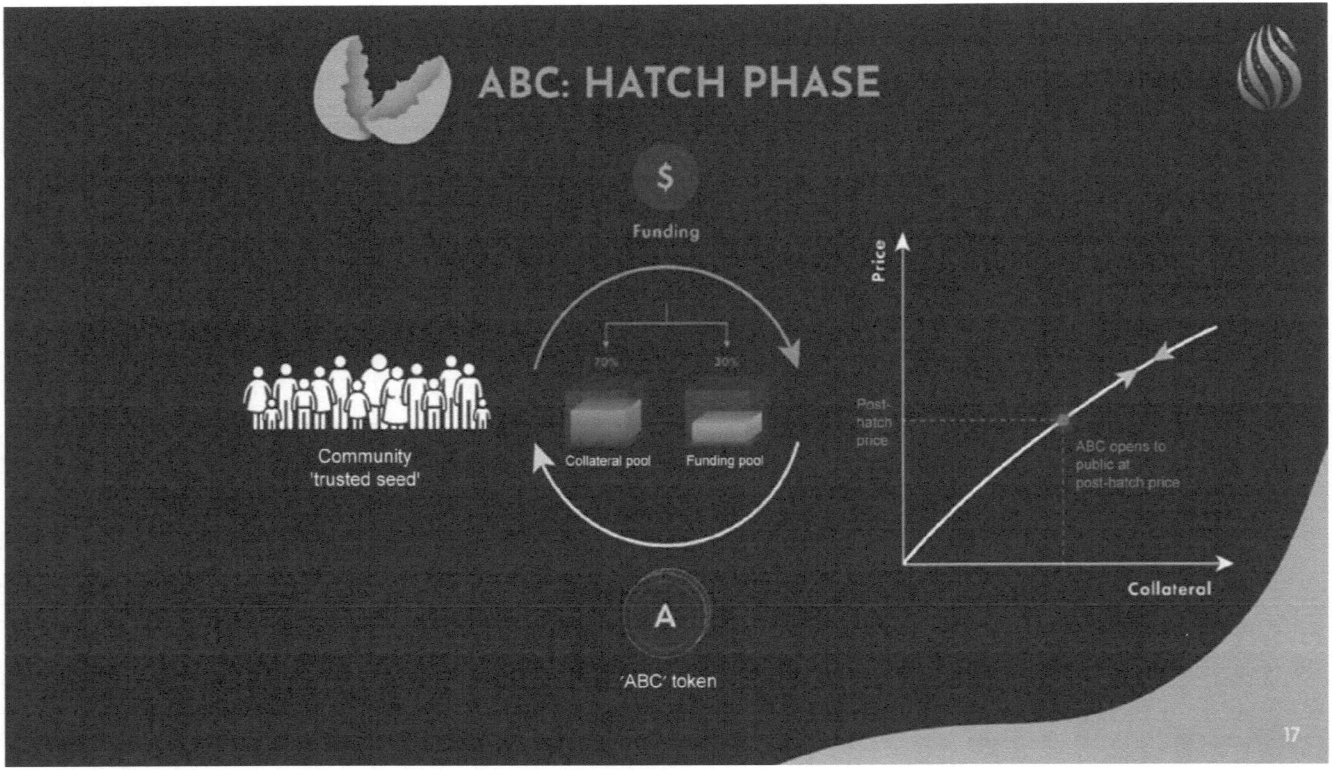

Figure 4.3 The ABC Hatch Phase

Source: Commons Stack website.

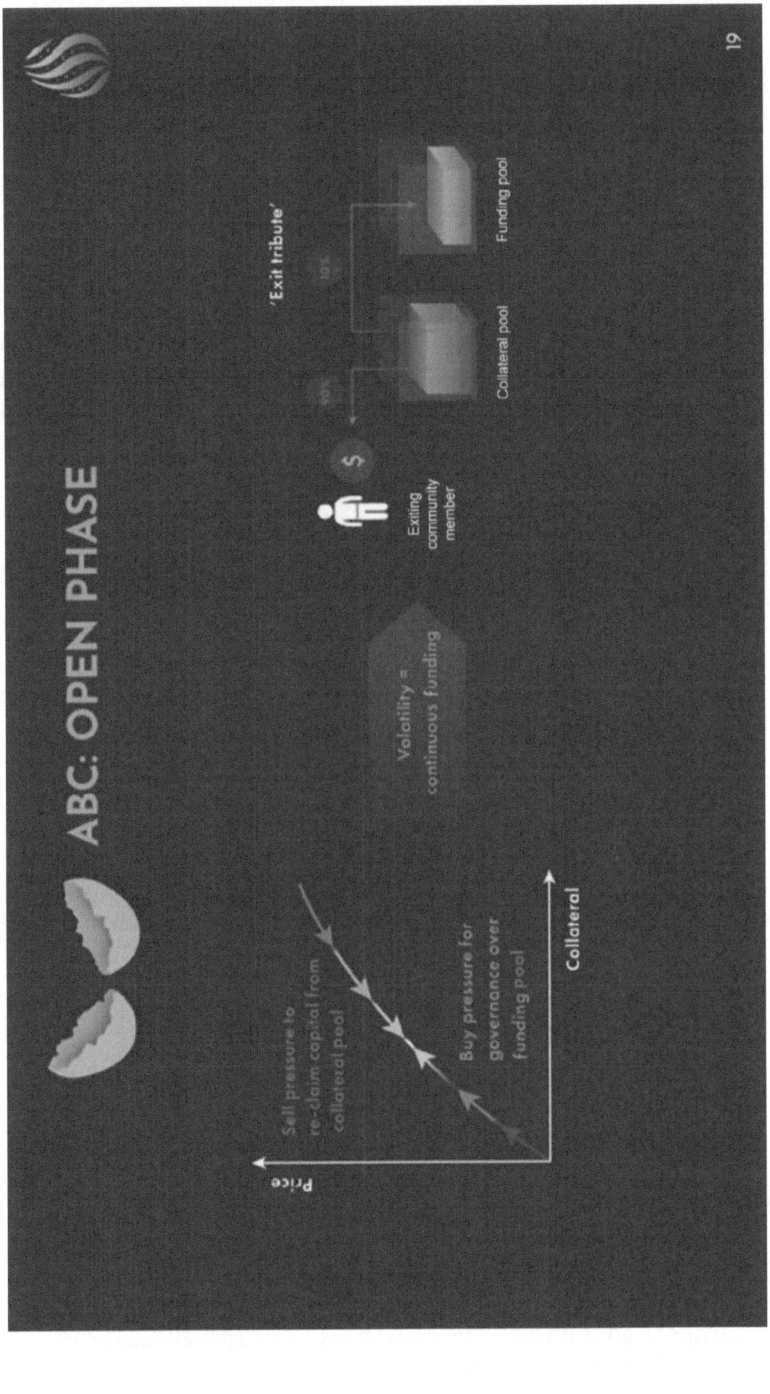

Figure 4.4 The ABC Open Phase

Source: Commons Stack website.

The hatchers' tokens locked in the reserve pool are slowly unlocked in correlation to how much capital has been decided, through conviction voting, to be allocated from the funding pool to the commons.

Whenever tokens are traded and burned (withdrawn for DAI → $), an exit tax is enacted on liquidation (Titcomb 2019). As members 'cash out' and liquidate their tokens for DAI, a small percentage of their returns are sent back to the funding pool, allowing for the simultaneous funding of the commons. When prices rise, speculators seek to sell to make profit, thereby contributing via the exit tax to a growing treasury. Conviction voting plugs in to help allocate funding for the commons. Common-pool funds are continuously allocated to community projects, bounties and proposals via participatory grant-making processes that use DAO token-weighted voting. When prices drop, members of the commons seek to buy to claim additional governance power over the growing treasury through conviction voting. The exit tax and conviction voting thus set up an interplay of interests between speculators and members of the commons that leverages speculation into a continuous source of income for the commons. The system always benefits, even if speculators are interested only in making returns.

In short, the ABC can be conceptualised as a typical bonding curve with the addition of a funding pool, a token lock-up/vesting mechanism, exit tax, conviction voting and inter-system feedback loops engineered by cadCAD. Members of the commons are incentivised to participate in conviction voting, along with early hatchers, to allocate funding to curated projects that may have a beneficial impact on the commons and, therefore, increase their share on the commons.

As Fritsch et al. (2021: 9) sum it up:

> By correlating the spot price of tokens with their quantity in speculation through the bonding curve, a speculative potential opens that rewards successful commons stewardship, leading to more participation in the shared cause and incentivising early participation in promising communities. At the same time, as market interaction with the ABC increases, the community funding pool benefits from additional tax revenue.

Primary and Secondary Markets

In effect, the ABC could be used by communities to tackle the tragedy of the commons by aligning individual profit-driven incentives with community projects, ensuring a sustainable funding mechanism for commons-based communities, and creating circular regenerative economies that can be used by any commons-based community. The ABC could allow the creation of business models around the commons that could disincentivise value extraction and incentivise value creation by compensating users appropriately (Emmett 2022). For example, a local neighbourhood DAO or a global healthcare DAO could apply to receive funding from the ABC with the aim of growing and sustaining its operations. DAO members could use their shares of tokens to vote on proposals not only within their DAO but across a federation of DAOs. Participants could enter or leave the glocal economy by contributing or withdrawing reserve assets in exchange for tokens. Exit is disincentivised via a tax used to create a continuous stream of funds for the commons. In addition, the exit tax provides a countervailing force against a 'run on the bank' scenario on the ABC, constantly pouring liquidity into the funding pool, thereby preventing the risk of capital flight from reserves due to sell pressure (Emmett 2022). In a nutshell, the ABC could be considered a stock market for the commons, utilising governance tokens to unite capital and labour under the commons goals.

The potential of micro-economies launched by the ABC should be further examined in tandem with the overall macro-structure of the economy. The ABC introduced by the Commons Stack could be considered a primary automated market maker, as opposed to secondary automated market makers such as Uniswap and SushiSwap operating on Blockchain. Although secondary automated markets combine existing assets such as Eth and DAI to create an LP (liquidity provider) token that can then be staked for liquidity mining or yield farming rewards, the ABC creates a market from scratch by minting new tokens backed by collateralised reserve assets such as DAI.

In times of crises and extreme market volatility such as bull and bear markets, the ABC could serve as a parachute amid price volatility. The collateral maintained in the funding pool via the exit tax would always prevent the price falling to zero. But, even so, the funding pool might not have enough to sustain operations within the commons in times of crises. Fragmentation due to decentralisation may be detrimental to the commons. Additional funding mechanisms would perhaps be necessary to inject capital into the commons markets in times of crises, just as the Federal Reserve in the United States injects money into the economy to keep it afloat. Several mechanisms could be put in place here, such as credit union DAOs and peer-to-peer lending, to enable the circulation of funds across the commons, just like water flowing from one pasture to the other in times of drought. Free-riding over commons funds could be disincentivised by some sort of 'proof of operation'. Thus, a commons/DAO mesh could dampen economic volatility through dynamic reinvestment into the network (interview with Jeff Emmett, 2021).

CADCAD

The Commons Stack makes use of the cadCAD[7] design and simulation tool to shift the ABC design from manual, experience-based trial and error to model-based simulation refined through complex systems design, interdisciplinary research and advances in data science (Zartler 2022). The cadCAD is the structural grammar of the ABC that mathematically pre-formulates conservation functions for the commons via constant feedback loops between initial engineering and empirical iterations (Figure 4.5).

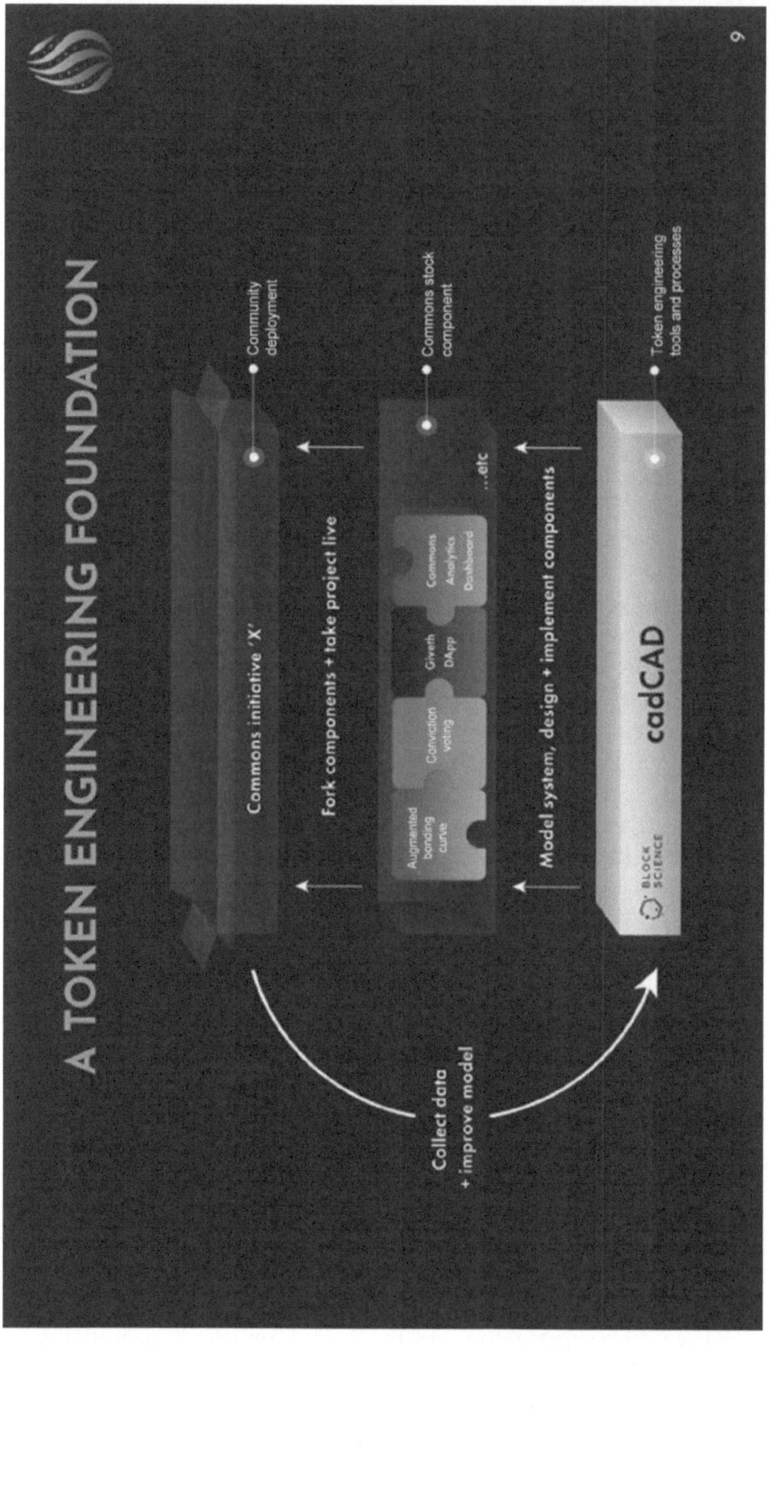

Figure 4.5 The cadCAD Module

Source: Commons Stack website.

CONVICTION VOTING

The token traded via the ABC represents the owner's quantified right to influence decision-making over expenditures by the funding pool by participating in the conviction voting tool. The concept of conviction voting draws on social choice theory, behavioural economics, evolutionary biology and political science. It stems from the work of Dr Michael Zargham (2018), who employs algorithmic design to shift social choice from one-shot voting games (as in the case of representative democracy) into an evolutionary Blockchain-based real-time participatory democracy, in which the actions of agents are signals and a Blockchain network serves the role of sensor. Algorithmic design research is undertaken as a means of formalising social choice as sensor fusion by aggregating agent preferences using tokenised assets traded via the ABC (Zhang, Zargham & Preciado 2020).

As with all other components, the Commons Stack adopts a biomimetic approach to collective decision-making, whereby governance is considered tantamount to the way natural ecosystems 'balance themselves because of carefully weighted signals which are constantly emitted by all agents to let the larger system adapt to external and internal changes. Some great examples we can observe are streams of nutrients in forests, communication of insects, electrical current in the bodies of animals and humans, etc.' (Gertler 2019). By analogy to continuous feedback mechanisms in nature, conviction voting is conceived as a decision-making tool that allows communities governing a shared resource to choose between a set of actions in a decentralised way.

Rather than voters casting votes in a single time-boxed session, as in the case of legacy majority systems, conviction voting aggregates individual preferences in a streamlined, continuous process that enables real-time feedback of human needs into governance systems (Emmett 2019c; Zargham, Shorish & Paruch 2020). Vote streaming allows for much richer signalling from a community as to its actual priorities. Contrary to legacy voting systems, which condemn vote buying, conviction voting allows vote buying. Contrary to 'one person, one vote' systems, in which a voter has to choose one proposal each time, conviction voting adopts 'one token, one vote' systems, which allow voters to display both the plurality and intensity of their preferences by voting more than one proposal at different proportions. Conviction voting is a combination of the amount of tokens staked at a proposal and the length of time they are staked for.

To tackle plutocracy and decentralise further, the Commons Stack experiments with quadratic measures and vote delegation/liquid democracy. Quadratic voting disincentivises plutocracy by rendering the cost of casting more than one vote for an issue quadratic (Buterin 2018, 2019; Wright 2019). Therefore, the marginal cost of each additional vote is equal to the square root of the token put into the vote. Let's say that voting towards an issue costs $1 and one has $100 of tokens. Casting one vote will cost $1 token. However, casting two votes for the same issue will cost $4 tokens, casting three votes will cost $9 tokens and casting ten votes will cost the entire $100 of tokens. Thus, quadratic voting lessens the influence of large token holders in comparison to smaller ones. As Fritsch et al. (2021: 9) point out:

> The inclusion of these mechanisms is an attempt to moderate voting power in token-based governance systems, both in space (in the case of QV), and in time (in the case of CV). The former reduces the relative impact of large token holders, the latter more fundamentally changes decision making toward continuous preference signalling, thus facilitating real time indicators of collective sentiment.

Additionally, liquid democracy[8] is a mixture of direct and representative democracy. Voters have the right to vote directly on all policy issues, *à la* direct democracy, but they also have the option to delegate their votes to someone who will vote on their behalf, *à la* representative democracy. Delegated conviction voting is a type of liquid democracy that adds token delegation functionality (Emmett 2022). It enables a grassroots representative system in which decision-making power is directly proportional to the trust built in a network. Delegation mitigates the overburdened attention issue caused by the information overload inherent in token-weighted voting systems.

Voters can alter their preferences at any time. However, the longer a preference is held for a proposal, the 'stronger' the conviction gets, thereby attributing to consistent preferences more influence over time. Voting power is executed gradually over time following logarithmic growth and decay functions. Thus, conviction voting replaces collective orientation towards the will of the majority with a shift towards 'sufficient support' for proposals. Communities may seek support for specific proposals without having the approval of the majority. Ultimately, conviction voting aggregates individual signals into a social sensor fusion that triggers action when a predetermined threshold has been reached for a funding proposal to be released to a community. This threshold is defined as the relative amount of the overall voting capacity that is proportional to the requested funding of a proposal as compared to the total funding pool.

The Commons Stack is agnostic as to whether voting rights are distributed in a plutocratic, meritocratic or democratic mode. Conviction voting applies to funding decisions and may be incorporated into the overall governance framework of the community, which may vary from community to community. For instance, vote buying may be prohibited by communities trading off egalitarianism against plutocracy. In any case, conviction voting is susceptible to several attack vectors present in on-chain time-boxed voting, such as vote buying, plutocracy, Sybil attacks, last-minute vote swings and on-chain voter apathy. Users can bribe other voters to vote a certain way, buy a significant amount of tokens to manipulate voting, use multiple accounts to gain undue influence or simply abstain from voting. Current delegated voting systems have a clunky token-staking UX, meaning a user experience wherein most people delegate all/some tokens to a single delegate. This creates centralised whale dynamics in voting.

By introducing logarithmic growth and decay functions in the execution of voting power, conviction voting raises the costs of influencing the system over long periods of time, thus reducing the vote-buying attack vector and increasing collusion resistance. It eliminates large token holders' ability to influence votes at the last minute, favouring long-standing minority positions against short-term majorities. By splitting up large token holdings into multiple accounts or assigning X per cent of voting power to each, delegated conviction voting prevents large token holders from gaining undue influence, thereby becoming Sybil-resistant. To avoid entrenchment, delegated conviction voting could enforce rotational cycles for delegates or continuous 'decay' on delegation (Emmett 2022). To tackle on-chain voter apathy, the ABC incentivises participants to maintaining their Commons by attracting new members. Moreover, conviction voting seeks to make voting as easy as possible by smoothing out user experience.

TAO VOTING (AKA DISPUTABLE VOTING)

The tao voting application adds mechanics to voting that include delegating votes, protection against last-minute vote result flipping and a framework for disputing proposals. Tao voting is a system of negative voting that could be employed to further democratise decision-making. Rather than voters being able to support or not support a proposal, they could also express disagreement by voting against a proposal. Negative voting could thus bring to the fore conflict, which lies at the heart of democratic politics. Disagreement could further deliberation, which could then lead to refined proposals.

Proposals can be disputed by a challenger; the proposer must respond by either negotiating a settlement or escalating the challenge to Celeste[9] or a form of court and must fork out a token fee to assign and pay jurors to mediate the dispute. Celeste is a fork of Aragon Court, created by 1hive for decentralised dispute resolution. It is a subjective oracle, enabling smart contracts to ask questions and receive answers. It can be used to resolve subjective disputes, settle prediction markets, moderate content, and more. The Commons Stack will be using Celeste to resolve potential disputes during tao voting. Relevant parameters of tao voting include a delegated voting period, a minimum quorum, a quiet ending period, a quiet ending extension, support required, vote duration and vote execution day.

THE GIVETH DAPP

The Giveth Proposal Engine (GPE)[10] is, essentially, the predecessor of the Commons Stack. It was developed between 2016 and 2019 as an Ethereum-based application that would cut out bureaucracy costs and offer transparency and accountability to philanthropic fund allocation. The GPE acts as a proposal framework for DAOs operating in the service of cyber-physical commons to request funding. It consists of a set of smart contracts that allows users to donate

Ether and DAI cryptocurrency to DAOs requesting funding. Currently, the GPE is in a closed beta testing. The three key building blocks of the GPE are decentralised altruistic communities (DACs), campaigns and milestones. DACs can fund and steer multiple campaigns, during which funds are distributed upon successful completion of milestones. Every milestone can be linked to exactly one campaign, but multiple milestones can exist in one campaign.

Seven basic roles are defined in the GPE system: givers, delegates, campaign managers, campaign reviewers, milestone managers, milestone reviewers, recipients. Givers can either donate anonymously directly to campaigns, specific milestones and DACs or pledge their Ether to a cause and have a delegate choose an appropriate campaign or milestone for them. By donating to DACs, givers automatically become members of the DACs. When a giver donates Ether, the coins are stored in a Solidity smart contract and cannot be removed without the owner's permission. Delegates are registered DAC members who take on the task of allocating funds to one or more campaign(s). Campaign managers create campaigns and allocate funding to completed milestones. Campaign reviewers are appointed by campaign managers to guarantee the legitimacy of the process. Milestone managers are nominated by campaign managers to oversee the orderly completion of milestones. Milestone reviewers confirm the orderly completion of milestones. In the event of the cancellation of a milestone or a campaign by the respective reviewer, the funds are reimbursed to their giver. Finally, recipients receive the funds upon the successful completion of a milestone. Every entity within the Giveth system is represented by an Ethereum address. Additionally, these roles could be supplemented by a multisig, oracle, DAO, etc.

The GPE integrates smoothly in the Commons Stack component library, wherein the production of public goods is launched in terms of campaigns, which further break down into milestones, to be produced by the respective communities. DACs are complemented by additional funds raised by ABC through taxation. The ABC can be considered a democratically run stock market providing funds for the commons. The allocation of funds is determined by token holders, who execute their governance rights through conviction voting, which installs a form of direct democracy in terms of continuous preference signalling. Conviction voting expresses support for and eventually triggers payment to a campaign (or milestone). As soon as one milestone of a campaign has been funded, either by an individual, a DAC or an ABC, production of the milestone may begin. CadCAD is further employed, to provide simulation-based parameter optimisation and customisation to context-specific use cases. Ultimately, the goal is to transform centralised donations into token-engineered decentralised circular economies around the commons.

Let's assume, for example, that there is a community of activists who clean up beaches and self-organise around a DAC called 'Trash Heroes'. They raise 100,000 xDAI by members and stakeholders and lock them into the smart contract of the ABC; 50,000 are sent to the Trash Heroes Commons pool and 50,000 are used to create 5 million tokens sent to the funding pool. These tokens are sold to the public and are locked until the Commons raise 150,000 xDAI to spend on projects. As soon as the Commons raises 150,000 xDAI, the Trash Heroes project can initialise. Spending goes through milestones created in the GPE. A milestone may be the cleaning of 5 km of coast from plastic and waste. As soon as the gathering of three tons of plastic and waste is documented in pictures and videos, the xDAI locked in the smart contract will be sent to the token bonding curve and Trash Heroes will mint Trash Hero tokens, which they can decide to burn – cash out – immediately. After initialisation, the token holders can burn newly minted tokens and unlocked tokens for 98 per cent of the current minting cost, and the extra 2 per cent is sent to the Commons. Speculators and secondary markets may be involved around the Commons, with the trading volume hopefully creating an extra flow of funds to go back into the pool as taxation fees. Every participant – whether an initial crowdfunder, a regular giver or a speculator – should and will act in her own self-interest, which is steering the Commons to become a success, with everyone's incentives aligned.

THE COMMONS ANALYTIC DASHBOARD

The Commons Analytic Dashboard is the digital twin of the system. It is a mathematical representation coded in cadCAD, which is an open-source Python package that assists in the processes of designing, testing and validating complex systems through simulation. CadCAD supports different system-modelling approaches by allowing communities to change initial parameters and run simulation tests. Communities can use cadCAD to set key parameters, such as the hatch rate percentage of the funding pool, the hatch token price, the post-hatch token price, the vesting process (the ABC opening price and reserve ratio, the exit tax, token freeze and token thaw), etc.[11] Designing these key parameters ex ante provides communities with unique strategy combinations to incentivise participation, and establish the foundations for the long-term sustainability of the ABC.

CadCAD can provide additional parameterisations by displaying data generated by user communities via the Commons Stack modules in the form of system health metrics, such as user interaction, accepted versus non-accepted proposals, the degree of conflict, reputation, transactions, etc.

A number of trade-offs come up when voting on the parameters of the ABC. Let's take, for example, the parameters of token freeze and token thaw. The token freeze parameter is the duration in weeks that the community's tokens are locked within a smart contract before they are released to token holders. The token thaw parameter is the duration it takes for 100 per cent of the community tokens to be released to all token holders. If the community chooses a small duration (four to 16 weeks) for token freeze, it limits economic activity, since tokens may be cashed out soon. If the community chooses a large duration (208 weeks), it increases economic activity, but risks losing the participation of community investors (token holders) and limits the capital being available for use on secondary markets and other use cases. Similarly, if the community chooses a short duration (two to 16 weeks) for token thaw, it risks significant price volatility for the community token during that time period, as more tokens are released and available to sell back into the ABC. If the community chooses a long duration (208 weeks), it provides a slow and steady stream of tokens to be released, but limits the capital being available for use on secondary markets and other use cases.

The Governance Layer

Whereas the design layer refers to the technical build phase, during which the software is mathematically designed and written in smart contracts, the governance layer corresponds to the cultural build phase, during which the community, which will test the components in beta, discusses and establishes their Commons goals and best practices. To help the Commons scale from the local level into cyber-physical commons operating at a glocal level, the Commons Stack attempts to apply Elinor Ostrom's design principles to the Blockchain space (Emmett 2019b). Ostrom identified eight design principles of sustainable commons management. Next I illustrate how the design layer of the Commons Stack applies Ostrom's eight principles of sustainable commons management to the governance layer of cyber-physical commons.

Clearly defined community boundaries

The commons need to have clear boundaries to prevent free riders from (over-) using the shared resource and avoid the tragedy of the commons. Tokenisation via the ABC satisfies Ostrom's first principle by demarcating a clearly defined system boundary and specifying who are authorised to use the commons (Emmett 2019b). Only token holders of the Trusted Seed can be part of communities launching cyber-physical commons, using the ABC as a funding mechanism that insulates the internal economy of the commons from speculators. Tokens may represent both financial and non-financial contributions to a community, granting access rights, decision-making power and fractional ownership to community members. The Trusted Seed defines group boundaries by limiting access to governance decisions to token holders aligned with the goals of the commons.

Congruence between rules and local conditions

The Commons Stack supports localism by offering communities a series of customisable tools to support funding, governance, monitoring, etc. (Emmett 2019b). The interoperable and modular nature of the Commons Stack components allows them to be combined, parameterised and simulated to suit a wide range of different contexts. The ABC helps communities decide what funding streams are appropriate for their specific context. Conviction voting allows communities to choose an appropriate governance template. CadCAD can run a series of simulations that fit the community in question. Thus, the Commons Stack library is designed to meet the varied needs of diverse communities, thereby satisfying Ostrom's second principle of adaptability to fit local conditions.

Collective choice arrangements

The Commons Stack employs Blockchain technology to tokenise voting and governance rights and allow for large-scale community decision-making (Emmett 2019b). Conviction voting offers community members, who contribute either money or time to the commons, the option to have a say over governance. The ABC increases voter engagement by incentivising long-term commitment to a community cause. The longer a conviction holds over a proposal, the more governance power there is over the commons in question and, potentially, the more financial returns from the long-term sustainability of a project. Therefore, the Commons Stack library satisfies Ostrom's third principle of including stakeholders in decision-making processes.

Monitoring

The Giveth Proposal Engine brings accountability and transparency to funding proposals for the commons, and the Commons Analytics Dashboard measures impact through metrics fully available to the community (Emmett 2019b). Members who submit proposals are paid out for their efforts on verified milestone completion, with the impact of each milestone completion being reported to the members of the community. Thus, the Commons Stack toolkit provides a highly effective monitoring mechanism that satisfies Ostrom's fourth principle.

Graduated sanctions

The Commons Stack toolkit offers communities a wide array of choices for applying graduated sanctions to members, whether through reputation systems, blacklisting or relevant metrics (Emmett 2019b). CadCAD helps estimate the systemic impact of particular sanctions through the holistic simulation of agents' interaction. If the Commons Stack Association suspects that the motivation of a member of the Trusted Seed is to extract value from the community rather than to nurture it, then graduated sanctions may be applied to the member in question, the most severe of which would be the burning of that person's CSTK tokens. The sanction(s) will be carried out with maximum transparency and community consultation. Thus, the Commons Stack library satisfies Ostrom's sixth principle of graduated sanctions.

Conflict resolution mechanisms

Blockchain-based smart contracts are a cheap and easy means to mitigate the threat of 'contract breaking' that initiates conflict between community members (Emmett 2019b). However, conflict may not always be resolved via smart contracts. The Commons Stack is pioneering a set of cultural best practices, including a deliberative 'space' for conflict resolution. Communities can use the Commons Stack to apply tailor-made solutions in their own projects. Tao voting, for example, could be an instance of conflict resolution. Multiple signatures to sign off on completed tasks might be another instance of ensuring a higher degree of accountability when it comes to the quality of the work delivered by community members. Conflict could also be handled through graduated levels of future decentralised court systems, such as Celeste, with escalation to real-world legal systems when necessary. In short, multiple tools in the Commons Stack library satisfy Ostrom's sixth principle of accessible and low-cost conflict resolution.

Local enforcement of local rules

The Commons Stack will offer the communities that use the Commons Stack library the appropriate legal structure for their jurisdiction and use case (Emmett 2019b). For example, DAOs using the Commons Stack library will have the option to register internationally as a legal entity, which would limit liability for participants. Thus, the Commons Stack satisfies Ostrom's seventh principle of commons receiving legal recognition.

Multiple layers of nested enterprises

The Commons Stack library intends to create a federated community structure wherein commons may have nested layers of decision-making, expanding jurisdiction from local to broader levels of governance (rural, urban, global) (Emmett 2019b). A federated community structure facilitates polycentric governance, enabling flexible decision-making networks of nested responsibility that could operate under a hierarchical structure, a horizontal 'leaderless' structure or anything in between. The ABC and conviction voting modules serve the interoperability among various commons. Thus, the Commons Stack infrastructure seeks to sustain an ecosystem of Commons via a fractal design pattern that satisfies Ostrom's eighth principle of nested commons.

Organisational Structure

The Commons Stack partners with several other projects working on token engineering, such as the TEC, the Token Engineering Academy, the Regen Network, ixo Foundation and BlockScience. The TEC is the first commons launched by the Commons Stack. It is currently in the process of deploying the

Commons Stack toolkit to forward token engineering. The Token Engineering Academy is a larger community, which BlockScience feeds into with theoretical and applied research translated into token engineering components standardised through cadCad and open-sourced for communities to employ in their own projects.

The Commons Stack consists of eight full-time members, who also act as stewards of the various working groups; 15 part-time members; and some 300 to 400 contributors. Around 30 to 40 per cent of the members are women, and members are mostly of international origin, thus forming a transnational community (interview with Chuy Garcia, 2022). People interested in working for the Commons Stack must be part of the Trusted Seed and pass an onboarding process. If they successfully pass the onboarding process, they get a contract licensed under the Commons Stack Swiss Association (interview with Maria Cordova, 2021). This onboarding process is accompanied by monthly reviews and is similar to the job trial periods of ordinary companies. However, it has been described as a more humane process compared to the progress reports and performance criteria required by capitalist company structures (interview with Maria Cordova, 2021)

The Commons Stack is funded principally by its founder, Griff Green, as well as through crowdfunding, membership dues, donations and grants deriving from Gitcoin and community members. Funds are transparently kept in Excel files available in the Giveth DApp.[12] One major issue that remains to be seen is if and to what extent the Commons Stack can be financially sustainable in the long term and achieve its goal of providing continuous funding to its members. The Commons Stack is a multidimensional project in progress, constantly experimenting with its organisational structure and exploring different design patterns. Currently the Commons Stack is organised around seven working groups (Zartler & Emmett 2021).

THE TRUSTED SEED

To understand how the components of the Commons Stack toolkit interoperate, it is crucial that we embark upon the Trusted Seed layer, which lays the foundation for the Commons Stack community build-up (Emmett 2019d). The Trusted Seed is a key cultural initialisation tool that sets the parameters for designing a commons from the bottom up. Although anyone can contribute time and/or money to the build of the Commons Stack, the Trusted Seed consists of experienced community members who are offering more than just contributions to the Commons Stack. They form a reputable network of trusted actors with skin in the game, who will use their expertise to help steward sustainably funded Commons ecosystems.

Members of the Trusted Seed will be invited to participate in the hatch phases of various field test Commons. Setting up a commons will involve fine-tuning the Commons Stack components to suit the needs of the community. Thus, members of the Trusted Seed need to have a comprehensive knowledge of how the various Commons Stack components interoperate. The goal is to protect the launch of an augmented bonding curve from profit-seeking speculators and guide communities to make good decisions in the early stages of any Commons' governance.

Anyone can apply to become a member of the Trusted Seed as long as they are aligned with the Commons Stack mission and have some sort of experience in the fields of Blockchain tech, decentralised governance, token engineering and/or grassroots organising. One formally activates one's membership in the Trusted Seed by paying dues in DAI to join the Swiss association that underpins the organisation. If paying dues is a financial burden, successful applicants to the Trusted Seed may apply for a scholarship. Recently the Trusted Seed counted 334 members (interview with Maria Cordova, 2021).

The Commons Stack uses Giveth to provide transparent tracking on the use of membership dues. Members of the Trusted Seed can accumulate CSTK tokens based on the amount of time and/or additional funds contributed to the build of the Commons Stack project and tools. Their CSTK score is represented on the xDAI chain by a non-transferable token, meaning that it has no monetary value. CSTK tokens denote reputation in the Commons Stack (Reese 2020). Members of the Trusted Seed can use the CSTK tokens to vote over the pre-hatch conditions for a Commons and are not attached to a bonding curve, unlike the tokens for any individual Commons, which are able to be minted and burned only using an augmented bonding curve.

Members join the Trusted Seed's Swiss Association, which gives them legal protection against issues that can arise from DAOs being classified as 'general partnerships' legally. Many DAO participants unknowingly enter into general partnerships, which come with their own set of requirements. DAO members could be held individually liable for actions of other DAO members that are done in the name of the DAO. By joining the Trusted Seed's legal Swiss Association, members are protected from some of the potential risk involved with a general partnership. Members of the Trusted Seed could prove unreliable, and, in these extreme circumstances, the Commons Stack Association has the ability to engage graduated sanctions, the most severe of which would be the burning of CSTK tokens.

COMMONS DEPLOYMENT SUPPORT

The goal of the Commons Stack is to build tools that can be deployed by other commons to develop their projects. The Commons Stack is supporting the incubation phase of the various commons with seed funding via donations, administration, development and advisory support.

DECENTRALISED DEVELOPMENT TEAM

The Commons Stack tech team builds, documents and maintains the Commons Stack toolkit. Several designers and developers have emerged around the

Swiss membership DApp, the Commons simulator, the hatch and Commons Configuration Dashboard and the Commons Swarm, which is a sum of efforts between 1hive and the Commons Stack to create and fund public goods using an augmented bonding curve and conviction voting.

This team of designers and developers are pioneers in the field of token engineering and they share knowledge and resources on the GitHub platform, which hosts open-source projects. The Commons Swarm currently develops and audits the smart contracts for Iteration 0 of the Commons Stack design pattern that the TEC will deploy as the first Commons. This will be the first reference implementation of the augmented bonding curve, governed via real-time conviction voting. The Commons Swarm also develops the Hatch Configuration Dashboard, which can be customised by other commons opting to model their parameters for their token economy.

PUBLIC GOODS ECOSYSTEM ACCELERATOR

The Public Goods Ecosystem Accelerator helps communities building open-source public goods get funding by using existing platforms and tools, such as Giveth, Gitcoin Grants, Panvala and Stakes.social, among others. Apart from fundraising, this node of the Commons Stack facilitates partnerships, coordinates inter-organisational DAO2DAO collaborations, produces and participates in events and engages in multimedia production and distribution, public relations and community care work. It also encourages knowledge and resource sharing and promotes research collaboration and educational opportunities.

COMMUNICATIONS AND LEGAL

This group runs the communication platforms, including newsletters, publication and distribution management, promotion and media production. It works to communicate ideas, research and development in the Commons Stack across many communities scattered around in academia, the cryptosphere, community currency organisations, and more. It also supports cross-communication between various ecosystems. In addition, this group supports the Commons Stack legal innovation and infrastructure. It works to ensure that members of the Commons Stack are compliant with regulations and legal requirements.

KNOWLEDGE COMMONS

The Knowledge Commons group documents the ongoing academic research on the commons and applied case studies, with the aim of creating an info repository and a commons handbook as an open source of commons education for communities looking to use those tools to launch their own commons.

RESEARCH LAB

The Research Lab engages in collaborative research with ecosystem partners such as BlockScience, 1hive, Curve Labs, ixo Foundation, Regen Network and cadCAD. The objective is to advance open-source scientific knowledge of token engineering primitives by producing research digests and academic papers, walkthroughs of cadCAD modes, and more. Topics of interest range from dynamic and risk-adjusted bonding curves and computer-aided governance to the invisible economy and feminist economics.

The Production Layer

Tracking and quantifying 'labour' on the Blockchain is one of the major challenges of crypto-commons. The idea here is simple: to tune online and offline labour with metrics and compensate contributors accordingly. DAOs such as Coordinape,[13] SourceCred[14] and the Commons Stack are currently experimenting with various models. The Commons Stack has introduced the Contributor Praise,[15] which is a tool to measure contributions in the Commons Stack build. Contributions range widely, from writing code or posting an article to assisting members or simply participating in the forum and the discussions. Anyone can dish praise on someone else's contribution in the main Commons Stack Telegram and Discord channels. Praise dishing is done on a monthly cycle. Before the 15th of every month the Commons Stack Association analyses the praise awarded from the month before. Praise is transparent and recorded in a sheet in terms of quantifiable impact hours (IHs), which then turn into CSTK tokens that have no monetary value but denote reputation earned in the Trusted Seed. CTSK tokens are non-transferrable, meaning that one cannot sell them. CSTK tokens can be used to give access to members of the Trusted Seed to the launch of future commons.

However, the Contributor Praise has run into problems inherent in quantifying labour on the Blockchain. 'Objective' metrics are too gamable, and a lot of work is not captured by the metrics. Subjective metrics such as contributors reviewing each other or rating each contribution are biased and cannot scale, let alone connect to the real economy. As Emmet admits:

> The praise system is kind of a side-show to the larger cyber physical commons – in my experience it has done little more than capture ephemeral/'surface level' participation, and routinely undervalues deeper, less visible infrastructural work. It is unfortunate, because this also happens to be the core of what we are doing – many infrastructures are public goods, and if we can't reward them internally with these systems, we won't reward them externally with them either. It is easy to get caught up in the details of various mechanisms (praise, SourceCred, Coordinape, etc.) and lose sight that this is just an over-engineered and underperforming quantification tool.
>
> (interview with Jeff Emmett, 2021)

When referring to contributions, the Commons Stack deliberately abstains from any classical, or even neoclassical, political economy framework. There is no mention of production, labour, salaries, working rights, etc. An elementary division of labour exists among core team members, who are being paid a salary out of the community budget, funded principally by Griff Green, the founder of Giveth and the Commons Stack. Full transparency of the community budget is documented, with detailed analytics available on the Giveth platform. Core team members are the stewards of the working groups, which consist of volunteers who contribute time and effort and/or money. Stewards act mostly as coordinators and advisors of the working groups. Anyone can contribute to any layer at any time. Contributions are assessed collectively by the community ex post.

However, this model reproduces a contradiction most prominent within open-source projects between core team member paid a salary and volunteers earning reputation. Some value is recognised among the community in monetary terms and some value is not recognised in monetary terms or not recognised at all. Some value, therefore, gets extracted, wasted or misrecognised. The Commons Stack has recently launched the TEC, which is innovating rapidly on the next steps to improve on the above deficiencies of the praise system.

The Finance Layer

The finance layer consists of decentralised mechanisms to pool capital into the commons, such as crowdfunding, donations and grants. It introduces taxation through the ABC as a monetary tool to support the commons financially. The Giveth DApp[16] in particular provides an alternative to traditional donations, since donors receive GIVbacks, GIVdrops and GIV rewards from their donations and staking, respectively, that allow them to vote on proposals.[17]

The First Hatch: the Token Engineering Commons

The TEC[18] is the first deployment of the Commons Stack pattern. The TEC is a DAO that is emerging out of the Commons Stack. It is an open-source and collectively governed project that aims to create a token economy to accelerate the token engineering field through the ethical creation of public goods. Token engineering projects eligible for funding via the ABC module include cadCAD development, DAO/commons modules, governance tools and models, iterations of market mechanisms and components, bonding curve innovation, crypto-economic building blocks for Web 3.0, legal research, academic papers, articles, courses, books, conferences, presentations, talks, and more.

The Commons Stack assumes the role of building out the baseline technical and cultural processes associated with hatching a Commons. The token engineering community is utilising the Commons Stack toolkit to launch the TEC. The TEC community voted to have the Trusted Seed to act as founding members in its hatch. This ensures that hatchers have reputation at stake and a legal structure to protect them individually, while allowing the TEC to avoid a formal legal structure that would restrict its ability to evolve. The TEC community is the first of, hopefully, many communities that will partner with the Commons Stack to launch their commons.

TEC Hatch Phases

As mentioned earlier, the ABC launches a commons in two phases: the hatch phase (Figure 4.6) and the open phase (Figure 4.7). It is useful here to go briefly through the hatch phases of the TEC, which can serve as a customisable model for launching other commons in the future. The intention of the Commons Stack and the TEC was to launch first the TEC hatch as a DAO and then upgrade to a Commons, which will initialise the ABC and conviction voting. The hatch phase of the TEC hatch DAO splits into three phases: the pre-hatch phase, the post-hatch phase and the open phase.

Pre-Hatch Phase

In the pre-hatch phase, the founding community members from both the Commons Stack (Trusted Seed) and the TEC (builders) collectively decide and vote on the design parameters (Params Dashboard) for deploying the TEC hatch DAO (hatch period, hatch minimum goal, hatch maximum goal, hatch tribute, vote duration, minimum quorum, and more). Builders are awarded impact hours tokens in proportion to their contribution for setting the parameters for the pre-hatch phase. Members of the Trusted Seed and builders utilise their CSTK tokens and impact hour tokens, respectively, to vote through the Tokenlog[19] application, which is a governance tool that creates token-weighted backlogs. Tokenlog allows projects to continuously gather feedback from their token holders, who actively signal which items matter to them rather than just vote on single proposals.

The pre-hatch vote determined a duration time of 30 days for hatchers to co-vest funds into the hatch raise, during which period the hatchers sent wxDAI (1 wxDAI = 1 xDAI = 1 DAI = 1 US dollar) in exchange for TEC hatch (TEC-H) tokens, which represent voting power in the post-hatch phase. TEC-H token holders would be able at any time to rage-quit and pull out their proportional share of the wxDai collected in the redeemable pool. Eventually, the hatch managed to raise 1.5 million xDAI out of 472 hatchers, which was allocated in a temporary reserve.[20] Twenty-five per cent of all the newly minted TEC-H tokens were awarded to the builders in proportion to their impact hours.

Post-Hatch Phase

During the post-hatch phase TEC-H token holders (hatchers) used the Commons Config Dashboard to propose economic designs for the TEC. They used quadratic voting to vote on Tokenlog on the governance parameters of

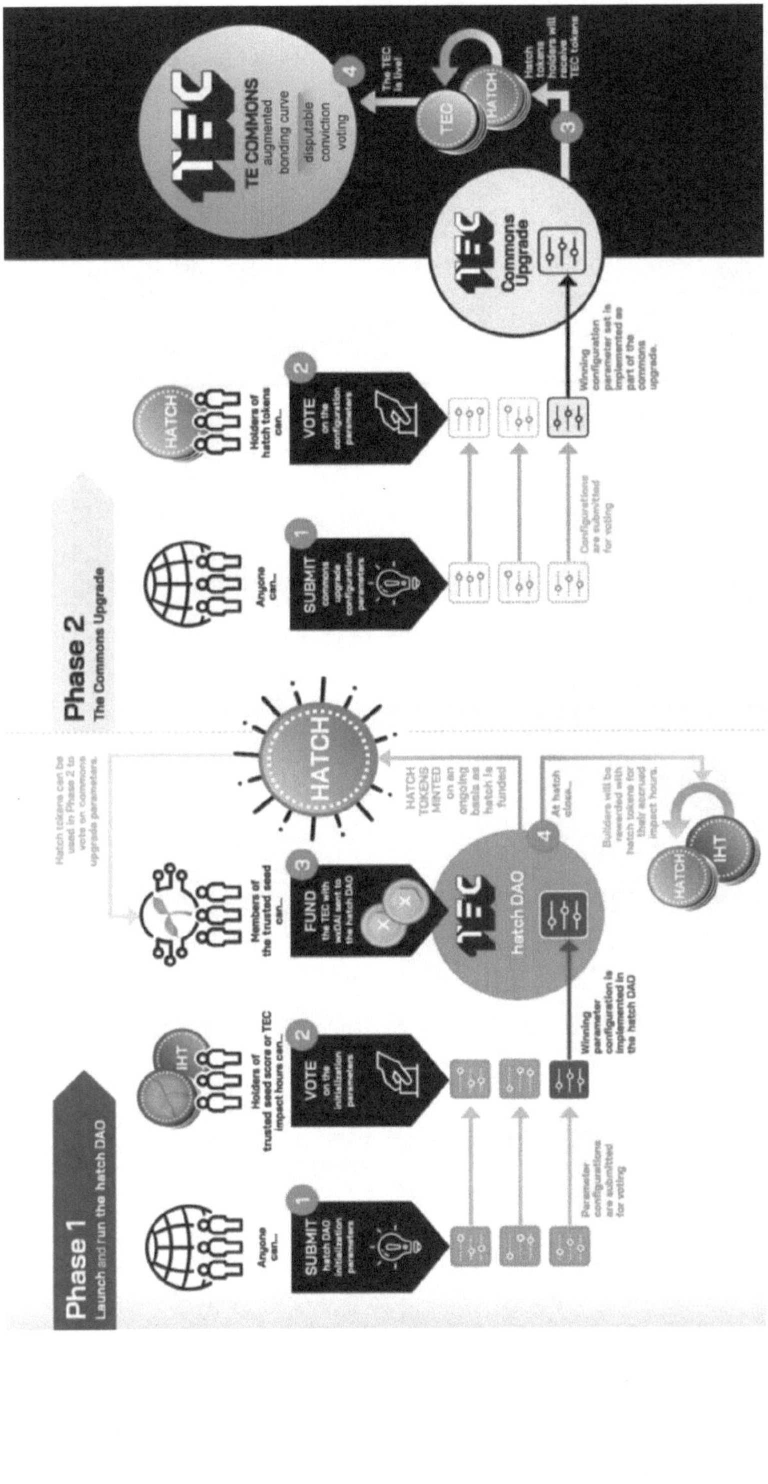

Figure 4.6 The Hatch Phase

Source: TEC website.

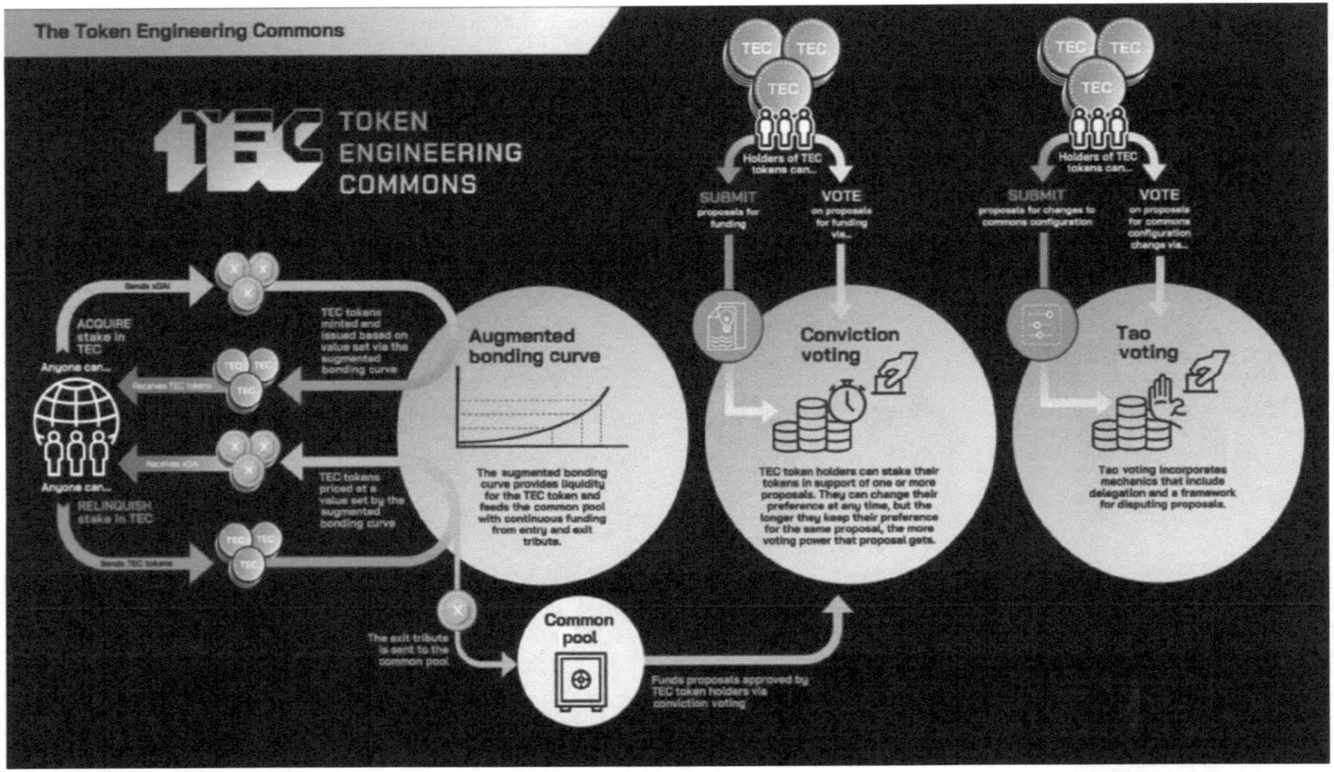

Figure 4.7 The Open Phase

Source: TEC website.

the ABC, conviction voting and tao voting. Relevant parameters included the support required, minimum quorum, vote duration, tollgate fee, vote proposal buffer, vote execution delay and rage-quit period.[21] Eventually, 82 out of the total 472 Hatchers participated in the vote in Snapshot[22] for the final parameters of the ABC. At the end of the voting period all funds were sent to the smart contracts, which converted TEC-H tokens into TEC tokens, and the final TEC DAO entered the open phase and went live on 13 January 2022. Tokens minted in the hatch are locked, so they cannot be sold or transferred, but have all voting powers. Some of the final parameters of the ABC are listed below.

TOKEN FREEZE AND TOKEN THAW

- **Token freeze**: **26 weeks**, meaning that 100 per cent of the TEC tokens minted for hatchers will remain locked from being sold or transferred for 26 weeks. They can still be used to vote while frozen.
- **Token thaw**: **52 weeks**, meaning that the hatchers' frozen tokens will start to become transferable at a steady rate starting at the end of token freeze and ending 52 weeks later.
- **Opening price**: **1 wxDAI**, meaning that, for the initial buy, the first TEC minted by the augmented bonding curve will be priced at 1 wxDAI, making it the price floor during the token freeze.

AUGMENTED BONDING CURVE

- **Commons tribute**: **69.00 per cent**, which means that 69.00 per cent of the hatch funds (870244.26 wxDAI) will go to the common pool and 31.00 per cent (390979.31 wxDAI) will go to the ABC's reserve.
- **Entry tribute**: **22.00 per cent**, meaning that, from every 'Buy' order on the ABC, 22.00 per cent of the order value in wxDAI is subtracted and sent to the common pool.
- **Exit tribute**: **2.00 per cent**, meaning that, from every 'Sell' order on the ABC, 2.00 per cent of the order value in wxDAI is subtracted and sent to the common pool.

CONVICTION VOTING

- **Conviction growth**: seven day(s), meaning that voting power will increase by 50 per cent every seven days that they are staked behind a proposal, so that, after ten days, a voter's voting power will have reached 75 per cent of its maximum capacity.
- **Minimum conviction**: **4.0 per cent**, meaning that, to pass any funding request, it will take at least 4.0 per cent of the actively voting TEC tokens.
- **Spending limit**: **11.0 per cent**, which means that no more than 11.0 per cent of the total funds in the common pool can be funded for a single proposal.

OPEN PHASE

As mentioned above, the TEC Commons entered the open phase on 13 January 2022 with an initial buy-in price of $1. At the time of writing (11 February 2022) the TEC token is priced at $2.934 (TEC/wxDAI), with 382 backers holding tokens. It has a total pool value (circulating supply) of 2,071,027 tokens, with $1,110,187 allocated in the reserve pool and $960,840 in the common pool value.[23] Anyone can buy tokens and provide funding for R&D grants and vote on projects to be funded. Anyone can apply for a grant and become a recipient of funds oriented towards the research and development of token engineering projects focused on the creation of public goods. However, the open phase currently serves as a way for the TEC to self-fund the operations of the working groups for the period of the next six months, after which all tokens will be gradually unlocked and the CV platform will go live for relevant proposals.

Stakeholders and Tokenomics

It is useful to clarify here the stakeholders and the tokenomics involved in the TEC hatch (Voshmgir 2021).

PRE-HATCH PHASE

Stakeholders

- The Commons Stack: incubator role.
- Builders: the members of the Trusted Seed and the TEC who have contributed to the design and implementation of the hatch.
- Future grant recipients: communities that want to use the Commons Stack toolkit to launch their commons (TEC showcase).

Tokenomics

- Impact hour tokens: reputation tokens that are rewarded to builders in proportion to their contributions measured by the Commons Stack praise system. If the hatch is successful, IH tokens will turn into TEC-H tokens, which come with voting rights and a monetary value, the price of which will depend on total fundraising during the hatch.
- CSTK tokens: reputation tokens that determine the eligibility to participate in the hatch. They give access and voting rights in the pre-hatch phase. They are used mainly for legal reasons, since CSTK requires membership in the Trusted Seed Association, which will give limited liability to the hatchers. They also serve as an additional entry point for people who want to fund the commons but have no time to contribute, and cannot therefore collect impact hours. If the hatch is successful, CSTK tokens have no utility in the next phase.

- wxDAI tokens: payment tokens that hatchers use to fund the TEC hatch DAO and acquire TEC-H tokens. They serve as a property right.

POST-HATCH PHASE

Stakeholders

- Commons Stack: incubator role.
- Hatchers: people who have contributed time or money, including builders. Hatchers will need to make key decisions regarding the parameters of the Hatch DAO and how the Commons upgrade (the opening phase of the TEC DAO) will occur. Hatchers will provide funding for the initialisation of the augmented bonding curve and will have significant influence on the direction of the TEC once the hatch process is over.
- Future grant recipients: communities that want to use the Commons Stack toolkit to launch their commons (TEC showcase).

Tokenomics

- TEC hatch token (TEC-H): an investment token that is minted during the creation of the hatch DAO. It grants governance rights to vote on the parameters of the final TEC DAO. Twenty-five per cent of the TEC-H tokens are awarded to the builders in proportion to the impact hours they collected. TEC-H tokens convert into TEC tokens when the TEC DAO goes live.
- wxDAI token: payment token that hatchers use to fund the TEC Hatch DAO and acquire TEC-H tokens. It serves as a property right.

OPEN PHASE

Stakeholders

- Commons Stack: will still provide legal entity for members of the Trusted Seed and protect their liability status.
- Backers: investors who fund the TEC DAO and receive TEC tokens in proportion to the money they invest.
- Builders: will continue to manage the TEC DAO and continue research and development of community governance tools.
- Grant recipients: TEC showcase.

Tokenomics

- TEC token: an investment and governance token to vote on funding individual projects via conviction voting and disputable voting. Supply, price stability and rights are to be defined and chosen in the post-hatch phase by all hatchers, along with the final parameters of the ABC.

- wxDAI token: a payment token that backers use to fund the TEC DAO and acquire TEC tokens. It serves as a property right.

The TEC Organisational Structure

The TEC's organisational structure breaks down into ten working groups[24] and three main roles: (1) the stewards of the working groups, who are also in charge of the advice process; (2) community members, who volunteer on small or big tasks, make proposals and vote on proposals on the TEC website and Snapshot; and (3) token holders (Table 4.1). Roles often overlap, since stewards

Table 4.1 The TEC DAO governance model

Off-chain governance	*On-chain governance*
Value proposition	
The creation of open-source software based on the Commons Stack toolkit for the advancement of the commons	Smart-contracts applied on top of the Ethereum platform Github cadCAD
Principles	
Ostrom's eight principles Non-hierarchical grassroots democracy Do-ocracy Transparency Accountability	Decentralisation DAO2DAO interoperability Commons fractalisation
Roles/stakeholders	
Working groups (self-sustained DAOs) Community members/contributors Token holders buying tokens either through the ABC or through secondary markets Trusted Seed members	Programmers Software engineers Design architects Experts/researchers Social scientists
Funding model	
Donations Gitcoin grants Trusted Seed membership dues Salaries for regular contributors	Crowdfunding Token issuance through the ABC The Giveth DApp
Incentives	
Cultural build Reputation gained for contributions/labour through the praise system and SourceCred	Alliance of profit-driven individual incentives and commons-driven goals Proposals receive funding from the common pool
Membership/partnerships	
Trusted Seed members Community members/contributors Experts/researchers	BlockScience Commons Stack Token engineering Experts/researchers

Table 4.1 Cont.

Off-chain governance	*On-chain governance*
Communication	
Communications Working Group	Blockchain interoperability:
Posts in the TEC forum	GitHub
Community calls in Discord	Aragon
Group chat in Telegram	1hive gardens
Twitter account	Ethereum
	Gnosis
	MakerDAO (DAI)
Decision-making	
Advice process	Changes to smart contracts
Proposal submission by token holders	Funding
Voting on proposal via Tokenlog, Snapshot, conviction voting, tao voting (delegation), token-weighted quadratic voting	Large impact cultural decisions
	Automatically executed funding proposals via conviction voting, tao voting, quadratic voting
	Arbitration/dispute resolution via Celeste
Legal foundation	
No legal entity	GPL v3.0 and MIT
Commons Stack Swiss Association to provide funding to TEC members up to Swiss franc 10,000 in legal defence	

Source: Adapted from van Pelt et al. (2021: 31).

and community members can be token holders and vice versa. Some token holders as well as some stewards who have helped launch the TEC Commons are part of the Commons Stack Trusted Seed.

The TEC currently consists of 14 stewards, 20 to 30 community members and 383 token holders (interview with Chuy Garcia, 2022). The TEC lacks well-developed, detailed and accurate analytics and metrics with regard to the precise number of community members. However, it is evident by following the discussions in the forum and the community calls that there are a significant number of women participating, as well as people of international origin. It is important to note also that, with the exception of a few community members and stewards who are paid a salary for contributing regularly in the build-up of the TEC, all other community members are gaining reputation tokens for their contributions, which can be variously redeemed down the road.

The TEC lacks the skills, tools and resources available to organisations such as states and corporations (Table 4.2). Furthermore, one should not conflate the structure of the TEC DAO with the development or advancement of actual token engineering in practice (Voshmgir 2020: 318–327). Token engineering is, basically, identified with companies, such as BlockScience, that develop abstract mathematical models to be applied in code written to steer commons-based

Table 4.2 State, Corporation and TEC DAO

DAO	*State*	*Corporation*	*TEC*
Token	Fiat money (US dollar, euro)	Fiat money (US dollar, euro)	Algorithmic money (TEC token)
Governance	Autocracy, oligarchy, democracy	Hierarchical top-down management	On-chain and off-chain governance complying with Ostrom's design principles
Agents	Citizens, politicians, parties, civil servants	Shareholders, boards of directors, employees	Stewards, community members, token holders
Funding	Taxation, debt, lobbying, public–private partnerships	Stock market, venture capital, government subsidies	Crowdfunding, donations, grants, DAO2DAO partnerships
Labour	Distribution of labour through hierarchical top-down management	Distribution of labour through hierarchical top-down management	Horizontalism, do-ocracy, stigmergy, equipotentiality
Compensation	Tax-based salaries for politicians and civil servants	Salaries, stock options	Salaries, pay per task, reputation
Law	Constitution	Types of legal entities: limited company, public limited company, for-profit, not-for-profit, etc.	Algorithmic consensus protocols, smart contracts, conviction voting, liquid democracy, tao voting
Dispute resolution	Court	Court or internal dispute settlement	Decentralised arbitration service (Celeste), retroactive change in the ledger with hard-fork or on-chain governance
Identification	Citizenship, birth certificate, national identity card, passport	National ID card, work permit, social security number	Wallet address, IP addresses of the server, all with multi-sig accounts and digital signatures
Incentives	Taxation, penalty systems, nudging	Salaries, bonuses, return on investment	Token price appreciation, reputation, cultural build

Source: Adapted from Voshmgir (2020: 130–131).

communities, whereas the TEC is a commons DAO implementing some tools built by BlockScience and the Commons Stack, such as the ABC and conviction voting, to fund the creation of open-source software and relevant tools to be used by other communities. Whereas BlockScience is a professional organisation consisting of experts and computer scientists, the TEC consists basically of the work of non-experts and volunteers who collaborate for a common cause, implementing Ostrom's principles for the purpose of creating open-source software. As Emmett contends:

> The TEC is a socio-political experiment in itself. It has been interesting to witness the interplay of various microcosms or political movements play out even in small, purportedly aligned communities. Beyond just the application of new tools, it has been educational to witness differing personal ideologies lead to various levels of individualistic vs collectivist sentiment in some proposals, even within an organisation aiming to run as a commons.
>
> (interview with Jeff Emmett, 2022)

The core values of the TEC are open sourcing, non-hierarchy, transparency and accountability. We can see below how the cultural practices of the TEC intersect with some of the working groups that comprise their governance model.

1. Gratitude: the TEC upgrades the praise system, which derives from Giveth and the Commons Stack, to reward contributions, acknowledge unseen care work and ensure accountability.[25] Contributions are classified into objective ones such as posts, tweets, likes, comments, replies on GitHub, Discourse, Discord and Twitter and subjective ones such as kindness, care, commitment, support, volunteering, etc. The TEC incorporates the SourceCred rewards system, which employs the Google PageRank algorithm to reward objective contributions. Instead of webpages voting for each other on hyperlinks, contributors and contributions are voting on each other based on interactions. Objective contributions are automatically tracked and quantified by SourceCred and subjective contributions are manually praised and quantified via the Commons Stack praise system, used by randomly selected members of the community named as quantifiers. A Fibonacci sequence will be used as the incremental factor for quantifying. Contributions are quantified in terms of effort, impact and uniqueness. Quantifiers will be provided a 'Rules of Praise' (WIP) document, which will help them navigate the quantification process. A percentage of the common pool will be requested from the TEC treasury for funding rewards. This percentage will vary between 0.3 per cent and 1.5 per cent. Reward allocations are valued in DAI, but paid out in TEC. The initial allocation distribution will be 50 per cent of the allocation value

to SourceCred, and the other 50 per cent goes to praise. A Reward Board will be responsible of inspecting the distribution and releasing the funds. The Reward Board establishes an allocation distribution of 88 per cent to contributors, 10 per cent to quantifiers, 2 per cent to the Reward Board. The final distribution and allocation of funds must be approved by a community vote. Thus, the community will act as the backstop in instances of collusion or poor judgement from the Reward Board. A Blockchain ledger of final praise distributions will be maintained by the Reward Board and made publicly available.

2. Celebration: online meetings begin with opening questions that foster intimacy and playfulness among participants. Meetings turn into parties, at which participants dish praise on each other on account of bi-weekly accomplishments. This helps maintain a friendly and celebratory atmosphere.
3. Do-ocracy: anyone has the agency to work on a task. An advice process helps members and contributors navigate within the broader ecosystem without creating chaos.
4. Stewardship: stewards lead working groups and are responsible for planning and managing the resources. Stewards are the super-spreaders of the core values, of the advice process and of the shared vision. Stewards coordinate via open weekly community calls that offer transparency, accountability and brainstorming for future actions.
5. Participatory decision-making: grassroots democracy begins with the question of how to decide on what to decide. Therefore, it is a digital version of an informal procedural democracy activated by discussions on Discord channel, poll voting in the forums or Telegram and quadratic voting. The cultural build of the Commons Stack seeks to tackle heterogeneity, pluralism and conflict within a DAO before even proceeding into setting the parameters of ABC and conviction voting.
6. Inclusion: no prerequisites exist for participation in the community. However, a certain level of trust needs to be fact-checked before any member is free to interact in the community.
7. Transparency: the Commons Stack uses a springboard to keep track of who is doing what. Working group calls take place daily on Discord. All the community calls are recorded and uploaded on YouTube. Praise quantification is open to active participants. Each working group is audited and given a transparency score.
8. Education: there are various education initiatives, such as the TE Academy, TEC labs, Graviton training, Book Club, TEC dashboards, TE Spotlight (TokenSpice/Ocean Protocol, Metagame, Opolis, Near Protocol, Grassroots Economics).
9. Conflict management: Graviton trains people to be the harmony keepers of the community by using non-violent communication. Graduated sanctions apply when issues happen to scale.

Technical and Social Challenges

The Commons Stack and the TEC comply with most of the commons principles, beginning with Ostrom's design principles and expanding to the organisational principles of the digital commons. Democracy, holoptism, transparency, equipotentiality, stigmergy, modularity, openness, sharing, do-ocracy, sustainability, the equitable distribution of value – all are amply showcased in the Commons Stack. Alongside collaborative economics and the relevant techno-economic innovations, astonishing is the so-called cultural build: the spirit of democratic deliberation, conviviality and cooperation that nurtures the values of the Commons Stack's and the TEC's operations. The Commons Stack and the TEC seek to infuse a friendly atmosphere across the distributed 'workplace' and decision-making space, where like-minded people come together to co-create for the sake of a common good.

However, the Commons Stack narrative is problematic. The Commons Stack adopts Ostrom's neo-institutional framework for addressing collective action problems, manifested most prominently in the provision of public goods, ranging from climate change to open-source software. Yet the very term 'public goods' limits the commons to the ones administered by the state or self-managed by Ostrom's limited-access communities, while the term 'polycentric governance' brings into the self-management of common pool resources libertarian actors along with commoners, thereby aiming to reconcile different power dynamics in the ever-growing loop of the commons, propelled by the ABC and conviction voting. This contradiction is offset through the tax imposed on transactions, which in turn aims to align incentives and secure the sustainability of cyber-physical commons.

The Commons Stack narrative rests on a vague 'good-doerism', which is characteristic of the republican libertarianism that Vitalik Buterin famously espouses, when he champions the use of Blockchain to create a better world. This programmatic vagueness is reproduced by the term 'collaborative economics', introduced by Griff Green, the founder of the Commons Stack, who follows in the footsteps of Buterin to introduce a sort of computer-aided participatory crypto-economics. In this framework, it is presumed that the means of socio-economic arrangement are mathematically designed ex ante by experts and are separate from the ends of the commons, which are context-dependent. Code is retroactive to the needs of the commons but, nevertheless, the commons remain free-floating on the emptiness of ends, which are supposed to be democratically agreed upon by community members ex post. This context-specific presumption of public goods reproduces the liberal misconception that technology is value-free and devoid of normative assumptions, which fall, instead, in the jurisdiction of the pluralism of ethics. However, technology is an ethic in itself, encoded into algorithms that flirt with technocracy when they are not democratically designed. Eventually, economism lurks in the high burden of techno-econometrics weighing down on the socio-political foundation of collaboration. On the one hand, exhaustive design is inevitable, to secure the commons against speculators. On the other, a simpler design would perhaps attract more users.

The Commons Stack focuses on addressing climate change and free riding in open-source software, following on Buterin's narrative to promote the creation of public goods on the Blockchain. However, this narrative does not touch upon either the commons or the contradictions inherent in the capitalist production of private goods, such as the extraction of rent (surplus value) from workers, and the power asymmetries between managers and workers, capital and labour, the elites and the people. The limitation of the commons to public goods indirectly legitimises the capitalist expropriation of common wealth and, as such, is detrimental to the evolution of the commons into a broader socio-political movement that expands way beyond context-specific public goods and open-source software. The Commons Stack and the DAOs ecosystem as a whole would potentially attract more users by opening up their narrative to encompass all types of commons, from local to global commons.

In addition, it is not clear how open-source software and token engineering alone can tackle climate change. The very idea of tokenising nature is the worst nightmare of crypto-biotech neoliberalism commercialising natural resources. By limiting the scope of their narrative to public goods and climate change, the Commons Stack risks falling prey to the sirens of techno-economism, oscillating between crypto-libertarianism and crypto-commonism rather than adopting a clear post-capitalist perspective that clashes head-on with the capitalist system and paves the way for a more holistic paradigm shift from the current neoliberal status quo.

The Commons Stack and the TEC are at an early stage of development, and they face numerous challenges. They coalesce around several DAOs currently experimenting with Blockchain-based funding and governance tools to create decentralised micro-economies. Their development is co-emergent with the Blockchain Web3 ecosystem, which will take time to reach mainstream adoption, if ever. The technical infrastructure of the Commons Stack and the TEC is embedded in smart contracts built on Ethereum. Blockchain's decentralised infrastructure, especially for DAOs, is not yet ready for large-scale deployment. Myriad technical issues are yet to be resolved, such as the scalability of Ethereum, high transaction fees, the standardisation and interoperability across Blockchains and with existing systems, the usability by non-geeks, large-scale fair governance issues, legal issues, a profound shortage of trained Blockchain developers, environmental concerns with proof of work algorithms, applications in the real economy, state regulation, and so on (Hassan et al. 2020: 103).

Much of the Blockchain hype has been built upon the concept of trust guaranteed by mathematics and computer code. However, trust in the Blockchain technology is constantly undermined by flaws in the code, hack attacks, frauds, Ponzi schemes, and so on. Global digital illiteracy makes people still rely on centralised institutions. It will take time for Blockchain technology to become more environmentally friendly, robust and secure, thereby potentially reaching mainstream adoption. Till then people will most likely continue to trust central authorities to protect their money, rather than an algorithm on a computer that can be hacked at any time. Crypto-volatility and bear markets also weigh heavily on people investing time and effort and/or money on cryptocurrencies and DAOs.

Despite the current frenzy with Blockchain, DAOs still have a limited user base. The most important techno-social challenge of DAOs' operation is their application to the real economy. There remains little connection to start-ups or cooperatives building value propositions for the real economy with the aim of creating a more humane, ethical, democratic, environment-friendly and equitable collaborative economy, let alone the numerous socio-political and legal implications. How would self-governance work for thousands or millions of users online? How would DAOs address the contradictions of online versus offline inter-operation; the digital versus the physical space; algorithmic centralisation versus decentralisation; the tyranny of structurelessness versus grassroots democracy; exploration versus efficiency; paid labour versus reputation; complexity versus simplicity; commerciality versus non-commerciality; fragmentation versus coordination; liminality versus legality; and so on?

We can see some of these contradictions playing out in the Commons Stack and the TEC, where, for instance, some people are paid a salary and some people are gaining reputation tokens. The Commons Stack and the TEC have hundreds of members, but only a fraction of them participate in the community calls and only a dozen or so of them vote on proposals. Procedures, tools and platforms are complex for non-geeks to cope with and participate in. In the quest for decentralisation, tools and mechanisms span multiple websites and platforms, becoming overwhelming even for experts to go through. Polycentrism would prevent the chaos of complexity and noise featuring in DAOs by deploying user-friendly interfaces and holistic coordination mechanisms – DAO2DAO interoperability – able to reach a critical mass. A major challenge therefore remains for DAOs to balance holistic design, coordination, simplicity and decentralisation.

Eventually, the majority of issues in the TEC are mostly debated by a minority of ten to 15 people – the so-called stewards and advisors – who have the knowledge and the skills necessary to prefigure the best solutions available to highly complex issues. It is still unknown how democracy would operate with hundreds or even thousands of members willing to participate in community calls. How would online operations connect to offline operations? Garcia calls for the Ostrom's principles fostered by conviction voting and liquid democracy to widen democracy both online and offline (interview with Chuy Garcia, 2022). Ostrom's polycentric model of governance can, indeed, account for the diverse motivations of the actors involved in the self-management of common pool resources (states, companies, NGOs) but it does not question the power asymmetries inherent in the actors themselves. Ostrom's principles are not sufficient to sustain a broader democratic movement inasmuch as they do not clash head-on with the contradictions of capitalism and the state – that is, the power asymmetries between directors and executants, managers and workers, the elites and the people. To be fair, the Commons Stack and the TEC are pioneers in building up a promising small-scale grassroots democratic culture on Web3. The question is: how can this culture connect to the real economy and scale to broader democratic procedures that could involve millions of people?

The Commons Stack, therefore, seems to fall into the trap of neo-institutional economics, swinging back and forth radicalism and conservatism. The Commons Stack diverts from crypto-libertarianism in that it introduces a tax to private goods (tokens), which is channelled via club goods (the reserve pool) into common goods (the common pool) to eventually produce public goods. But, ultimately, the Commons Stack introduces a liberal version of a cyber-physical commons that still cannot address the equitable distribution of value amid open-sourced production – let alone the application of the ABC to the rest of the economy. Additional mechanisms should be explored for contributors to be paid the full value of their labour and have a say in the production process, irrespective of stake. To avoid free riding over resources, capital should pay a fee if it is intended to commercialise resources for profit (copyfair licence).

A number of additional philosophical and ethical issues arise with regard to the blending of Blockchain with AI and the IoT. To what degree are humans willing to employ technology to cooperate and communicate? How do we strike a balance between online and offline life? To what degree do humans want to financialise life? To what degree do humans want to tokenise value? To what degree do humans want to delegate politics and justice to smart contracts?

These are complex political issues, and they cannot be dealt with in a computer-based decentralised fashion but need to be discussed in both physical and digital space, employing all possible coordination mechanisms necessary to broaden democratic procedures. To facilitate the federated scaling of the commons, intermediate nodes (DAOs, associations, state delegates, institutions, etc.) are a *sine qua non* for coordinating democracy and preventing chaos arising from socio-economic and ecological waste and noise. To avoid reproducing the capitalist survival of the fittest among DAOs and the commons, a holistic coordination mechanism would unite dispersed initiatives under the post-hegemony of the commons.

Notes

1 See https://1hive.org.
2 See https://aragon.org.
3 See https://sourcecred.io.
4 See www.molochdao.com.
5 See https://commonsstack.org.
6 See www.crypto-commons.org.
7 See http://cadcad.org.

8 See https://en.wikipedia.org/wiki/Liquid_democracy.
9 See https://token-engineering-commons.gitbook.io/tec-handbook/governance/celeste.
10 See https://giveth.io.
11 See https://commonsstack.org/abc#simulation.
12 See https://trace.giveth.io/campaign/commons-stack-association.
13 See https://coordinape.com.
14 See https://sourcecred.io.
15 See https://wiki.commonsstack.org/contributors-guide.
16 See https://docs.giveth.io/whatisgiveth.
17 See https://giv.giveth.io.
18 See https://tecommons.org.
19 See https://tokenlog.xyz/CommonsBuild/commons-config-proposals.
20 See https://hatch.tecommons.org.
21 See https://github.com/CommonsBuild/commons-config-proposals/issues/127.
22 See https://snapshot.org/#. Snapshot is a voting tool based on the IPFS decentralised storage system, used by many crypto-projects to poll their user bases. Because Snapshot does not use 'on-chain' verification, any votes are essentially fee-less.
23 See https://dune.xyz/tecommons/TECommons.
24 See https://token-engineering-commons.gitbook.io/tec-source.
25 See https://forum.tecommons.org/t/outlining-the-rewards-system-process-v2/646.

5 The Post-Hegemony of the Commons

A recent intellectual exchange between Nathan Schneider and Vitalik Buterin over democratic politics and the Blockchain will be a useful lens to walk us through the last chapter of this book.

Schneider (2021b) outlines the pros and cons of crypto-economics. By introducing novel tools of funding, voting, dispute resolution and collective resource management, crypto-economics can advance democratic traditions and reduce reliance on military or police power (Schneider 2021b: 24). However, if considered alone, crypto-economics is an extension of neoliberalism on Blockchain that seeks to replace politics with economics. Schneider (2021b: 14–17) highlights three key problems inherent in crypto-economics: (1) plutocracy; (2) the crowding out of intrinsic motivations (ethics) by extrinsic motivations (money); and (3) positive (free riding in public goods) and negative (crypto-energy use) externalities. To tackle these problems, Schneider (2021b: 20–25) advances the renewal of liberal democratic theory to encompass hybrid post-capitalist models of production, which merge traditional and platform cooperatives with DAOs within the overall structure of current representative democracy.

> A napkin sketch of classical, never-quite-achieved liberal democracy (Brown 2015) would depict a market (governed through economic incentives) enclosed in politics (governed through the deliberation on the common good) … Whereas democracy through state regulation would likely come from outside the network, cooperative democracy depends on network participants to invest in egalitarian spaces – as those in some crypto-economic projects already have.
>
> (Schneider 2021b:19, 21)

Schneider (2022b) takes a step forward by making a series of policy proposals for the coordination and democratisation of DAOs, such as:

- smart-contract-enhanced decentralisation and transparency;
- cross-platform DAO governance standards (e.g. PrimeDAO, Metagov[1]);

DOI: 10.4324/9781003039723-5

- protocol-enabled protection of labour from capital (e.g. Source Cred contribution tracking) coupled with identity verification tools, such as Proof of Humanity;[2]
- protocol taxes (e.g. from Zcash's[3] built-in Development Fund and Optimism's[4] investment in retroactive public goods to the Commons Stack's ABC entry and exit tribute);
- insurance pools, medical coverage, education;
- the creation of an enforcement market that punishes network nodes using carbon-emitting energy sources;
- built-in universal basic income distributing tokens equally to all users via reparations (e.g. Circles[5]); and
- protocol-enabled human rights enforcement that can reverse transactions provably tied to abuses, preventing even powerful entities from carrying them out.

Buterin (2021c) goes along with Schneider's liberal democratic sketch. He puts forth a game-theoretical conceptualisation, piecing together communitarian and libertarian elements to describe politics as the management of coordination. Politics turns into finance, and vice versa, when it cannot prevent collusion, which leads to the perennial overrepresentation of concentrated and concerted interests (lobbies, bankers, corporations, crypto-whales, states, parties, and so on).

> Finance can be viewed as a set of patterns that naturally emerge in many kinds of systems that do not attempt to prevent collusion. Any system which claims to be nonfinance, but does not actually makes an effort to prevent collusion, will eventually acquire the characteristic of finance, if not something worse … When a system does not prevent collusion, it cannot treat different individuals differently, or even different number of individuals differently: whenever a 'position' to exert influence exists, the owner of that position can just sell it to the highest bidder.
>
> (Buterin 2021c)

Essentially, Buterin departs from the Hobbesian conception of individuals clashing with each other to mix libertarianism with digital republicanism under the banner of mathematics and computer code, which can be used for the betterment of society and the planet. To the extent that Buterin offers a fair depiction of everyday libertarianism lying at the core of the central social imaginary of our times, his mathematical rigour, along with his digital republicanism, could occupy a distinct place within Schneider's liberal democratic sketch to help tilt neoliberal state capitalism towards the post-capitalism of the commons.

CBPP, platform co-ops and DAOs face numerous challenges and obstacles, which reproduce a number of internal and external contradictions: commerciality versus non-commerciality, competition versus cooperation, transparency versus privacy, private property versus common property, exchange value versus use value, centralisation versus decentralisation, exclusion versus inclusion, individuality versus communality, localism versus globalism, fragmentation versus scale, and so on.

The Commons Stack and the TEC, along with other DAOs in the Web3 ecosystem, form a constellation of Blockchain-based initiatives that have the potential to tackle some of the contradictions of the commons, such as the lack of coordination and funding, mismanagement, unrecognised labour and fragmentation. DAOs use Blockchain, crypto-economics and token engineering to experiment with funding tools, reputation tools, governance tools, signalling tools, voting tools, capital accumulation and distribution tools, which all have the potential to merge with local commons and platform co-ops to sustain a commons-based collaborative economy.

For example, the Commons Stack's ABC and conviction voting tools are designed to align individual and collective incentives, create a continuous crowdfunded stream of income democratically allocated to the commons, allow for pluralism with regard to commons value propositions and bootstrap a prediction market that could help the commons scale up into a federated ecosystem. The praise system is an attempt, albeit immature, to quantify reputation and unrecognised labour on the Blockchain and perhaps spread outside Blockchain. However, attention should be drawn not to the tools themselves but to the social relations of production that these tools can support. The cultural build of the Commons Stack is an admirable, but limited in scope, experiment in commoning.

Technology alone cannot sustain a commons-oriented eco-techno-social transformation. CBPP, platform co-ops and DAOs are but scattered islands on the ocean of capitalism, under constant threat of being submerged under the forces of profit, exploitation, co-optation, precariousness, climate change and competition. The contradictions of the commons reflect the lack of the political – that is, a holistic coordination mechanism aiming to unite local and global commons, platform co-ops, DAOs, ethical market entities and institutions under a post-hegemonic networked ecosystem of value creation that would alter the social relations of production and mutualise knowledge and resources in a mission to transform capitalism into the post-capitalism of the commons.

Complementary to Schneider's political topology would be a radical critique and truly liberal reformation of representative democracy, the real deepening of democracy across all spheres of society, along with the reconstruction of a collective subject that conceives politics as the self-management of society as a whole. Post-hegemonic politics, as such, is the pendulum of 'centralised' nodes of consensus and 'decentralised' forces of conflict in the constant co-creation of the political. Post-hegemonic politics forms a chain of equivalence that builds on a theory of the commons to accommodate particular commons interests into a holistic strategy capable of challenging neoliberalism. Rather than relying on fragmented commons that strive for survival in the jungle of the fittest, the post-hegemonic dialectics of consensus and conflict would unite the spontaneous plurality of the commons under a chain of equivalence that would reconcile pluralism and equality, individuality and communality, commerciality and non-commerciality, exchange and use value, private and common property, and so on.

Post-hegemony seeks to do away with socialist versions of hegemony that concentrate power in the state. Rather, post-hegemony seeks to distribute power to the people via the commonification of the state and the market. A chain of equivalence is crucial, in that it brings to the fore a 'collective subject' that transforms society on the principles of the commons and sustainability science. A 'collective subject' incarnates a novel anthropological type that respects nature and the principles of the commons. Rather than relying on a representative democracy that is prone to bureaucracy, elitism, corruption and inefficiency, the 'collective subject' of the commons would disperse into an economic democracy that gives real power to the people.

Irrespective of whether the state comes first or follows social change, its role is paramount in setting up the macro and meso structures necessary to bootstrap the bottom-up self-organisation of commons-based micro-economies. Contrary to leftist versions of the state that condemn cooperativism and decentralisation as inefficient and susceptible to capitalist co-optation, a partner state could operate as the enabler of the commons, safeguarding the latter against capitalism. The advantage of the state vis-à-vis loose decentralisation is the ability to holistically coordinate large-scale targeted incentives, as well as to directly regulate capitalism to the benefit of the commons. During this transition one could imagine crypto-economics variously interacting with the commons, including the right of individuals and communities to opt out of money and techno-science whenever they see fit.

Post-hegemony, in practice, would translate into the post-capitalist eco-techno-social transformation of both the means and social relations of production, along with commons-based intra-regenerative flows of culture, capital, knowledge and resources self-governed by communities. Proper incentive schemes, well-designed policies, financial mechanisms, law reforms, affordable housing, education and sustainability science are all part and parcel of a holistic post-hegemonic strategy aiming to transform neoliberalism into the post-capitalism of the commons, supported by a partner state that represents the interests of the people rather than elites.

Notes

1 See https://metagov.org.
2 See www.proofofhumanity.id.
3 See https://z.cash.
4 See www.optimism.io.
5 See https://joincircles.net.

References

Agbo Cornelius C., Mahmoud Qusay H. and Eklund J. Mikael. 2019. 'Blockchain Technology in Healthcare: A Systematic Review'. *Healthcare* 7 (2). DOI: 10.3390/healthcare7020056.

Akins Benjamin W., Chapman Jennifer L. and Gordon Jason M. 2014. 'A Whole New World: Income Tax Considerations of the Bitcoin Economy'. *Pittsburgh Tax Review* 12 (1): 25–56.

Alchian Armen A. and Demsetz Harold. 1972. 'Production, Information Costs, and Economic Organisation'. *American Economic Review* 62 (5): 777–795.

Alizart Marc. 2020. *Cryptocommunism*. Cambridge: Polity Press.

Atzori Marcella. 2017. 'Blockchain Technology and Decentralized Governance: Is the State Still Necessary?'. *Journal of Governance and Regulation* 6 (1): 45–62.

Arp Laurie Gemmill, Forbes Megan, Cartolano Robert T., Cramer Tom, Kimpton Michele, Skinner Katherine and Whiteside Ann Baird. 2018. 'It Takes a Village: Open Source Software Sustainability'. Atlanta: LYRASIS.

Arrow Kenneth. 1950. 'A Difficulty in the Concept of Social Welfare'. *Journal of Political Economy* 58 (4): 328–346.

Arrow Kenneth. 1962. 'Economic Welfare and the Allocation of Resources for Invention'. In Robert Nelson (ed.), *The Rate and Direction of Inventive Activity: Economic and Social Factors*, 609–626. Princeton, NJ: Princeton University Press.

Arrow Kenneth and Debreu Gerard. 1954. 'Existence of an Equilibrium for a Competitive Economy'. *Econometrica* 22 (3): 265–290.

Arterton Christopher. 1987. *Teledemocracy: Can Technology Protect Democracy?* Newbury Park, CA: SAGE.

Arvidsson Adam and Peitersen Nicolai. 2013. *The Ethical Economy: Rebuilding Value after the Crisis*. New York: Columbia University Press.

Balasanov Slava. 2018. 'Bonding Curves in Depth: Intuition and Parametrization'. Relevant, 13 December. Available at: https://blog.relevant.community/bonding-curves-in-depth-intuition-parametrization-d3905a681e0a.

Balibar Etienne and Wallerstein Immanuel. 1991. *Race, Nation, Class: Ambiguous Identities*. London: Verso Books.

Barbereau Tom, Smethurst Reilly, Papageorgiou Orestis, Sedlmeir Johannes and Fridgen Gilbert. 2022. 'Decentralised Finance's Unregulated Governance: Minority Rule in the Digital Wild West'. Available at: https://ssrn.com/abstract=4001891.

Barbrook Richard. 1998. 'The High-Tech Gift Economy'. *First Monday* 3 (12). DOI: 10.5210/fm.v3i12.631.

Barnett Jeremy and Treleaven Philip. 2018. 'Algorithmic Dispute Resolution: The Automation of Professional Dispute Resolution Using AI and Blockchain Technologies'. *The Computer Journal* 61 (3): 399–408.

Bauwens Michel and Kostakis Vasilis. 2014. 'From the Communism of Capital to Capital for the Commons: Towards an Open Co-operativism'. *tripleC: Communication Capitalism & Critique* 12 (1): 356–361.

Bauwens Michel and Niaros Vasilis. 2017a. 'Value in the Commons Economy: Developments in Open and Contributory Value Accounting'. Berlin: Heinrich Böll Stiftung.

Bauwens Michel and Niaros Vasilis. 2017b. 'Changing Societies through Urban Commons Transitions'. Berlin: Heinrich Böll Stiftung.

Bauwens Michel and Pantazis Alekos. 2018. 'The Ecosystem of Commons-Based Peer Production and Its Transformative Dynamics'. *Sociological Review Monographs* 66 (2): 302–319.

Bauwens Michel, Kostakis Vasilis and Pazaitis Alex. 2019. *Peer to Peer: The Commons Manifesto*. London: University of Westminster Press.

Beck Roman, Müller-Bloch Christoph and King John Leslie. 2018. 'Governance in the Blockchain Economy: A Framework and Research Agenda'. *Journal of the Association for Information Systems* 19 (10): 1020–1034.

Benkler Yochai. 2002. 'Coase's Penguin, or, Linux and the Nature of the Firm'. *Yale Law Journal* 112 (3): 349–466.

Benkler Yochai. 2006. *The Wealth of Networks: How Social Production Transforms Markets and Freedom*. New Haven, CT: Yale University Press.

Benkler Yochai. 2017. 'Peer Production, the Commons, and the Future of the Firm'. *Strategic Organisation* 15 (2): 264–274.

Benkler Yochai, Shaw Aaron and Hill Benjamin Mako. 2015. 'Peer Production: A Form of Collective Intelligence'. In Thomas Malone and Michael Bernstein (eds.), *Handbook of Collective Intelligence*, 1–28. Cambridge, MA: MIT Press.

Berg Chris, Davidson Sinclair and Potts Jason. 2017. 'The Blockchain Economy: A Beginner's Guide to Institutional Cryptoeconomics'. Medium, 27 September. Available at: https://medium.com/cryptoeconomics-australia/the-blockchain-economy-a-beginners-guide-to-institutional-cryptoeconomics-64bf2f2beec4.

Birchall Johnston. 2017. *The Governance of Large Co-operative Businesses*, 2nd edn. Manchester: Co-operatives UK.

Birkinbine Ben. 2020. *Incorporating the Digital Commons. Corporate Involvement in Free and Open-Source Software*. London: University of Westminster Press.

Bollier David. 2015. 'The Blockchain: A Promising New Infrastructure for Online Commons'. Bollier.org, 4 March. Available at: www.bollier.org/blog/blockchain-promising-new-infrastructure-online-commons.

Bollier David and Helfrich Silke. 2012. *The Wealth of the Commons: A World beyond Market and State*. Amherst, MA: Levellers Press.

Bollier David and Helfrich Silke. 2015. *Patterns of Commoning*. Amherst, MA: Levellers Press.

Bollier David and Helfrich Silke. 2019. *Free, Fair and Alive. The Insurgent Power of the Commons*. Gabriola Island, Canada: New Society Publishers.

Bowles Samuel and Gintis Herbert. 2011. *A Cooperative Species: Human Reciprocity and Its Evolution*. Princeton, NJ: Princeton University Press.

Brabham Daren C. 2013. *Crowdsourcing*. Cambridge, MA: MIT Press.

Braun-Dubler Nils, Gier Hans-Peter, Bulatnikova Tetiana, Langhart Manuel, Merki Manuela, Roth Florian, Burret Antoine and Perdrisat Simon. 2020. *Blockchain: Capabilities, Economic Viability, and the Socio-Technical Environment*. Zürich: vdf.

Bronkema Wietze. 2020. 'Introduction to Multisig Contracts'. Medium, 15 January. Available at: https://medium.com/mycrypto/introduction-to-multisig-contracts-33d5b25134b2.

Brousseau Eric and Curien Nicolas (eds.). 2007. *Internet and Digital Economics: Principles, Methods and Applications*. Cambridge: Cambridge University Press.

Brown Wendy. 2015. *Undoing the Demos: Neoliberalism's Stealth Revolution*. New York: Zone Books.

Buchanan James M. and Tullock Gordon. 1962. *The Calculus of Consent: Logical Foundations of Constitutional Democracy*. Indianapolis: Liberty Fund.

Buterin Vitalik. 2014. 'DAOs, DACs, DAs and More: An Incomplete Terminology Guide'. Ethereum.org, 6 May. Available at: https://blog.ethereum.org/2014/05/06/daos-dacs-das-and-more-an-incomplete-terminology-guide.

Buterin Vitalik. 2015. 'On Public and Private Blockchains'. Ethereum.org, 7 August. Available at: https://blog.ethereum.org/2015/08/07/on-public-and-private-blockchains.

Buterin Vitalik. 2017. 'Ethereum Whitepaper'. Ethereum.org, 26 October. Available at: https://ethereum.org/en/whitepaper.

Buterin Vitalik. 2018. 'Governance, Part 2: Plutocracy Is Still Bad'. Vitalik.ca, 28 March. Available at: https://vitalik.ca/general/2018/03/28/plutocracy.html.

Buterin Vitalik. 2019. 'Quadratic Payments: A Primer'. Vitalik.ca, 7 December. Available at: https://vitalik.ca/general/2019/12/07/quadratic.html.

Buterin Vitalik and Weyl Eric Glen. 2018. 'Liberation through Radical Decentralisation'. Medium, 21 May. Available at: https://medium.com/@VitalikButerin/liberation-through-radical-decentralization-22fc4bedc2ac.

Buterin Vitalik. 2020. 'Why Proof of Stake'. Vitalik.ca, 6 November. Available at: https://vitalik.ca/general/2020/11/06/pos2020.html.

Buterin Vitalik. 2021a. 'An Incomplete Guide to Rollups'. Vitalik.ca, 5 January. Available at: https://vitalik.ca/general/2021/01/05/rollup.html.

Buterin Vitalik. 2021b. 'Why Sharding Is Great: Demystifying the Technical Properties'. Vitalik.ca, 7 April. Available at: https://vitalik.ca/general/2021/04/07/sharding.html.

Buterin Vitalik. 2021c. 'On Nathan Schneider on the Limits of Cryptoeconomics'. Vitalik.ca, 26 September. Available at: https://vitalik.ca/general/2021/09/26/limits.html.

Caffentzis George. 2013. *In Letters of Blood and Fire: Work, Machines and the Crisis of Capitalism*. Oakland, CA: PM Press.

Casey Michael J. 2021. 'NFTs Are an Internet Game-Changer'. Yahoo!, 15 October. Available at: https://finance.yahoo.com/news/nfts-internet-game-changer-172540069.html.

Castells Manuel. 2007. 'Communication, Power and Counter-Power in the Network Society'. *International Journal of Communication* 1: 238–266.

Catalini Christian. 2017. 'The Firm as a Nexus of Smart Contracts? How Blockchain and Cryptocurrencies Can Transform the Digital Economy', blog. Yale Journal on Regulation, 7 June. Available at: www.yalejreg.com/nc/the-firm-as-a-nexus-of-smart-contracts-how-blockchain-and-cryptocurrencies-can-transform-the-digital-economy-by-christian-catalini.

Catalini Christian and Gans Joshua S. 2019. 'Some Simple Economics of the Blockchain', Working Paper 22952. Cambridge, MA: National Bureau of Economic Research.
Chohan Ushman W. 2021. 'Non-Fungible Tokens: Blockchains, Scarcity, and Value', discussion paper. Islamabad: Critical Blockchain Research Initiative.
Cila Nazli, Ferri Gabriele, de Waal Martijn, Gloerich Inte and Karpinski Tara. 2020. 'The Blockchain and the Commons: Dilemmas in the Design of Local Platforms'. Association for Computing Machinery, 23 April. DOI: 10.1145/3313831.3376660.
Coase Ronald. 1937. 'The Nature of the Firm'. *Economica* 4 (16): 386–405.
Coase Ronald. 1998. 'The New Institutional Economics'. *American Economic Review* 88 (2): 72–74.
Codagnone Christiano, Biagi Fabienne and Abadie Federico. 2016. 'The Future of Work in the "Sharing Economy": Market Efficiencies and Equitable Opportunities or Unfair Precarisation?'. Luxembourg: Publications Office of the European Union.
Cole George D. H. 2011 [1920]. *Guild Socialism Restated.* London: Routledge.
Coleman Stephen and Gotze John. 2001. 'Bowling Together: Online Public Engagement in Policy Deliberation'. *Information Polity* 7 (4): 247–252.
Conway Luke. 2021. 'Bitcoin Halving'. Investopedia, 29 November. Available at: www.investopedia.com/bitcoin-halving-4843769.
Dardot Pierre and Laval Christian. 2014. *Commun: Essais sur la révolution au XXIe siècle.* Paris: La Découverte.
Davidson Sinclair, De Filippi Primavera and Potts Jason. 2016. 'Economics of Blockchain'. Available at: https://ssrn.com/abstract=2744751.
Davidson Sinclair, De Filippi Primavera and Potts Jason. 2018. 'Blockchains and the Economic Institutions of Capitalism'. *Journal of Institutional Economics* 14 (4): 639–658.
Davila Joshua. 2021. 'Decentralisation at Work: Cooperatives on the Blockchain'. dGen.org, 27 May. Available at: www.dgen.org/blog/decentralisation-at-work-cooperatives-on-blockchain.
Dean Jodi. 2009. *Democracy and Other Neoliberal Fantasies. Communicative Capitalism and Left Politics.* Durham, NC: Duke University Press.
Dean Jodi. 2012. *The Communist Horizon.* London: Verso Books.
De Angelis Massimo. 2017. *Omnia Sunt Communia: On the Commons and the Transformation to Postcapitalism.* London: Zed Books.
De Filippi Primavera. 2019. 'Blockchain Technology and Decentralised Governance: The Pitfalls of a Trustless Dream'. DOI: 10.2139/ssrn.3524352.
De Filippi Primavera, Loveluck Benjamin, Niaros Vasilis, Pantazis Alekos and Fuster Morell Mayo. 2013. 'Best Practices for CBPP Communities and Policy Recommendations'. P2PValue. Available at: https://p2pvalue.eu/wp-content/uploads/2013/07/Deliverable_2.3-updated.pdf.
De Filippi Primavera and Hassan Samer. 2014. 'Measuring Value in the Commons-Based Ecosystem: Bridging the Gap between the Commons and the Market'. MoneyLab Reader, Institute of Network Cultures, University of Warwick. Available at: https://papers.ssrn.com/sol3/papers.cfm?abstract_id=2725399.
De Filippi Primavera and Loveluck Benjamin. 2016. 'The Invisible Politics of Bitcoin: Governance Crisis of a Decentralized Infrastructure'. *Internet Policy Review* 5 (3). DOI: 10.14763/2016.3.427.
De Filippi Primavera and Wright Aaron. 2018. *Blockchain and the Law. The Rule of Code.* Cambridge, MA: Harvard University Press.

De Filippi Primavera and Hassan Samer. 2018. 'Blockchain Technology as a Regulatory Technology: From Code Is Law to Law Is Code'. DOI: 10.5210/fm.v21i12.7113.

De Filippi Primavera, Mannan Morshed and Reijers Wessel. 2020. 'The Problem of Trust and Challenges of Governance'. *Technology in Society* 62. DOI: 10.1016/j.techsoc.2020.101284.

De Filippi Primavera, Mannan Morshed and Reijers Wessel. 2022. 'The Alegality of Blockchain Technology'. *Policy and Society* 41 (3): 358–372.

De Lautour Vassili Joannides and Cortese L. Corinne. 2016. 'Cooperatives: Governance and Accountability Systems for a Better World?' *Journal of Accounting and Organisational Change* 12 (1): 1–9.

De la Rouviere Simon. 2017a. 'Tokens 2.0: Curved Token Bonding in Curation Markets'. Medium, 21 November. Available at: https://medium.com/@simondlr/tokens-2-0-curved-token-bonding-in-curation-markets-1764a2e0bee5.

De la Rouviere Simon. 2017b. 'A Bonded Curation Community'. Medium, 10 March. Available at: https://medium.com/@simondlr/a-bonded-curation-community-247f14a6de04.

De la Rouviere Simon. 2017c. 'Introducing Curation Markets: Trade Popularity of Memes & Information (with Code)!'. Medium, 22 May. Available at: https://medium.com/@simondlr/introducing-curation-markets-trade-popularity-of-memes-information-with-code-70bf6fed9881.

De la Rouviere Simon. 2018. 'Tokens 2.0: Bancor's Smart Tokens vs Token Bonding Curves'. Medium, 13 November. Available at: https://medium.com/@simondlr/bancors-smart-tokens-vs-token-bonding-curves-a4f0cdfd3388.

Di Zerega Gus. 2013 'Turning the Tables: The Pathologies and Unrealized Promise of Libertarianism'. In Kelly Georgia (ed.), *Uncivil Liberties: Deconstructing Libertarianism*, 56–112. New York: Praxis Peace Institute.

Dicker Jarrod. 2021. 'Cities of Ghosts Await Their DAO Revival'. Dark Star, 2 June. Available at: https://darkstar.mirror.xyz/eYRttcLec0IXODpzLFsHZTRdzuWosBwfyVKnSc93NdA.

Duffy Kim Hamilton. 2017. 'The Time for Self-Sovereign Identity Is Now'. Medium, 7 November. Available at: https://medium.com/learningmachine-blog/the-time-for-self-sovereign-identity-is-now-222aab97041b.

Dunn Jarett. 2021. 'The Eternal Battle of Collectivism vs Individualism'. Hackernoon, 22 February. Available at: https://hackernoon.com/the-eternal-battle-of-collectivism-vs-individualism-wx223330.

Dyer-Witheford Nick. 1999. *Cyber-Marx: Cycles and Circuits of Struggle in High-Technology Capitalism*. Urbana, IL: University of Illinois Press.

Dyer-Witheford Nick. 2006. 'The Circulation of the Common'. Paper presented at 'Immaterial Labour, Multitudes and New Social Subjects: Class Composition in Cognitive Capitalism' conference, Cambridge, 30 April. Available at: https://dlc.dlib.indiana.edu/dlc/bitstream/handle/10535/4519/circulation%20of%20the%20common.pdf?sequence=1.

Dyer-Witheford Nick. 2015. *Cyber-Proletariat: Global Labour in the Digital Vortex*. London: Pluto Press.

Eghbal Nadia. 2020. *Working in Public: The Making and Maintenance of Open Source Software*. San Francisco: Stripe Press.

Emmett Jeff. 2019a. 'Introducing the Commons Stack: Infrastructure for Scalable Community Collaboration'. Medium, 18 November. Available at: https://medium.com/commonsstack/introducing-the-commons-stack-infrastructure-for-scalable-community-collaboration-f0d4a459b313.

Emmett Jeff. 2019b. 'Automating Ostrom for Effective DAO Management'. Medium, 23 December. Available at: https://medium.com/commonsstack/automating-ostrom-for-effective-dao-management-cfe7a7aea138.

Emmett Jeff. 2019c. 'Conviction Voting: A Novel Continuous Decision Making Alternative to Governance'. Medium, 18 November. Available at: https://medium.com/commonsstack/conviction-voting-a-novel-continuousdecision-makingalternative-to-governance-62e215ad2b3d.

Emmett Jeff. 2019d. 'The Trusted Seed of the Commons Stack'. Medium, 28 October. Available at: https://medium.com/giveth/the-trusted-seed-of-the-commons-stack-5af6fb04cd30.

Emmett Jeff. 2020. 'Architecting the Cyber-Physical Commons'. Medium, 27 February. Available at: https://medium.com/commonsstack/architecting-the-cyber-physical-commons-a294d88b5415.

Emmett Jeff. 2022. 'Augmented Bonding Curves as Common Market Makers (CMMs)'. Presentation to RMIT University, Melbourne, 30 January. Available at: www.youtube.com/watch?v=ZJqXeQYfJiw.

Faqir-Rhazoui Youssef, Arroyo Gallardo Javier and Hassan Samer. 2020. 'An Overview of Decentralised Autonomous Organisations on the Blockchain'. OpenSym, 25 August. Available at: https://opensym.org/wp-content/uploads/2020/08/os20-paper-a11-el-faqir.pdf.

Faqir-Rhazoui Youssef, Arroyo Gallardo Javier and Hassan Samer. 2021. 'A Comparative Analysis of the Adoption of Decentralized Governance in the Blockchain through DAOs'. Research Square, 4 February. Available at: https://assets.researchsquare.com/files/rs-1166470/v1_covered.pdf?c=1631852800.

Faustino Sandra. 2019. 'How Metaphors Matter: An Ethnography of Blockchain-Based Re-Descriptions of the World'. *Journal of Cultural Economy* 12 (6): 478–90.

Federici Silvia. 2012. *Revolution at Point Zero: Housework, Reproduction, and Feminist Struggle*. Oakland, CA: PM Press.

Ferraro Fabrizio, Pfeffer Jeffrey and Sutton Robert I. 2005. 'Economics Language and Assumptions: How Theories Can Become Self-Fulfilling'. *Academy of Management Review* 30 (1): 8–24.

Foucault Michel. 1978. *The History of Sexuality*, vol. 1, *An Introduction*. New York: Pantheon Books.

Fourier Charles. 1971. *Design for Utopia: Selected Writings*. New York: Schocken.

Frank Sam. 2015. 'Come With Us If You Want to Live'. *Harper's Magazine*, January: 26–36.

Fritsch Felix, Emmett Jeff, Friedman Emaline, Kranjc Rok, Manski Sarah, Zargham Michael and Bauwens Michel. 2021. 'Challenges and Approaches to Scaling the Global Commons'. *Frontiers in Blockchain* 4. DOI: 10.3389/fbloc.2021.578721.

Frenken Koen. 2017. 'Political Economies and Environmental Futures for the Sharing Economy'. *Philosophical Transactions of the Royal Society A* 375. DOI: 10.1098/rsta.2016.0367.

Freund Andreas and Stanko Danielle. 2018. 'The Wolf and the Caribou: Coexistence of Decentralised Economies and Competitive Markets'. *Journal of Risk and Financial Management* 11 (2). DOI: 10.3390/jrfm11020026.

Forte Andrea, Larco Vanessa and Bruckman Amy. 2009. 'Decentralisation in Wikipedia Governance'. *Journal of Management Information Systems* 26 (1): 49–72.

Foster Sheila and Iaione Christian. 2016. 'The City as a Commons'. *Yale Law & Policy Review* 34 (2): 281–349.

Fuchs Christian. 2008. *Internet and Society: Social Theory in the Information Age*. Abingdon: Routledge.

Fuchs Christian. 2011. *Foundations of Critical Media and Information Studies*. Abingdon: Routledge.

Fuchs Christian. 2014. *Digital Labour and Karl Marx*. Abingdon: Routledge.

Fuster Morell Mayo. 2010. 'Governance of Online Creation Communities: Provision of Infrastructure for the Building of Digital Commons', doctoral dissertation, European University Institute. Available at: http://cadmus.eui.eu//handle/1814/14709.

Fuster Morell Mayo, Smichowski Bruno Carballa, Smorto Guido, Espelt Ricard, Imperatore Paola, Rebordosa Manel, Rocas Marc, Rodriguez Natalia, Senabre Enric and Ciurcina Marco. 2017. 'Multidisciplinary Framework on Commons Collaborative Economy'. Luxembourg: Publications Office of the European Union.

García-Siñeriz Mateo Peyrouzet. 2018. '*In Blockchain They Trust: Now, Power to the People or to the Invisible Hand?*', doctoral dissertation, University of Exeter. Available at: www.academia.edu/38081197/In_blockchain_they_trust_Now_power_to_the_people_or_to_the_invisible_hand.

Garrod Joel Z. 2016. 'The Real World of the Decentralised Autonomous Society'. *tripleC: Communication Capitalism & Critique* 14 (1): 62–77.

Gensler Gary. 2018. 'Blockchain and Money', OpenCourseWare. Massachusetts Institute of Technology. Available at: https://ocw.mit.edu/courses/15-s12-blockchain-and-money-fall-2018.

Gerard David. 2018. 'The Promise of the Blockchain Technology'. Economist, 30 August. Available at: www.economist.com/technology-quarterly/2018/08/30/the-promise-of-the-blockchain-technology.

Gertler Kay. 2019. 'Conviction Voting: From Ad-Hoc Voting to Continuous Voting'. Medium, 29 May. Available at: https://medium.com/giveth/conviction-voting-34019bd17b10.

Gibson Katharine and Graham Julie. 1996. *The End of Capitalism (As We Knew It): A Feminist Critique of Political Economy*. Minneapolis: University of Minnesota Press.

Gibson Katharine and Graham Julie. 2006. *A Postcapitalist Politics*. Minneapolis: University of Minnesota Press.

Gillmor Dan. 2004. *We the Media: Grassroots Journalism, By the People, For the People*. Sebastopol, CA: O'Reilly.

Giotitsas Chris and Ramos Jose. 2017. *A New Model of Production for a New Economy: Two Cases of Agricultural Communities*. London: New Economics Foundation.

Gorz André. 1980. *Farewell to the Working Class*. London: Pluto Press.

Grossman Lawrence K. 1995. *The Electronic Republic: Reshaping Democracy in the Information Age*. New York: Viking.

Habermas Jürgen. 1996. *Between Facts and Norms: Contributions to a Discourse Theory of Law and Democracy*. Cambridge, MA: MIT Press.

Hague Barry N. and Loader Brian D. 1999. *Digital Democracy, Discourse and Decision Making in the Information Age*. London: Routledge.

Hardin Garrett. 1968. 'The Tragedy of the Commons'. *Science* 162: 1243–1248.

Hardt Michael and Negri Antonio. 2000. *Empire*. Cambridge, MA: Harvard University Press.

Hardt Michael and Negri Antonio. 2004. *Multitude: War and Democracy in the Age of Empire*. London: Penguin Books.

Hardt Michael and Negri Antonio. 2009. *Commonwealth*. Cambridge, MA: Belknap Press.

Harvey David. 2003. *The New Imperialism*. Oxford: Oxford University Press.

Harvey David. 2005. *A Brief History of Neoliberalism*. Oxford: Oxford University Press.

Harvey David. 2010. *The Enigma of Capital and the Crises of Capitalism*. Oxford: Oxford University Press.

Hassan Samer, Brekke Jaya K., Atzori Marcella, Bodó Balatz, Meiklejohn Sarah, De Filippi Primavera, Beecroft Kate, Rozas David, Orgaz Alonso Christian, Martínez Vicente Elena, Lopéz Morales Genoveva and Figueras Aguilar Abel. 2020. *Scanning the European Ecosystem of Distributed Ledger Technologies for Social and Public Good: What, Why, Where, How, and Ways to Move Forward*. Luxembourg: Publications Office of the European Union.

Hassan Samer and De Filippi Primavera. 2021. 'Decentralized Autonomous Organization'. *Internet Policy Review* 10 (2). DOI: 10.14763/2021.2.1556.

Hayek Friedrich. 1944. *The Road to Serfdom*. London: Routledge.

Hayes Adam. 2016. 'Decentralised Banking: Monetary Technocracy in the Digital Age'. AIS eLibrary, 26 October. Available at: https://aisel.aisnet.org/mcis2016/3.

Heilweil Rebecca. 2020. 'Why Algorithms Can Be Racist and Sexist'. Vox, 18 February. Available at: www.vox.com/recode/2020/2/18/21121286/algorithms-bias-discrimination-facial-recognition-transparency.

Hess Charlotte. 2008. 'Mapping the New Commons'. Available at: https://ssrn.com/abstract=1356835.

Hess Charlotte and Ostrom Elinor. 2007. 'Introduction: An Overview of the Knowledge Commons'. In Charlotte Hess and Elinor Ostrom (eds.), *Understanding Knowledge as a Commons: From Theory to Practice*, 3–26, Cambridge, MA: MIT Press.

Hill Kevin and Hughes John. 1998. *Cyberpolitics: Citizen Activism in the Age of the Internet*. Oxford: Rowman & Littlefield.

Hu Yining, Seneviratne Suranga, Thilakarathna Kanchana, Fukuda Kensuke and Seneviratne Aruna. 2019. 'Characterizing and Detecting Money Laundering Activities on the Bitcoin Network'. DOI: 10.48550/arXiv.1912.12060.

Husain Syed Omer, Franklin Alex and Roep Dirk. 2020. 'The Political Imaginaries of Blockchain Projects: Discerning the Expressions of an Emerging Ecosystem'. *Sustainability Science* 15: 379–394.

Huws Ursula. 2003. *The Making of a Cybertariat: Virtual Work in a Real World*. New York: Monthly Review.

Huws Ursula. 2014. *Labour in the Global Digital Economy: The Cybertariat Comes of Age*. New York: Monthly Review.

Jacobs Michael and Mazzucato Mariana (eds.). 2016. *Rethinking Capitalism: Economics and Policy for Sustainable and Inclusive Growth*. Oxford: Wiley-Blackwell.

Jenkins Henry. 2006. *Convergence Culture: Where Old and New Media Collide*. New York: New York University Press.

Kallis Giorgos, Kostakis Vasilis, Lange Steffen, Muraca Barbara, Paulson Susan and Schmelzer Matthias. 2018. 'Research on Degrowth'. *Annual Review of Environment and Resources* 43: 291–316.

Karjalainen Risto. 2020. 'Governance in Decentralised Networks'. Streamr Network, 5 March. DOI: 10.2139/ssrn.3551099.

Kia Solmaz S., Van Scoy Bryan, Cortes Jorge, Freeman Randy A., Lynch Kevin M. and Martinez Sonia. 2019. 'Tutorial on Dynamic Average Consensus: The Problem, Its Applications, and the Algorithms'. *IEEE Control Systems Magazine* 39 (3): 40–72.

Klein Mark, Sayama Hiroki, Faratin Peyman and Bar-Yam Yaneer. 2001. 'What Complex Systems Research Can Teach Us about Collaborative Design'. DOI: 10.1109/CSCWD.2001.942221.

Kleiner Dmytri. 2018. 'The Face Value of Bitcoin: Proof of Work and the Labour Theory of Value'. NewsClick, 3 February. Available at: www.newsclick.in/face-value-bitcoin-proof-work-and-labour-theory-value.

Kim Seong-Kyu, Kim Ung-Mo and Huh Jun-Ho. 2019. 'A Study on Improvement of Blockchain Application to Overcome Vulnerability of IoT Multiplatform Security'. *Energies* 12 (3). DOI: 10.3390/en12030402.

Kioupkiolis Alexandros. 2019. *The Common and Counter-Hegemonic Policies.* Edinburgh: Edinburgh University Press.

Kioupkiolis Alexandros. Forthcoming. 'Digital Commons, the Political and Social Change: Towards an Integrated Strategy of Counter-Hegemony Furthering the Commons'. *Ephemera.*

Kohlhaas Paul. 2018. 'Token Bonding Curves in Practice: Exploring a Universal Distribution of IP via NFTs + Curation Markets'. Token Economy, 27 August. Available at: https://tokeneconomy.co/token-bonding-curves-in-practice-3eb90 4720cb8.

Kohlhaas Paul. 2019. 'Token Bonding Curve Design Parameters'. Medium, 8 January. Available at: https://medium.com/molecule-blog/token-bonding-curve-design-par ameters-95d365cbec4f.

Kostakis Vasilis and Bauwens Michel. 2014. *Network Society and Future Scenarios for a Collaborative Economy.* London: Palgrave Macmillan.

Kostakis Vasilis and Giotitsas Chris. 2014. 'The (A)Political Economy of Bitcoin'. *tripleC: Communication Capitalism & Critique* 12 (2): 431–440.

Kostakis Vasilis, Niaros Vasilis, Dafermos George and Bauwens Michel. 2015. 'Design Global Manufacture Local: Exploring the Contours of an Emerging Productive Model'. *Futures* 73: 126–135.

Kreutler Kei. 2021. 'A Prehistory of DAOs'. Gnosis Guild, 21 July. Available at: https://gnosisguild.mirror.xyz/t4F5rItMw4mlpLZf5JQhElbDfQ2JRVKAzEpanyxW1Q.

Krugman Paul. 2018. 'Transaction Costs and Tethers: Why I'm a Crypto Skeptic'. *New York Times*, 31 July. Available at: www.nytimes.com/2018/07/31/opinion/tran saction-costs-and-tethers-why-im-a-crypto-skeptic.html.

Laclau Ernesto and Mouffe Chantal. 1985. *Hegemony and Socialist Strategy: Towards a Radical Democratic Politics.* London: Verso Books.

Lakhani Karim R. and Wolf Robert G. 2005. 'Why Hackers Do What They Do: Understanding Motivation and Effort in Free/Open-Source Software Projects'. In Joseph Feller, Brian Fitzgerald, Scott A. Hissam and Karim R. Lakhani (eds.), *Perspectives on Free and Open Source Software*, 3–22. Cambridge, MA: MIT Press.

Laul Mario. 2019. 'Blockchain Networks Are Bureaucracies par Excellence'. Medium, 6 May. Available at: https://mariolaul.medium.com/blockchains-arebureaucracies-par-excellence-db39cfda7ea9.

Leach Darcy K. 2013. 'Prefigurative Politics'. In David A. Snow, Donatella della Porta, Bert Klandermans and Doug McAdam (eds.), *The Wiley-Blackwell Encyclopedia of Social and Political Movements*, 1004–1006. Oxford: Wiley-Blackwell.

Lee Allen. 2021. 'How Linus Torvalds Achieved a Net Worth of $150 Million'. Money Inc, 8 February. Available at: https://moneyinc.com/linus-torvalds-net-worth.

Lenin Vladimir. 1961. *Collected Works.* Moscow: Foreign Languages Publishing House.

Lerner Josh and Tirole Jean. 2002. 'Some Simple Economics of Open Source'. *Journal of Industrial Economics* 50 (2): 197–234.

Lessig Lawrence. 2001. *The Future of Ideas: The Fate of the Commons in a Connected World.* New York: Random House.

Lessig Lawrence. 2004. *Free Culture: The Nature and Future of Creativity*. New York: Penguin Books.

Lewis Lynne, Owen Jane, Fraser Hamish and Dighe Rohit. 2021. 'Non-Fungible Tokens (NFTs) and Copyright Law'. Bird & Bird, 2 June. Available at: www.twobirds.com/en/news/articles/2021/australia/non-fungible-tokens-nfts-and-copyright-law.

Linares Julio. 2021. 'The Promise of People Powered Money with CirclesUBI', podcast. The Blockchain Socialist, 11 April. Available at: https://theblockchainsocialist.com/the-promise-of-people-powered-money-with-circlesubi.

Locke John. 1975 [1690]. *An Essay Concerning Human Understanding*. Oxford: Oxford University Press.

Magnuson William. 2020. *Blockchain Democracy: Technology, Law and the Rule of the Crowd*. Cambridge: Cambridge University Press.

Malta Mariana Curado, Bandeira Ana Maria, Bertuzi Rui, Castro Conceição, Meira Deolinda, Pereira Denise, Pereira Inês, Vieira Isabel and Tomé Brízida. 2020. 'A Framework for Cooperatives' Transparency: A Linked Data Approach'. Valencia: CIRIEC–España. Available at: http://ciriec.es/wp-content/uploads/2020/09/COMUN-087-T16-CURADO-BANDEIRA-et-al-ok.pdf.

Mannan Morshed. 2018. 'Fostering Worker Cooperatives with Blockchain Technology: Lessons from the Colony Project'. *Erasmus Law Review* 11 (3): 190–203.

Manski Sarah and Manski Ben. 2018. 'No Gods, No Masters, No Coders? The Future of Sovereignty in a Blockchain World'. *Law and Critique* 29 (2): 151–162.

Manski Sarah and Bauwens Michel. 2020. 'Reimagining New Socio-Technical Economics through the Application of Distributed Ledger Technologies'. *Frontiers in Blockchain* 2. DOI: 10.3389/fbloc.2019.00029.

Maples Mike. 2018. 'Crypto Commons'. Medium, 28 June. Available at: https://medium.com/@m2jr/crypto-commons-da602fb98138.

Marden Peter. 2003. *The Decline of Politics: Governance, Globalization and the Public Sphere*. Aldershot: Ashgate.

Marshall Alfred. 2013 [1890]. *Principles of Economics*. New York: Palgrave Macmillan.

Marx Karl. 1993 [1858]. *Grundrisse*. London: Penguin Books.

Mason Paul. 2015. *Postcapitalism: A Guide to Our Future*. London: Allen Lane.

Mazzucato Mariana. 2013. *The Entrepreneurial State: Debunking Public vs Private Sector Myths*. New York: Anthem Press.

Mazzucato Mariana. 2018. *The Value of Everything: Making and Taking in the Global Economy*. London: Penguin Books.

McCann Duncan and Yazici Edanur. 2018. *Disrupting Together: The Challenges (and Opportunities) for Platform Co-operatives*. London: New Economics Foundation.

Metcalfe Bob. 1995. 'Metcalfe's Law: A Network Becomes More Valuable as It Reaches More Users'. InfoWorld, 2 October.

Mohamad Maslinawati, Othman Waheedah Intan and Mohamed Arun. 2013. 'Accountability Issues and Challenges: The Scenario for Malaysian Cooperative Movement'. *World Academy of Science, Engineering and Technology International Journal of Economics and Management Engineering* 7 (6): 1503–1508.

Muldoon James. 2022. *Platform Socialism: How to Reclaim Our Digital Future from Big Tech*. London: Pluto Press.

Murdock Graham. 2013. 'Communication in Common'. *International Journal of Communication* 7: 154–172.

Nabben Kelsie. 2021a. 'Resilience as "Political Decentralization": An Alternate History of the Cypherpunks Origins of Decentralised Technology'. 7 October. Available at: https://ssrn.com/abstract=3938626.

Nabben Kelsie. 2021b. 'Experiments in Algorithmic Governance Continue'. Substack, 29 July. Available at: https://kelsienabben.substack.com/p/experiments-in-algorithmic-governance.

Nabben Kelsie, Puspasari Novita, Kelleher Megan and Sanjay Sadhana. 2021. 'Grounding Decentralised Technologies in Cooperative Principles: What Can "Decentralised Autonomous Organisations" (DAOs) and Platform Cooperatives Learn from Each Other?', working paper. New York: New School Platform Cooperativism Consortium. Available at: file:///C:/Users/Michael/Downloads/SSRN-id3979223.pdf.

Nabben Kelsie and Zargham Michael. 2021. '"Permissionlessness": Exploring a Commonly Misconceived and Convoluted Term'. Substack, 22 April. Available at: https://kelsienabben.substack.com/p/permissionlessness-exploring-a-commonly.

Nadini Matthieu, Alessandretti Laura, Di Giacinto Flavio, Martino Mauro, Aiello Maria Luca and Baronchelli Andrea. 2021. 'Mapping the NFT Revolution: Market Trends, Trade Networks, and Visual Features'. *Scientific Reports* 11. DOI: 10.1038/s41598-021-00053-8.

Nafus Dawn. 2011. '"Partners Don't Have Gender": What Is Not Open in Source Software'. *New Media & Society* 14 (4): 669–683.

Nakamoto Satoshi. 2008. 'Bitcoin: A Peer-to-Peer Electronic Cash System'. Satoshi Nakamoto Institute, 31 October. Available at: https://nakamotoinstitute.org/bitcoin.

Nascimento Susana and Pólvora Alexandre (eds.). 2019. *Blockchain Now and Tomorrow: Assessing Multidimensional Aspects of Distributed Ledger Technologies*. Luxembourg: Publications Office of the European Union.

Nguyen Quoc Khanh. 2016. 'Blockchain: A Financial Technology for Future Sustainable Development'. DOI: 10.1109/GTSD.2016.22.

Nizzoli Leonardo, Tardelli Serena, Avvenuti Marco, Cresci Stefano, Tesconi Maurizio and Ferrara Emilio. 2020. 'Charting the Landscape of Online Cryptocurrency Manipulation'. *IEEE Access* 8. DOI: 10.1109/ACCESS.2020.3003370.

Odiljon Atabaev and Gai Keke. 2019. 'Efficiency Issues and Solutions in Blockchain: A Survey'. In Meikang Qiu (ed.), *Smart Blockchain*, 76–86. Berlin: Springer.

O'Dwyer Rachel. 2015. 'The Revolution Will (Not) Be Decentralised: Blockchains'. P2P Foundation, 23 March. Available at: http://blog.p2pfoundation.net/the-revolution-will-not-be-decentralised/2015/03/23.

Olson Mancur. 1965. *The Logic of Collective Action: Public Goods and the Theory of Groups*. Cambridge, MA: Harvard University Press.

Ostrom Elinor. 1990. *Governing the Commons: The Evolution of Institutions for Collective Action*. Cambridge: Cambridge University Press.

Ospina Daniel. 2021. 'Minimum Viable Salaries for a Fairer Web3'. Mirror.xyz, 13 December. Available at: https://mirror.xyz/0x8B580433568E521ad351b92b98150c0C65ce69B7/aKI_cniOIsTcxNz4xC0EqzlXDDykwLw6geEc0ipFvIs.

Owen Robert. 1991 [1813]. *A New View of Society*. London: Penguin Books.

Papadimitropoulos Vangelis. 2017. 'From the Crisis of Democracy to the Commons'. *Socialism and Democracy* 31 (3): 110–122.

Papadimitropoulos Vangelis. 2018. 'Reflections on the Contradictions of the Commons'. *Review of Radical Political Economics* 50 (2): 317–331.

Papadimitropoulos Vangelis. 2020. *The Commons: Economic Alternatives in the Digital Age*. London: University of Westminster Press.

Patron Travis. 2014. *The Bitcoin Revolution: An Internet of Money*. Toronto: Diginomics.

Pazaitis Alex. 2020. 'Breaking the Chains of Open Innovation: Post-Blockchain and the Case of Sensorica'. *Information* 11 (2). DOI: 10.3390/info11020104.

Pazaitis Alex, De Filippi Primavera and Kostakis Vasilis. 2017. 'Blockchain and Value Systems in the Sharing Economy: The Illustrative Case of Backfeed'. *Technological Forecasting and Social Change* 125: 105–115.

Pazaitis Alex, Kostakis Vasilis and Bauwens Michel. 2017. 'Digital Economy and the Rise of Open Cooperativism: the Case of Enspiral Network'. *Transfer: European Review of Labour and Research* 23 (2): 1–16.

Philipp Peter, Hermes Sebastian, Schreieck Maximilian and Böhm Markus. 2021. 'Challenges and Success Potentials of Platform Cooperatives: Insights from a Multiple Case Study', Research Paper 1375. Atlanta: Association for Information Systems.

Proudhon Pierre-Joseph. 1944. *What Is Property?* Cambridge: Cambridge University Press.

Puri Drona Lal and Walsh John. 2018. 'Impact of Good Governance on Performance of Cooperatives in Nepal'. *Management & Marketing* 16 (2): 208–224.

Quilligan James B. 2012. 'Why Distinguish Common Goods from Public Goods?'. In David Bollier and Silke Helfrich (eds.), *The Wealth of the Commons: A World beyond Market and State*, 73–81. Amherst, MA: Levellers Press.

Quiniou Matthieu. 2019. *Blockchain: The Advent of Disintermediation*. London: ISTE.

Raymond Eric. 1999. *The Cathedral and the Bazaar*. Sebastopol, CA: O'Reilly.

Raymond Robert. 2021. 'The DAO of Decentralization: Can Co-ops Thrive on the Blockchain?'. Shareable, 21 December. Available at: www.shareable.net/the-dao-of-decentralization-can-co-ops-thrive-on-the-blockchain.

Reese Adam. 2020. 'CSTK Score: The "Trust Score" of Commons Stack'. Medium, 30 June. Available at: https://medium.com/commonsstack/cstk-the-token-of-the-commons-stack-trusted-seed-931978625c61.

Reijers Wessel, Iris Wuisman, Morshed Mannan, Primavera De Filippi, Christopher Wray, Vienna Rae-Looi, Angela Cubillos Vélez and Liav Orgad. 2021. 'Now the Code Runs Itself: On-Chain and Off-Chain Governance of Blockchain Technologies'. *TOPOI: International Review of Philosophy* 40 (4): 821–831.

Restakis John. 2010. *Humanising the Economy: Co-operatives in the Age of Capital*. Gabriola Island, Canada: New Society Publishers.

Rheingold Howard. 2003. *Smart Mobs: The Next Social Revolution*. Cambridge, MA: Perseus.

Rifkin Jeremy. 2014. *The Zero Marginal Cost Society: The Internet of Things, the Collaborative Commons, and the Eclipse of Capitalism*. New York: Palgrave Macmillan.

Robey Austin. 2021. 'Ways to Improve the Ownership Economy'. Forefront, 5 July. Available at: https://ff.mirror.xyz/ZRsr5HZMfbHOEe2lIYoWinRCI65NlvDW_QzEu1rn7As.

Robey Austin. 2022. 'What Co-ops and DAOs Can Learn from Each Other'. Friends With Benefits, 13 January. Available at: www.fwb.help/wip/what-co-ops-and-daos-can-learn-from-each-other.

Robinson Chris. 2015. 'The Decentralisation Mega-Trend and the Future of the Species'. N-o-d-e.net, 28 September. Available at: http://n-o-d-e.net/post/109307736436/the-decentralization-mega-trend-and-the-future-of.

Rochet Jean-Charles and Tirole Jean. 2003. 'Platform Competition in Two-Sided Markets'. *Journal of the European Economic Association* 1 (4): 990–1029.

Roubini Nouriel. 2021. 'Bitcoin Is Not a Hedge against Tail Risk'. *Financial Times*, 10 February. Available at: www.ft.com/content/9be5ad05-b17a-4449-807b-5dbcb5ef8170.

Rose Carol. 1986. 'The Comedy of the Commons: Commerce, Custom and Inherently Public Property'. *University of Chicago Law Review* 53 (3): 711–781.

Rozas David. 2017. 'Self-Organisation in Commons-Based Peer Production: Drupal: "The Drop Is Always Moving"', doctoral dissertation, University of Surrey. Available at: http://openresearch.surrey.ac.uk/esploro/outputs/doctoral/Self-organisation-in-commons-based-peer-production--Drupal--the-drop-is-always-moving/99512497702346.

Rozas David, Tenorio-Fornés Antonio, Díaz-Molina Silvia and Samer Hassan. 2021. 'When Ostrom Meets Blockchain: Exploring the Potentials of Blockchain for Commons Governance'. *SAGE Open* 11 (1): 1–14.

Rozas David, Tenorio-Fornés Antonio and Samer Hassan. 2021. 'Analysis of the Potentials of Blockchain for the Governance of Global Digital Commons'. *Frontiers in Blockchain* 4. DOI: 10.3389/fbloc.2021.577680.

Rushkoff Douglas. 2016. *Throwing Rocks at the Google Bus: How Growth Became the Enemy of Prosperity*. New York: Penguin Books.

Samman George and Freuden David. 2020. 'DAO: A Decentralized Governance Layer for the Internet ofValue'. Sydney: Monsterplay.

Sedlmeir Johannes, Bulh Hans Ulrish, Fridhen Gilbert and Keller Robert. 2020. 'The Energy Consumption of Blockchain Technology: Beyond Myth'. *Business & Information Systems Engineering* 62 (6): 599–608.

Schär Fabien. 2021. 'Decentralized Finance: On Blockchain- and Smart Contract-Based Financial Markets'. *Federal Reserve Bank of St. Louis Review* 103 (2): 153–174.

Schär Fabien and Berentsen Aleksander. 2020. *Bitcoin, Blockchain, and Cryptoassets: A Comprehensive Introduction*. Cambridge, MA: MIT Press.

Schneider Nathan. 2021a. 'The Tyranny of Openness: What Happened to Peer Production?'. *Feminist Media Studies*. DOI: 10.1080/14680777.2021.1890183.

Schneider Nathan. 2021b. 'Cryptoeconomics as a Limitation on Governance', working paper. Boulder, CO: University of Colorado.

Schneider Nathan. 2022a. 'Governable Stacks against Digital Colonialism'. *tripleC: Communication Capitalism & Critique* 20 (1): 19–36.

Schneider Nathan. 2022b. 'Policy Proposals for Crypto Protocols to Make Them Less Dystopic and More Inclusive'. Hackernoon, 7 January. Available at: https://hackernoon.com/policy-proposals-for-crypto-protocols-to-make-them-less-dystopic-and-more-inclusive.

Schneider Nathan, De Filippi Primavera , Frey Seth, Tan Joshua Z. and Zhang Amy X. 2021. 'Modular Politics: Toward a Governance Layer for Online Communities'. Association for Computing Machinery, 22 April. DOI: 10.1145/3449090.

Scholz Trebor. 2012. *Digital Labor: The Internet as Playground and Factory*. New York: Routledge.

Scholz Trebor. 2016. *Platform Cooperativism: Challenging the Corporate Sharing Economy*. New York: Rosa Luxemburg Stiftung.

Scholz Trebor and Schneider Nathan (eds.). 2016. *Ours to Hack and to Own: The Rise of Platform Cooperativism, a New Vision for the Future of Work and a Fairer Internet*. New York: Or Books.

Schonberger Jennifer. 2022. 'SEC's Gensler Wants Crypto Exchange Regulation in 2022, Warns on Stablecoin'. Yahoo!, 20 January. Available at: https://finance.yahoo.com/news/se-cs-gensler-wants-crypto-exchange-regulation-in-2022-warns-on-stablecoin-risks-130254530.html.

Schor Juliet B. 2016. 'Old Exclusion in Emergent Spaces'. In Trebor Scholz and Nathan Schneider (eds.), *Ours to Hack and to Own: The Rise of Platform Cooperativism, a New Vision for the Future of Work and a Fairer Internet*, 38–42. New York: Or Books.

Shaikh Anwar. 2016. *Capitalism, Competition, Conflict, Crises*. New York: Oxford University Press.

Shah Alkesh and Moss Andrew. 2021. *Global Cryptocurrencies and Digital Assets*. Charlotte, NC: BofA Securities.

Sharon Tamar and Zandbergen Dorien. 2017. 'From Data Fetishism to Quantifying Selves: Self-Tracking Practices and the Other Values of Data'. *New Media & Society* 19 (11): 1695–1709.

Shaw Aaron and Hill Benjamin M. 2014. 'Laboratories of Oligarchy? How the Iron Law Extends to Peer Production'. *Journal of Communication* 64 (2): 215–238.

Shirky Clay. 2008. *Here Comes Everybody: The Power of Organizing without Organizations*. New York: Penguin Books.

Shrivastava Gulshan, Le Dac-Nhuong and Sharma Kavita. 2020. *Cryptocurrencies and Blockchain Technology Applications*. Beverly, MA: Scrivener Publishing.

Simon H. William. 2019. 'Economic Democracy and Enterprise Form in Finance'. *Politics & Society* 47 (4): 557–571.

Smith Adam. 1977 [1776]. *An Inquiry into the Nature and Causes of the Wealth of Nations*. Chicago: University of Chicago Press.

Smythe Dallas W. 1977. 'Communications: Blindspot of Western Marxism'. *Canadian Journal of Political and Social Theory* 1 (3): 1–27.

Smythe Dallas W. 1981. *Dependency Road: Communications, Capitalism, Consciousness, and Canada*. Norwood, NJ: Ablex.

Söderberg Johan. 2008. *Hacking Capitalism: The Free and Open-Source Software Movement*. New York: Routledge.

Srnicek Nick. 2017. *Platform Capitalism*. Cambridge: Polity Press.

Staggs Kendra. 2020. 'Game Theory and Bitcoin: The Miners' Perspective'. SALT, 19 November. Available at: https://saltlending.com/game-theory-and-bitcoin.

Stallman Richard. 2002. *Free Software, Free Society*. Boston: GNU Press.

Standing Guy. 2011. *The Precariat: The Dangerous Class*. London: Bloomsbury.

Stiglitz Joseph E. 2016. *Rewriting the Rules of the American Economy*. New York: W.W. Norton.

Surowiecki James. 2004. *The Wisdom of Crowds: Why the Many Are Smarter than the Few*. New York: Little, Brown.

Swan Melanie. 2015. *Blockchain: Blueprint for a New Economy*. Sebastopol, CA: O'Reilly.

Swartz Lana. 2017. 'Blockchain Dreams: Imagining Techno-Economic Alternatives after Bitcoin'. In Manuel Castells (ed.), *Another Economy Is Possible: Culture and Economy in a Time of Crisis*, 82–105. Cambridge: Polity Press.

Swift Adam. 2006. *Political Philosophy: A Beginners' Guide for Students and Politicians*. Cambridge: Polity Press.

Szabo Nico. 1997. 'Formalising and Securing Relationships on Public Networks'. *First Monday* 2 (9). DOI: 10.5210/fm.v2i9.548.

Tai Kevin. 2022. 'DAOs Are Meant to Be Completely Autonomous and Decentralized, but Are They?'. Cointelegraph, 5 February. Available at: https://cointelegraph.com/news/daos-are-meant-to-be-completely-autonomous-and-decentralized-but-are-they.

Tan Joshua. 2022. 'Where Do You Belong in Crypto? Results from the Cryptopolitical Typology Quiz'. Medium, 11 January. Available at: https://medium.com/metagov/the-political-landscape-of-crypto-f440d521f411.

Tapscott Don and Tapscott Alex. 2016. *Blockchain Revolution: How the Technology Behind Bitcoin Is Changing Money, Business, and the World*. New York: Penguin Books.

Titcomb Abbey. 2019. 'Deep Dive: Augmented Bonding Curves'. Medium, 2 December. Available at: https://medium.com/commonsstack/deep-dive-augmented-bonding-curves-b5ca4fad4436.

Thorp Noah. 2015. 'How Society Will Be Transformed by Cryptoeconomics'. Medium, 18 May. Available at: https://medium.com/@noahthorp/how-society-will-be-transformed-by-crypto-economics-b02b6765ca8c.

Toffler Alvin. 1980. *The Third Wave*. New York: Bantam Books.

Torpey Kyle. 2019. 'Bitcoin Mining Centralization Is "Quite Alarming", but a Solution Is in the Works'. Forbes, 28 July. Available at: www.forbes.com/sites/ktorpey/2019/07/28/bitcoin-mining-centralization-is-quite-alarming-but-a-solution-is-in-the-works.

Tronti Mario. 2019 [1962]. *Workers and Capital*. London: Verso Books.

Truby Jon. 2018. 'Decarbonizing Bitcoin: Law and Policy Choices for Reducing the Energy Consumption of Blockchain Technologies and Digital Currencies'. *Energy Research and Social Science* 44: 399–410.

Truong David. 2018. 'Dynamic Token Bonding Curves'. Token Economy, 5 September. Available at: https://tokeneconomy.co/dynamic-token-bonding-curves-41d36e43befa.

Van Dijk Jan. 2006. *The Network Society: Social Aspects of New Media*. London: SAGE.

Van Pelt Rowan, Jansen Slinger, Baars Djuri and Overbeek Sietse. 2021. 'Defining Blockchain Governance: A Framework for Analysis and Comparison'. *Information Systems Management* 38 (1): 21–41.

Varoufakis Yanis. 2017. *Talking to My Daughter about the Economy: A Brief History of Capitalism*. London: Bodley Head.

Varoufakis Yanis. 2022. 'On Crypto, the Left and Techno-Feudalism'. DiEM25, 27 January. Available at: https://diem25.org/yanis-varoufakis-crypto-the-left-and-techno-feudalism/?fbclid=IwAR0IeImkSt5rq_2_X4mQJAT8QOvVNKJaxRt95Wh5C0oU9gj3uRsh6-57ag.

Vasek Marie and Moore Tyler. 2018. 'Analysing the Bitcoin Ponzi Scheme Ecosystem'. In Aviv Zohar, Ittay Eyal and Vanessa Teague (eds.), *Financial Cryptography and Data Security*, 110–112. Berlin: Springer.

Vercellone Carlo. 2013. 'The Becoming Rent of Profit? The New Articulation of Wage, Rent and Profit'. *Knowledge Cultures* 1 (2): 25–32.

Vesnic-Alujevic Lucia, Stoermer Eckard, Rudkin Jennifer Ellen, Scapolo Fabiana and Kimbell Lucy. 2019. *The Future of Government 2030+: A Citizen-Centric Perspective on New Government Models*. Luxembourg: Publications Office of the European Union.

Viégas Fernanda B., Wattenberg Martin and McKeon Matthew M. 2007. 'The Hidden Order of Wikipedia'. In Schuler Douglas (ed.), *OCSC 2007: Online Communities and Social Computing – Second International Conference*, 445–454. Berlin: Springer.

Vigna Paul. 2021. 'Bitcoin's "One Percent" Controls Lion's Share of the Cryptocurrency's Wealth'. *Wall Street Journal*, 20 December. Available at: www.wsj.com/amp/articles/bitcoins-one-percent-controls-lions-share-of-the-cryptocurrencys-wealth-11639996204?fbclid=IwAR2Vr4GKqdW0ywbg0QzwhRmF5ymRLB9TUe9GqLDQYfjkEZh7Gz4bvBMH5Ko.

Virtanen Marianna, Kivimäki Mika, Joensuu Matti, Virtanen Pekka, Elovainio Marco and Vahtera Jussi. 2005. 'Temporary Employment and Health: A Review'. *International Journal of Epidemiology* 34 (3): 610–622.

Voshmgir Shermin and Zargham Michael. 2020. 'Foundations of Cryptoeconomic Systems', Working Paper 1/2020. Vienna: Vienna University of Economics and Business.

Voshmgir Shermin. 2020. *Token Economy: How the Web3 Reinvents the Internet.* Berlin: Blockchain Hub.

Voshmgir Shermin. 2021. 'Token Engineering Commons'. Medium, 10 July. https://medium.com/token-engineering-commons/token-engineering-commons-69398048209a.

Ward Michael. 1996. 'The Effect of the Internet on Political Institutions'. *Industrial and Corporate Change* 5 (4): 1127–1142.

Weber Steven. 2004. *The Success of Open Source.* Cambridge, MA: Harvard University Press.

Williamson Oliver E. 1985. *The Economic Institutions of Capitalism.* New York: Free Press.

Wilser Jeff. 2021. '15 NFT Use Cases that Could Go Mainstream'. CoinDesk, 14 October. Available at: www.coindesk.com/business/2021/10/14/15-nft-use-cases-that-could-go-mainstream.

Wright Del Jr. 2019. 'Quadratic Voting and Blockchain Governance'. *UMKC Law Review* 88 (2): 475–496.

Wright, Erik Olin. 2009. *Envisioning Real Utopias.* London: Verso Books.

Wang Guizhou, Zhang Si , Yu Tao and Ning Yu. 2021. A Systematic Overview of Blockchain Research'. *Journal of Systems Science and Information* 9 (3): 205–238.

Zamfir Vlad. 2015. 'What Is Cryptoeconomics?'. Cryptocurrency Research Group Cryptoeconomicon, 28 January. Available at: https://youtu.be/9lw3s7iGUXQ?t=58.

Zargham Michael. 2018. 'Sensor Fusion and Social Choice'. GitHub, 28 March. Available at: https://github.com/BlockScience/conviction/blob/master/social-sensorfusion.pdf.

Zargham Michael, Shorish Jamsheed and Paruch Krzysztof. 2020. 'From Curved Bonding to Configuration Spaces', working paper. Vienna: Vienna University of Economics and Business.

Zartler Jessica. 2022. 'Announcing cadCAD 1.0: Foundations for a New Era of Open Modelling'. Medium, 1 February. Available at: https://medium.com/block-science/announcing-cadcad-1-0-foundations-for-a-new-era-of-open-modelling-ea636b64fda7.

Zartler Jessica and Emmett Jeff. 2021. 'Zen and the Art of Understanding Commons Stack'. Medium, 30 April. Available at: https://medium.com/commonsstack/zen-and-the-art-of-understanding-commons-stack-f5266b300912.

Zhang Zixuan, Zargham Michael and Preciado Victor M. 2020. 'On Modelling Blockchain-Enabled Economic Networks as Stochastic Dynamical Systems'. *Applied Network Science* 5 (1): 1–24.

Zhang Yu and Wen Jiangtao. 2015. 'An IoT Electric Business Model Based on the Protocol of Bitcoin'. In *Proceedings of 18th International Conference on Intelligence in Next Generation Networks (ICIN)*, 184–191. Piscataway, NJ: IEEE.

Zhu Jiang and Marjanovic Olivera. 2021. 'A Different Kind of Sharing Economy: A Literature Review of Platform Cooperatives'. University of Hawai'i. Available at: https://scholarspace.manoa.hawaii.edu/items/53742f09-a53a-48c5-8ee9-1c68460b88b8.

Žižek Slavoj. 2008. *In Defense of Lost Causes*. London: Verso Books.

Žižek Slavoj. 2010. 'How to Begin from the Beginning'. In Costas Douzinas and Slavoj Žižek (eds.), *The Idea of Communism*, 9–226. London: Verso Books.

Zuboff Shoshana. 2019. *The Age of Surveillance Capitalism: The Fight for a Human Future at the New Frontier of Power*. New York: Hachette.

Index

Note: Page numbers in *italic* denote figures and in **bold** denote tables.